SAN DIEGO
WORLD-CLASS CITY

By Tom Blair ■ *Profiles in Excellence by* Ron Donoho ■ *Captions by* Jacquelyn Landis

rt Direction by JIL FOUTCH ■ *Sponsored by the* GREATER SAN DIEGO CHAMBER OF COMMERCE

LIBRARY OF CONGRESS CATALOGING-IN-PUBLICATION DATA

Blair, Tom.
    San Diego : world-class city / by Tom Blair ; profiles in
excellence by Ron Donoho.
        p.   cm. — (Urban tapestry series)
    "Sponsored by the Greater San Diego Chamber of Commerce."
    Includes index.
    ISBN 1-881096-56-4 (alk. paper)
    1. San Diego (Calif.)—Civilization.   2. San Diego (Calif.)-
-Pictorial works.   3. San Diego (Calif.)—Economic conditions.
    4. Business enterprises—California—San Diego.   I. Donoho, Ron,
1965-   . II. Title.   III. Series.
F869.S22B58 1998
979.4'985—DC21
                                            98-3205
                                            CIP

Towery Publishing, Inc., 1835 Union Avenue, Memphis, TN 38104

URBAN
TAPESTRY
SERIES
TOWERY
PUBLISHING, INC.

Publisher: *J. Robert Towery*
Executive Publisher: *Jenny McDowell*
National Sales Manager: *Stephen Hung*
Marketing Director: *Carol Culpepper*
Project Directors: *Linda Frank, Ethan Kaskin, Karen Riva*
Executive Editor: *David B. Dawson*
Managing Editor: *Michael C. James*
Senior Editors: *Lynn Conlee, Carlisle Hacker*
Editors/Project Managers: *Lori Bond, Brian Johnston, Jennifer C. Pyron*
Staff Editors: *Mary Jane Adams, Jana Files, Susan Hesson*

Assistant Editors: *Becky Green, Allison Ring*
Editorial Contributors: *Kim Cromwell, Bradley Fikes, Eilene Zimmerman*
Creative Director: *Brian Groppe*
Profile Designers: *Laurie Beck, Kelley Pratt, Ann Ward*
Digital Color Supervisor: *Brenda Pattat*
Digital Color Technicians: *Jack Griffith, Darin Ipema, Jason Moak*
Production Resources Manager: *Dave Dunlap Jr.*
Production Assistants: *Geoffrey Ellis, Enrique Espinosa, Robin McGehee*
Print Coordinators: *Beverly Timmons, Tonda Thomas*

PAGES 4 AND 5: PHOTOS BY AL RODRÍGUEZ

CONTENTS

By Tom Blair

T HE REPORT HIT THE NEWS WIRES AND AIRWAVES IN SUMMER 1997: PHOENIX, the story went, had leapfrogged San Diego to become the sixth-largest city in the United States. The news was not greeted with universal dismay by San Diegans. Some surprise, perhaps, but not dismay. In San Diego, you see, quality of life has always been much more important than quantity.

Indeed, the fact that the news broke in midsummer—a time of year when most of Phoenix seems to escape to San Diego anyway—seemed cause for general amusement. A follow-up report noted that Arizona reporters were having some trouble tracking down the mayor of Phoenix for his reaction to the development. He was on vacation, it turned out. In San Diego.

In fact, the official word on the population race between San Diego and Phoenix won't come until the next official U.S. census. But if we do slip to seventh-largest city, or even eighth-largest, the final word may be met more by relief than any sense of wounded civic pride. San Diegans, by and large, fear growth. It threatens our idyllic quality of life—a life for which we pay dearly.

A sagacious old scribe once put it this way: "If Los Angeles is the city most Easterners think of when they think California, San Diego is the city they dream of when they dream California."

San Diegans need only look to the north for a lesson in what can go wrong when growth spins wildly out of control. A San Diego-based political action group calling itself PLAN (Prevent Los Angelization Now!) even spawned a candidate who gained instant credibility among the local populace—despite the fact that he sprang from the loins of sprawling Orange County, a massive bedroom community of 3 million that feeds the Los Angeles megalopolis of 9 million.

A CITY OF CONTRASTS, SAN Diego embraces the fast-paced businesses that punctuate its skyline, as well as the sun, surf, and sand of life's more leisurely side. A favorite pastime among locals is sailing, a sport that's both elevated and celebrated during the America's Cup race. A three-time winner of the prestigious contest, Dennis Conner proudly skippers the *Stars & Stripes* off the coast of San Diego (ABOVE).

This essentially one-issue candidate—a professor at the University of California, Irvine (in Orange County), and a champion of no-growth—ran for major political office in San Diego four times in the space of six years. He lost every time. But the point is that he always made a respectable showing, providing other local politicos with a valuable lesson: If you're going to pick one issue that is sure to fire up the San Diego electorate, pick growth.

TRANSPORTATION BECOMES A work of art in Greater San Diego, where cars along the Sassafras Street underpass inspire photographer Philipp Scholz Ritterman to create a whimsical "light drawing" (LEFT). Striking in its own beauty, the station at Kettner Boulevard is a main transfer hub for trolley cars that carry workers, shoppers, tourists, and serious revelers from points east through downtown and all the way to the U.S.-Mexico border (OPPOSITE).

The fact that tourism is the region's third-largest industry is no accident. The 14 million people who visit San Diego each year quickly discover what the nearly 3 million who live here already know: San Diego *is* the California dream. Tourists who make Los Angeles their vacation destination may wonder just what it was about California that attracted them, but if they happen to venture 100 miles down the freeway to San Diego, they'll find out. Most San Diegans *do* want tourists to find this corner of heaven. We just want them to find it, appreciate it, leave their money, and then go back to wherever they came from. In fact, one of the most popular bumper stickers in these parts reads Welcome to San Diego—Now Go Home!

SAN DIEGO—A WARM AND ARID COASTAL PARADISE BORDERING MEXICO—IS where California began. Then, as now, the city's story was a tale of growth versus no-growth. And it was a tale of tourism. ■ The first tourist to visit the city was Juan Rodríguez Cabrillo, who sailed into San Diego's natural harbor in 1542. He promptly claimed the area for Spain and christened it San Miguel. His proclamation must have amused the Diegueño Indians, who had occupied the land since 1000 B.C. and had never given it an official name other than "home."

Although Cabrillo praised San Miguel for its natural beauty and harbor, he quickly moved on in search of greater glory and a northwest passage linking the Atlantic and Pacific oceans. And so, the Diegueño Indians lived unmolested by tourists for 60 years longer, until another of Spain's intrepid explorers, Sebastián Vizcaíno, visited in 1602 with the intent of inspecting the motherland's holdings. Vizcaíno claimed his own share of history by renaming the land San Diego de Alcalá, after the Franciscan saint, St. Didacus of Alcalá.

Still, Spain showed little interest in San Diego until the mid-1700s, when it began to colonize Baja California and the rest of the state, mostly in an attempt to thwart Russian fur traders who were moving down the West Coast of North America. With Catalonian captain Don Gaspar de Portolá leading the military forces—and Franciscan mission priest Father Junípero Serra leading the charge for the church—the first of a string of presidios and missions, San Diego de Alcalá, was dedicated on July 16, 1769.

After that, San Diego slowly began to amass a population that, by 1846, totalled approximately 350, most of whom set up housekeeping at the foot of the mission. But it took yet another tourist, Alonzo Erastus Horton, to appreciate the value of San Diego's harbor and surrounding land and to dream of a great city.

WHILE THE TERRITORY SUR-rounding San Diego had been inhabited by the Diegueño Indians since 1000 B.C., credit for colonization is given to several Spaniards, whose influence is widely memorialized in today's metropolis. A statue of Juan Rodríguez Cabrillo, considered the discoverer of San Diego, stands tall at the tip of Point Loma (LEFT). Across town is Mission Basilica San Diego de Alcalá, the first of 21 Catholic missions established throughout California by Father Junípero Serra (OPPOSITE).

D ESPITE ITS SLOW-TO-GROW beginnings, by the 1920s, downtown San Diego boasted a few high-rises and a mixture of retail and commercial activity (TOP). Standing in contrast to the no-nonsense architectural styles that once characterized downtown is Villa Montezuma, an ornate Victorian mansion completed in 1887 (BOTTOM). Now a museum run by the San Diego Historical Society, the grand house was built by wealthy admirers of Jesse Shepard, an internationally renowned pianist and spiritualist, to lure him to San Diego.

A restless furniture dealer from San Francisco, Horton attended a lecture one night in 1867 about the ports of California and the prospects of San Diego. "I could not slee that night for thinking about San Diego," Horton said later. "In the morning, I said to my wife, 'I am going to sell my goods and go to San Diego and build a city.' "

Within three days, Horton had disposed of his stock of furniture and booked passage on a steamer. He disembarked at what is now the foot of Market Street on April 15, 1867, and, after surveying the dusty village with a fair amount of ill-disguised contempt, declared where he thought the city should lie—by the wharf. "I have been nearly all over the United States," he said, "and that is the prettiest place for a city I ever saw." Within a month Horton had bought up 960 acres for $265—approximately 27.5 cents an acre—and New Town was launched.

By 1870, New Town was no longer a dream, but a budding city, and Horton was selling up to $1,000 worth of

S ITUATED HIGH ABOVE TOWN in Presidio Park, the Junípero Serra Museum, dedicated on July 16, 1929, occupies the former site of Serra's first mission (TOP). The facility and surrounding park were donated to the city by businessman and San Diego Historical Society founder George W. Marston. Another local philanthropist, John D. Spreckels, was an early owner of the historic Hotel del Coronado (BOTTOM). Legends and rumors abound about the "Del," including tales of a ghost that haunts one of its guest rooms.

ts each day. The population reached an astonishing 2,301, and the county had a cool 2.3 million in property assessments.

For the next 20 years, the economy of San Diego—fueled mainly by land speculation—would fluctuate wildly between boom and bust. The 1872 promise of the arrival of the Texas and Pacific Railroad sparked a wildfire of speculation and building in San Diego. But that boom went bust when attempts to sell bonds to finance the railroad went for naught.

By the mid-1880s, San Diego was once again booming, mostly because the Santa Fe-Atlantic & Pacific Railroad had arrived. The city exploded, and the population soared to 35,000. But, as with the boom of the 1870s, the 1880s version was feeding on itself. San Diego's railroad had never become more than a spur line, and the real rail traffic went north to rival Los Angeles. By the late 1880s, San Diego had crashed again, losing half its population.

At the turn of the century, as the city struggled to recover its losses, sugar heir John . Spreckels rode into town and poured millions of his family's money into a city he ould virtually own for the next two decades. It was Spreckels who ran the streetcar sys- m, two of the town's three newspapers, most of Coronado and North Island across the ly, and the landmark Hotel del Coronado. And it was Spreckels who would eventually narantee, in 1919, the completion of the railroad San Diego had always wanted. Ironi- lly, in the end, it was not the railroad, but San Diego's natural attributes—namely, its imate and its harbor—that secured its destiny as a world-class city.

From that point on, a steady stream of events served to put San Diego on the prover- al map. The Panama-California Exposition of 1915-1916, celebrating the completion of ne Panama Canal, drew thousands of tourists, who later spread the word about the city's ace and beauty. That exposition was also responsible for building much of Balboa ark, which, by the early 1920s, had become home to the world-famous San Diego Zoo.

OPENED IN 1888, THE HOTEL del Coronado (OPPOSITE) was already a crowd favorite by the time the Panama-California Exposition of 1915-1916 came to town to commemorate the com- pletion of the Panama Canal. Held in what is now known as Balboa Park, the celebration drew visitors from around the world to this newly discovered tourist des- tination (LEFT).

GRUNION HUNTING HAS LONG been a popular summertime diversion in San Diego. In this 1949 photograph, hungry beachgoers find the mother lode near Scripps Institution of Oceanography, where thousands of the wriggly little fish are washed ashore to spawn in the sand.

In 1927, when Charles Lindbergh built his *Spirit of St. Louis* in San Diego, he planted the seeds for the city's fast-developing aircraft industry. Other aviation pioneers, such as T. Claude Ryan and B.F. Mahoney, were drawn here, and Reuben H. Fleet even moved his Consolidated Aircraft Corporation to town from Buffalo, thereby laying the foundation for the future Convair and General Dynamics Corporation and enhancing San Diego's position as a major contributor to the U.S. defense complex.

The two world wars did a lot to guarantee San Diego's future as a military town. In 1917, when Congress declared war on Germany, the army dug in at Camp Kearny and the navy laid claim to North Island. Then, during World War II, the military presence further increased, and after the war, many veterans decided to stay in San Diego. Most found jobs in the city's growing defense and aerospace industries, which fueled the local economy for the next two decades.

But history repeats itself, and by the 1960s, the local aerospace industry was in de-
line, prompting *Time* magazine to declare San Diego "Bust Town, USA." This time,
however, the seeds of the city's future economy would be found elsewhere. Two of
those seeds took root in La Jolla: the opening by Dr. Jonas Salk of his Salk Institute,
and the establishment of the University of California, San Diego (UCSD). By the 1970s
and 1980s, San Diego was once again enjoying a resurgence of real estate speculation.
That, coupled with an ever growing tourism industry and a still-strong military presence, produced continued growth and redevelopment.

As San Diego approaches the millennium, most experts and civic leaders agree on
the city's promising future. The real estate industry will continue to ebb and flow, but
land will always be of prime value (San Diego consistently ranks among the 10 most expensive cities in the United States, and its housing prices lead the cost index). And the
local economy will always be driven, to some degree, by real estate speculation.

HOME TO SUCH MYSTERIOUS
creatures as starfish, sea
urchins, and anemones, the tidal
pools off Sunset Cliffs and La
Jolla provide an endless source
of fascination for San Diego's
youngest citizens.

N THE EARLY 1990S, BEFORE THE NATIONAL RECESSION HAD TOUCHED SAN DIEGO'S economy, housing prices reached a zenith. San Diegans, believing the upward spiral would never cease, were willing to pay astonishingly inflated prices for a piece of the sod. One of them, a former San Diego State University (SDSU) administrator, still tells this story on herself:

A native who had grown up in the suburb of Coronado, she'd left the upscale village when she left the family nest and had never quite been able to afford to return. Finally, after 20 years of hard work and serious saving, she'd scraped together enough to make a sizable down payment on her own Coronado home. Her tiny house, located on a little bitty lot that fronted on an alley, had a $300,000 price tag.

As soon as escrow closed, buyer's remorse set in. "Have I made a mistake? Have I paid too much?" she asked anyone who'd listen. "No, never. You can't lose in real estate here," they reassured her.

And then, at a neighborhood party, a friend introduced her to the dean of Coronado Realtors.

"Oh," she said to the Realtor. "I just bought a house in Coronado, and I'm worried . . ."

"Stop right there," he said. "Let me tell you, you can always make a killing in Coronado real estate. Why, right around the corner here, some idiot just paid $300,000 for a tiny house, on a little bitty lot, fronting on an alley."

Just as San Diego will continue to be a magnet for real estate speculators, it will remain a mecca for tourists—there's just too much to do and see and feel about this city for it to be otherwise. And the military, though its

E CLECTIC ARCHITECTURAL styles dot the coastal village of La Jolla. But one thing is constant: If there's a view to be had, there'll be plenty of windows to take advantage of it.

umbers have taken a slight dip in recent years, will continue to be a major economic contributor. But the substance of the future economy will be in the city's burgeoning high-tech, biotech, and telecommunications industries. San Diego has caught the wave of technology and is riding it into the future with confidence.

A few years ago, *San Diego Magazine*, where I serve as editor, undertook a six-part series of articles in an attempt to redefine its hometown—to tally San Diego's human and economic resources and to assess its future. In the research and writing, the authors managed to debunk a few myths about the city and its citizens. Chief among them was the misconception that San Diegans are laid-back, which for some is a euphemism for "lazy."

San Diego does have 70 miles of inviting beaches and the most temperate climate in the United States, but San Diegans are not laid-back. Most of them work longer and harder, for less money, than their counterparts in other U.S. cities—all for a little slice of paradise. They care passionately about their quality of life, and they're willing to sacrifice for it.

SAN DIEGO'S BEACHES ARE an irresistible lure for one and all. Whether it's a sunset frolic by the water or a lazy day spent basking in the sun, the sandy shores and oceanfront parks are always inviting.

SAN DIEGANS TAKE THEIR
recreation seriously, as dare-
devil mountain bikers head for
the hills east of town to test their
mettle and surfers brave the steep
cliffs north of La Jolla Shores in
their quest for the tastiest waves.

Some 25 years ago, when I was an apprentice columnist for San Diego's *Evening Tribune*, I heard a story of a young bond broker named Kent Newmark, who worked for one of the big Los Angeles brokerage houses. Newmark had decided to accept a job with a fledgling outfit in San Diego. After he made his announcement, one of his colleagues was aggressively skeptical: "How in God's name could you possibly leave all this to go down to work in a little hick town like San Diego?"

"Well," Newmark replied, "they offered me a little less money and I grabbed it."

Another point offered as evidence of San Diegans' character is their less-than-rabid support for their hometown sports franchises. In actuality, San Diego sports fans *do* back the home teams—when the teams earn their respect. In 1995, the San Diego Chargers made it to their first Super Bowl in the team's 37-year history. When they did

WHEREVER THERE'S A PATCH of unoccupied grass, an impromptu game will likely break out. Oddly enough, hardly anyone ever remembers to keep score.

some 50,000 fans turned out to form a human lightning bolt in the parking lot at Qualcomm Stadium to send them off to battle with the San Francisco 49ers.

The Padres have made it to a World Series just once in the 31 years since the franchise went major league. And after that 1984 series ended in Detroit, more than 30,000 fans were waiting at Qualcomm Stadium, at midnight, to welcome the team home—in defeat

San Diegans play hard, and they expect their sports teams to play hard. When the teams don't measure up, San Diegans would rather play than watch—play golf, tennis, rugby, or soccer, that is. They'd rather go surfing, sailing, hang gliding, waterskiing, parasailing, or boogie-boarding.

EACH YEAR, AS FOOTBALL season approaches, Chargers mania builds. The team's fortunes are determined on warm fall afternoons at Qualcomm Stadium, otherwise known as "the Q," but win or lose, fans remain philosophical. After all, there's always the beach.

Chargers General Manager Bobby Beathard, considered by many to be a football genius, also a surfer of some considerable skill. And he understands the San Diego sports psyche. In fall 1997—with the Chargers in a rebuilding mode, and the team's pitiable record reflecting it—Beathard addressed a group of civic leaders at a University Club luncheon.

He didn't like it, Beathard said, but he could understand the lack of support from some fans: "There are just too many other things to do here. I was out surfing last Sunday morning, and the sun was shining and the waves were great. But it was time for me to leave. And the guys in the water next to me asked me, 'Are you gonna go to the Chargers game today?' "

SAN DIEGO MAYOR SUSAN GOLDING HAS TAKEN TO CALLING HER HOMETOWN "The First Great City of the 21st Century." Though it's a nice catchphrase, it turns out to be much more than that. In research labs and high-tech facilities that spill across the region's mesas and fill its canyons, the labors of thousands of software engineers, molecular biologists, computer scientists, communications experts, and electronics designers are, in the words of writer Rick Dower, "inventing little pieces of the future." And they're not just inventing the future. They're producing it, making manufacturing the region's top industry—followed, in order, by the military and tourism.

"You know, we're never going to be a Los Angeles or a New York," says Richard Atkinson, a former UCSD chancellor who's now president of the nine-campus University of California system. "But I'm not sure we want to be. We want to maintain the quality of life here, because in order to attract the kind of intellectual talent that creates this high-tech base of activity, you've got to have an attractive environment."

How did San Diego come to be in such an enviable position? With the ascendance of its three largest institutions of higher learning—SDSU, UCSD, and the University of San Diego—came an academic and scientific community that is saturated with brain power. Some 30 percent of San Diegans hold college degrees, and the region boasts more Ph.D.'s per capita than any other part of the country. This population of thinkers and doers has generated a new breed of civic and industry leaders to aptly guide San Diego into the information age.

San Diego's proximity to Mexico has been the cause of seemingly insurmountable calamity and controversy in recent years. The Tijuana-San Ysidro border crossing, just 5 minutes from downtown San Diego, is the busiest in the world. Illegal immigration from Mexico has contributed to increased crime and the taxing of local health systems

IN RECENT YEARS, LOCAL ARCHItecture has moved away from the square-box design that long dominated San Diego's buildings. As a result, the downtown skyline has seen such stunning additions as the Emerald Plaza, a collection of hexagonal towers perpetually reaching for the stars (OPPOSITE). Another standout is the Geisel Library, located at the University of California, San Diego. Named for the late Theodore "Dr. Seuss" Geisel, the geometric structure is visible from Interstate 5 and is a welcome beacon for San Diegans returning from out of town (ABOVE).

id educational institutions—very real problems for San Diego and all of California.

ill, many futurists see the Mexico connection as more of a blessing than a curse.

UCSD's Chuck Nathanson, whose San Diego Dialogue has done extensive research

to our regional economy, sees the emerging Mexico market as the key to the region's

:onomic future. San Diego may be one of the 10 largest cities in the United States, but

a market, it ranks closer to 24th. The addition of

ijuana's population base to San Diego's swells the re-

ional population from 2.8 million to nearly 4.5 million.

hat could bump San Diego up to the 10th-largest mar-

et area in the United States.

Rounding out San Diego's top five industries are con-

:ruction and—a surprise to some—agriculture. Not sur-

risingly, however, the top industries complement each

:her neatly. In fact, they cross-pollinate freely. San

iego, for example, is noted for its abundance of first-rate golf courses and resorts—

orrey Pines is one of the top public courses in the country. So it seems only natural

1at such companies as Callaway, Taylor Made, Aldila, and Ashworth—all titans in the

1anufacture of golf equipment and apparel—would base their operations in the San

)iego region. Golf courses and golfing equipment; tourism and manufacturing—

1ey're natural pairings in San Diego.

Manufacturing companies are not new to San Diego. Solar Turbines Incorporated,

mainstay since 1927, provides power-generation equipment to companies worldwide.

ony Corporation has long been making television sets in Rancho Bernardo. Cubic

:orporation is still producing ticket machines for the Bay Area's BART system and

Vashington, D.C.'s Metro.

But it's the relative newcomers that are capturing the most attention. Chief among

1em—or certainly the most visible—is Qualcomm, the ultimate economic case study in

an Diego. The company was founded by Irwin Jacobs, a former UCSD professor and

D ATING BACK TO THE EARLY days of Spanish coloniza-
tion, San Diego's Latino-Hispanic roots are widely celebrated in the city today. History buffs and tourists alike frequent Old Town, where colorful vendors fill the streets and plazas, displaying such traditional Mexican crafts as handmade paper flowers (OPPOSITE). Ethnic celebrations take place year-round, including the Norteño Music Festival, held in the Spreckels Organ Pavilion at Balboa Park (ABOVE).

entrepreneur who had a vision of better, more advanced communications systems. In recent years, Jacobs has grown that vision from a 30-employee start-up to a publicly traded corporation with a headquarters complex that sprawls across the Sorrento Valley and employs 10,000. Its two main products, a satellite-tracking system and code division multiple access (CDMA) technology for wireless communication, are finding markets all over the world.

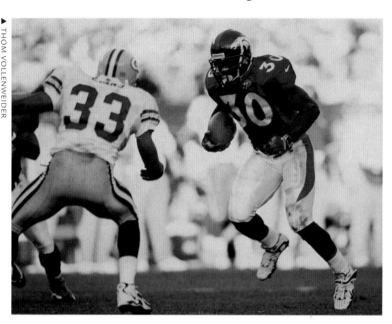

THOM VOLLENWEIDER

A model San Diegan, Jacobs isn't focusing only on improving and expanding his business—he's also committed to integrating Qualcomm into the community. When the recent publicly funded expansion of San Diego/Jack Murphy Stadium was about to be derailed because of lawsuits filed by opponents, Qualcomm stepped up to the plate, anted up the $18 million to fund the final phase of the expansion, and hit a home run with the citizens of San Diego.

Of course, this was not an entirely altruistic exercise.

WHILE THE CHARGERS FELL short of securing a bid for Super Bowl XXXII, San Diego received its share of glory from the game. Not only was the contest held at Qualcomm Stadium, but Denver Broncos running back Terrell Davis did his hometown proud by snagging the MVP award in his team's victory over the Green Bay Packers (ABOVE). Also home to Major League Baseball's San Diego Padres, the Q basks in a moment of calm as it patiently awaits the boys of summer (OPPOSITE).

As quid pro quo, the stadium now bears the Qualcomm name. Thus, the savvy Jacobs made his company an instant household name locally, and his company gets national exposure each time the Chargers or Padres throw the ball around on network TV.

Civic leaders know there are more Qualcomms out there, in different guises. In the telecommunications field alone, nearly 70 companies have already sprung up in the Sorrento Valley. Many believe that computer peripherals and software creators will break out next. Others look to biotechnology. An army of biotech researchers has already set up shop in San Diego to unravel the mysteries of myriad diseases. And from that research come new drugs produced by the multitude of pharmaceutical companies that now call San Diego home. Companies like Agouron, IDEC, and Alliance are just a few of the homegrown names that are becoming as familiar to San Diegans as Convair and General Dynamics were to generations past.

Whatever the next burgeoning industry, San Diego is poised to welcome it.

MINDFUL OF OUR SECOND-LARGEST INDUSTRY, THE MILITARY, SAN DIEGO has adjusted to the nationwide defense scale-backs with barely a blink. Gratefully, the city was spared the slash and burn of the Pacific Fleet suffered by San Francisco and Long Beach. Not that San Diego escaped unscathed: The Naval Training Center—long an institution in San Diego—began phasing out in 1993 and closed forever in 1997. Some 17 home-ported ships were also lost. But the city still has more than a dozen major military installations stretching from the marine corps base at Camp Pendleton, just south of the San Diego-Orange County line, to the navy's Ream Field, near the Mexican border.

The Department of Defense employs 136,000 active-duty personnel and civilian workers in San Diego. According to the Greater San Diego Chamber of Commerce, those jobs create another 60,000 within the region. The military's economic impact on San Diego is stunning: $1 million for every 36 military jobs. In 1996, the direct output from the military into the area was $9.61 billion.

As the 21st century looms, more changes are in store for San Diego's military sector. The Miramar Naval Air Station continues to operate, but no longer under the auspices of the navy. Top Gun has moved out, and the marines have moved in, changing the name to Marine Corps Air Station (MCAS) and bringing along even more marines than there were navy pilots and personnel.

EACH SUMMER, SAN DIEGANS are treated to a spectacular air show, courtesy of the Marine Corps Air Station. Featuring planes from the early days of military aviation, as well as an appearance by the U.S. Navy's Blue Angels, the event draws thousands of awestruck spectators (RIGHT). Especially impressive is the Red Baron Stearman Squadron, as it leaves a magnificent plume of vapor in the aftermath of a powerful vertical climb (OPPOSITE).

The navy's new high-tech Space and Naval Warfare Systems Command (SPAWAR) should be well entrenched in San Diego by the millennium. SPAWAR was created to help the military keep pace with evolving technology

MARINES AT CAMP PENDLETON go to great lengths to keep in shape—and occasionally have fun in the process. Part of their grueling routine includes the annual Mud Run, which draws some 2,500 hardy (or foolhardy) San Diegans to slip and slide toward the finish line.

in communications, computer intelligence, and electronic warfare. The good news for San Diego, aside from the romantic appeal, is that the program's total operating budget is $4.1 billion, most of which should be spent locally. Plus, SPAWAR should create hundreds of new jobs.

In yet another example of cross-pollination, the military's economic clout has a direct fallout on tourism and travel. The Department of Defense spends millions each year on business trips to San Diego, and the Convention & Visitors Bureau has developed sophisticated programs to encourage the practice.

Truly, San Diego has been a formidable tourist magnet since the Panama-California Exposition of 1915-1916—or, if you count those adventurous Spaniards, since 1542. And while some may grouse about the continual influx of wide-eyed, camera-toting escapees from less-pleasurable locales, it's probably more a conditioned reflex than a serious concern.

In actuality, tourists help polish San Diego's crown jewels. Balboa Park, with its world-famous San Diego Zoo, is the biggest and brightest. But Sea World, the Wild Animal Park, Hotel del Coronado, and Mission Bay Park are hardly lesser gems.

The zoo is not just a place where animals hang out—it's a renowned facility for research into animal behavior and preservation. Sea World and the Wild Animal Park enjoy similar distinction. Hotel del Coronado is a resort destination unto itself, drenching its guests in luxury and providing the ultimate San Diego experience. And Mission Bay—one of the most ambitious public water parks in the world—is about to undergo $200 million in improvements.

Showing an appreciation for both the whimsical and the financial, Legoland, America's first theme park to honor interlocking toys, will soon be open in neighboring Carlsbad. Among the colorful acres of commercial flower fields in San Diego's North County, the Danish toy company is building its only U.S. theme park—an attrac-

IN SEARCH OF THEIR OWN EXtremes, approximately 1,500 intrepid souls take a beating from the turbulent sea during the mile-long La Jolla Rough-Water Swim. Held each September since 1916, the event is the largest competition of its kind in the nation.

tion expected to draw nearly 2 million visitors each year. And at the south end of the county, the recently built Arco Olympic Training Center—the only permanent U.S. Olympic training facility—is already being promoted as a visitor attraction.

The San Diego Convention Center also draws a steadily increasing tide of tourist business. And when conventioneers are finished doing what they do, nightlife awaits in the Gaslamp Quarter, only a heartbeat away. Once San Diego's version of Skid Row, the Gaslamp now overflows with restaurants, nightclubs, and retail shops. On any night of the week, you're likely to see conventioneers sipping martinis elbow-to-elbow with the locals. Or cruising the cigar shops in search of the perfect stogie. When they do go home, they remember. And when they come back to visit again, they bring their families.

While the builders and the entrepreneurs are busy creating places for visitors to play, ·ty leaders and promoters are occupied with courting events. San Diego has hosted ·vo Super Bowls and expects to be in the regular rotation for future games. In 1996, ·ne city played host to the Republican National Convention, reaping the sort of inter-ational news coverage and visibility that simply can't be bought.

These are some of the reasons why—despite the best efforts of some to discourage ·—San Diego continues to grow. And the trend doesn't seem to be slowing: The county ·opulation is expected to reach 3.8 million by 2020, requiring more than 400,000 new ·ousing units. Phoenix, watch out!

Obviously, not everyone heeds our bumper sticker: Welcome to San Diego-Now Go ·Iome! And maybe we're all the better for it. ∎

WHETHER YOU'RE CHALLENG-ing the ocean head-on or chasing a vapor trail into the sun-set, the sandy shores of San Diego have a way of releasing the exuber-ance in everyone.

A CITY IN MOTION: HOMEBOUND commuters leave a colorful trail of light along Harbor Drive at dusk (OPPOSITE), while the city's signature red trolley cars, blurred by speed, create a show of their own (ABOVE).

I T HAS BEEN SAID THAT THE POWER of the world works in circles. Repeated frequently around town in art and architecture, perhaps these patterns also reflect the fullness of life in San Diego.

BY THEIR NATURE, CONVENTION centers tend to be inwardly focused. But San Diego's has massive overhead windows designed to bathe the interior in natural light (OPPOSITE). Further illustrating the city's love for the great outdoors is the facility's distinctive terrace, which hosts alfresco parties and events year-round (ABOVE).

E VERY BAYSIDE HOTEL WORTH
its salt has a marina to accommodate its waterborne guests.
The graceful contours of the San
Diego Marriott Hotel & Marina
seem to shelter visiting and resident boats in a warm embrace
(OPPOSITE). Mimicking the curves
of its neighbor, the amphitheater
at the San Diego Convention Center provides a welcome opportunity for joggers and strollers to
catch their breath and watch the
boats glide by (LEFT).

DAWN OR DUSK, THERE'S ALWAYS
a view to be found along
San Diego's shorelines, and most
locals have a favorite spot for a
romantic sunset picnic or an early
morning scenic run.

NESTLED AT THE FOOT OF THE skyline is bustling Seaport Village, which features the century-old Broadway Flying Horses Carousel among its 14 acres of attractions (PAGES 50 AND 51). A stone's throw from some of downtown's toniest hotels, this nostalgic collection of shops and restaurants has a bustling plaza where dancers, singers, and musicians represent the diverse cultures of San Diego.

NEW YEAR'S EVE AT SEAPORT
Village sparks a mammoth
celebration for local families. As
the fireworks display makes an
explosive finish overhead, there's
still time to grab one more snack
from the popcorn cart before
heading home.

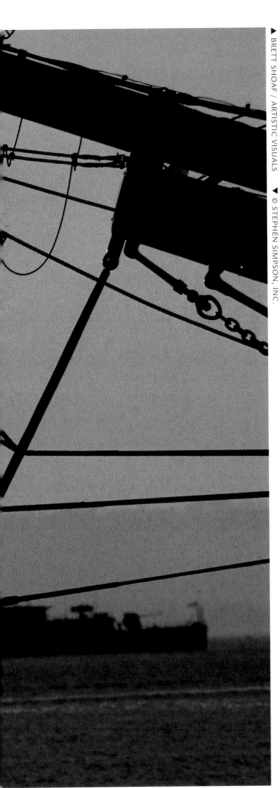

HEADING TO PORT, A NAVY vessel passes behind the bow of the historic *Star of India* (OPPOSITE). As the sky ignites with sunset fire, the *Star* stands stalwart, a patient parent welcoming home one of its brood (ABOVE).

BUILT IN 1863 AS AN IRON MER-
chant ship, the *Star of India*
was originally launched at the Isle
of Man and has circumnavigated
the globe 21 times. Currently
moored at the San Diego Maritime Museum, the venerable vessel is the world's oldest active ship.

THE OLD AND THE NEW: The 1898 *Berkeley*, now anchored at the Embarcadero as part of the city's maritime museum, spent most of its life as a ferryboat in San Francisco before moving permanently to San Diego in 1973 (PAGE 58). The ship's long history includes evacuating thousands of refugees to Oakland in the aftermath of the 1906 earthquake. In contrast, the *Island Princess*, an ultramodern cruise ship that boasts seven passenger decks, elegant lounges, a movie theater, and a casino, floats proudly against an ominous sky (PAGE 59).

O UT OF ITS NATURAL ELEMENT, a ship sits high and dry as it awaits repairs (PAGES 60 AND 61). Already bolstered by San Diego's proximity to the Pacific, the city's shipbuilding industry has actually benefited from the closure of naval bases elsewhere in the state, and the imminent arrival of even more aircraft carriers promises a healthy repair and maintenance business for years to come.

THE NUTS AND BOLTS OF KEEP-ing San Diego up and running are often tended to in out-of-the-way places or under the cover of night. Though it's innocent looking from the outside, this cement warehouse seems ready to burst at the seams (OPPOSITE).

Elsewhere, railway workers take advantage of the late-night lull between trains to repair a section of track (ABOVE).

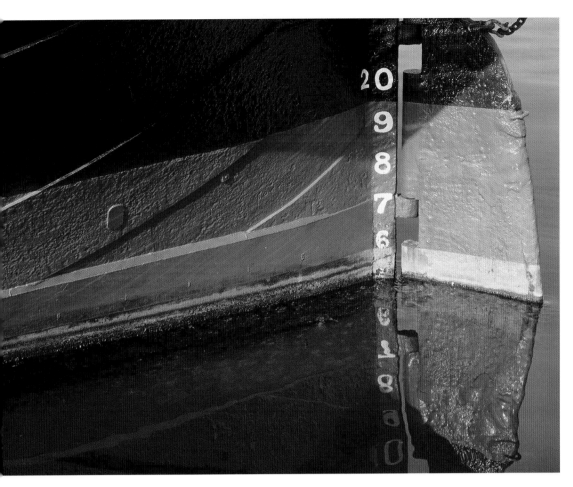

A TYPICAL MORNING ON THE Embarcadero finds workers minding the intricacies of the city's long-lived maritime industry—a vital business sector that continues to be a major employer.

SAN DIEG

ATERFRONT APPARITIONS:
Shifting light and fog
sometimes stir the imagination to
see what isn't there—or to question
what really is (LEFT). Perspectives
change as night descends on San
Diego Bay and the glittering skyline comes into clear focus (PAGES
68 AND 69).

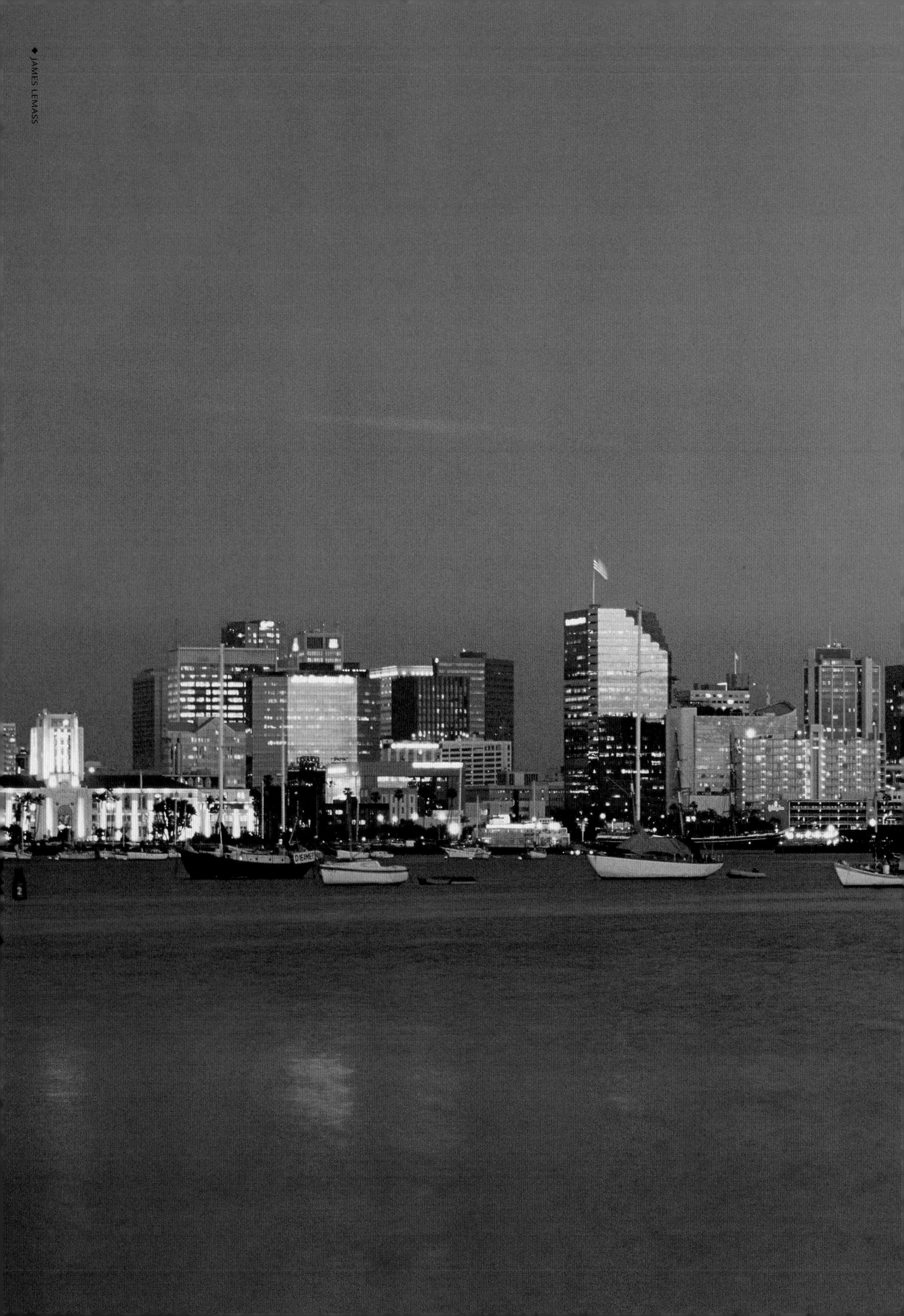

◆ JAMES LEMASS

MAJESTIC PALM TREES STAND sentinel outside area buildings. Of the countless varieties that dot the regional landscape, only one, the California fan palm, is native to San Diego County.

THANKS TO AN ABUNDANCE OF spectacular, sun-drenched vistas, windows are understandably plentiful in San Diego. Both the Koll Center on lower Broadway (OPPOSITE) and the San Diego Design Center in the Golden Triangle (ABOVE) know the value of unobstructed views.

RIGHT YELLOWS AND ORANGES adorn the exterior of the Village Hillcrest, home to a foreign- and art-film theater and an eclectic collection of restaurants (OPPOSITE). Similarly, the warm tones of the Aventine at La Jolla—with its offices, hotel, fitness center, and restaurants—reflect San Diego's temperate climate (LEFT).

AN UPWARD GLANCE IN SAN Diego is likely met with striking architectural details. While the giant glass triangles atop the San Diego Design Center flood the foyer with natural light (ABOVE), the atrium in the Wyndham Emerald Plaza boasts its own geometric forms that complement the hotel's hexagonal exterior (OPPOSITE).

ORNATE DETAILS ADD CHARAC-
ter to buildings old and
new. The facade of the downtown
YMCA reflects a time when more
attention was paid to exterior
embellishment (OPPOSITE). But
even today, who can resist the
comical character surveying the
scene at the Spreckels Theatre
(TOP) or the not-so-warm-and-
fuzzy gargoyle guarding the fountain at the Rancho Bernardo Inn
(BOTTOM)?

MOSAIC-TILED DOMES ARE AN oft-repeated theme among San Diego's historic, Spanish-style buildings. Among them are down-town's Santa Fe Depot (OPPOSITE), the Balboa Theatre in Horton Plaza (RIGHT), and Balboa Park's Casa del Prado (LEFT).

I F IT'S TRUE THAT ART GIVES THE highest quality to every moment, then moments spent admiring the water bearer in front of the art deco County Administration Building are to be cherished (OPPOSITE). Set your sights on Balboa Park, and you'll find the figure of an Aztec woman, resplendent on a base of Mexican tile (LEFT).

A S IF HAVING THE PACIFIC Ocean in our backyard weren't enough, ponds and fountains are abundant in San Diego, especially in beautiful Balboa Park (OPPOSITE). Its 1,174 acres are also home to the Botanical Building and Lily Pond, once used as a therapy pool for naval hospital patients during World War II (CENTER), as well as the House of Charm, site of the San Diego Art Institute Gallery (RIGHT).

YOU'LL ALMOST ALWAYS SPOT a creamy white blossom in the Lily Pond at Balboa Park (OPPOSITE). Alas, if none are to be found, stroll next door to the Museum of Art, which guarantees a few moments of peaceful appreciation while gazing at Georgia O'Keeffe's *The White Trumpet Flower* (ABOVE).

BALBOA PARK PROVIDES A BAN-
quet for the senses. Often
missed among all the other visual
delights are the beautiful architectural details on many of the park's
buildings. Look closely enough
and you'll spot a likeness of
Michelangelo's *David* on the
Museum of Art façade (OPPOSITE,
BOTTOM LEFT).

THE SPANISH ARCHITECTURE that began its proliferation during the Panama-California Exposition of 1915-1916 lives on in Balboa Park. As new buildings have been added and old ones restored, the expressive style, with its love of ornamentation, has been faithfully followed.

A SPIRIT OF CREATIVITY ABOUNDS in Balboa Park, where street musicians showcase their talents up and down El Prado and a grassy patch is the perfect site for an impromptu jam session (ABOVE). Nearby, a female form in contemplative repose provides inspiration for the many artists who create and sell their treasures in the Spanish Village Art Center (OPPOSITE).

IF DANCING IS TRULY THE LOFTIEST of arts, then Balboa Park is a lofty place indeed. Showcasing the many cultures of San Diego, a colorful dancer re-creates Mexico's Aztec beginnings (OPPOSITE LEFT), while an African troop taps out its own native steps (ABOVE). And just to make sure the rhythm never dies, a pair of Mexican dancers are forever fixed in curtsy and bow in a nearby mural (OPPOSITE RIGHT).

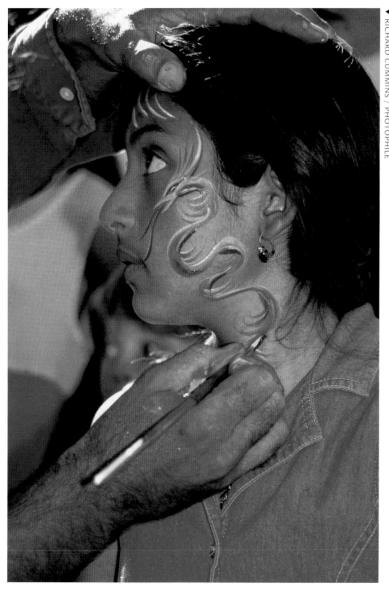

SIGHTS, SOUNDS, AND SMELLS: There's no need to wait for festival days to find entertainment in Old Town State Historic Park. Music and dance are everywhere, and the art of face painting has developed far beyond the traditional butterflies and flowers. Meanwhile, the aroma of home-made tortillas on the griddle is certain to lure folks to one of San Diego's countless Mexican restaurants.

As part of a Cinco de Mayo festival in Old Town State Historic Park, the Battle of Puebla is reenacted to commemorate Mexico's unlikely victory over France on May 5, 1862. Similar celebrations are held throughout San Diego and nearby Tijuana.

IMMIGRANTS ATTEMPTING TO FLEE Mexico face an uncertain future that is oftentimes belied by the cordial relations between San Diego and its neighbor to the south. The border fence stands as a stark reminder of the disparity between the two countries, and even those who successfully make the harrowing crossing must face a barrage of obstacles, including another man-made barrier—the freeway.

No OBJECT IS TOO OBSCURE or off-the-wall to become a work of art. Even the familiar form of the cactus, a denizen of the deserts of San Diego and Baja California, lends itself to adornment. With a little judiciously applied paint, the prickly plant trades its stark status for a chance to be someone's pièce de résistance.

A TRADITIONAL SPORT OF Mexico, bullfighting demands an acute mastery of skill and courage, not to mention an affinity for colorful costumes and capes. Tijuana's Bullring-by-the-Sea is among the local arenas that draw spectators from both sides of the border.

TAKE A STROLL THROUGH OLD Town State Historic Park and enjoy a journey back in time, when life was a little slower and long johns were the lingerie of choice. A smiling sun greets visitors to the six-block district, which includes the original Mason Street School, the city's first public schoolhouse.

R ECOGNIZING THE VALUE OF San Diego's architectural past, in 1971, the Save Our Heritage Organisation began moving several of the city's historic houses to Heritage Park in Old Town. Now open to the public, the restored Victorian structures have found new life as the ideal home for a variety of modern tenants, including shops, a synagogue, and a bed-and-breakfast.

A FEW SHORT YEARS AGO, THE turn-of-the-century buildings of the Gaslamp Quarter played host to a seedy assortment of questionable merchants and skid-row inhabitants. Today, with its restaurants, cigar shops, galleries, and retail establishments, the revitalized, 16.5-block district is home to more than 300 thriving businesses (PAGES 110 AND 111).

LIVE R&B [OPEN] DANCING

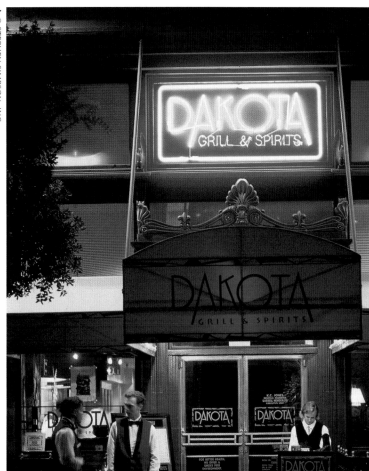

Restaurants and clubs, sushi bars and hotels, hardware stores and vintage clothing shops—all share space in the Gaslamp Quarter. After dark, the streets teem with locals and out-of-towners in search of the perfect martini, the finest meal, and the most aromatic cigar.

DINING BECOMES AN ART FORM in San Diego, as top chefs find ever more imaginative ways to present their culinary creations and please their patrons' palates. Here, Deborah Scott from Kemo Sabe shows off her delicious dish (TOP), while James Boyce from Loew's Coronado Bay Resort delights in the catch of the day (BOTTOM).

F ROM ONE END OF THE SPEC-
trum to the other, San
Diegans savor the local cuisine.
Dining alfresco with an ocean
view offers the ultimate gastro-
nomic and visual luxury (BOTTOM),
but just as satisfied is the hungry
lunchtime crowd that stretches
out the door and down the street
at Las Cuatro Milpas, a mainstay
in the city since 1933 (TOP).

CHEAP EATS WITH A FLAIR abound throughout the city. Eschewing subtlety, diners and delis announce themselves with bold neon greetings. But if a leisurely afternoon spent idling over food and wine is more to your taste, any number of restaurateurs are only too happy to oblige.

H ORTON PLAZA'S FESTIVE
atmosphere lures shoppers and theatergoers year-round
(PAGE 118), while the art deco Corvette Diner attracts its own share
of visitors, thanks to its Corvette
centerpiece, portraits of popular
singers, and soda-fountain fare
(PAGE 119).

NAMED FOR ALONZO ERASTUS Horton, one of the city's founding fathers, Horton Plaza is an 11.5-acre entertainment complex in the heart of downtown. With its shops, restaurants, and 14-screen cinema, it's a favorite destination for locals and visitors, who are frequently spotted looking for the perfect memento of their stay in San Diego.

A N EXPLOSION OF COLOR EN-
cased in neon lights bright-
ens the nighttime sky, enticing
revelers to cross the portals and
join the festivities inside (PAGES
122 AND 123).

THE CASINO AND AZTEC THE-aters sit patiently in the Gaslamp Quarter, awaiting an uncertain future. Remnants of a time before multiplex cinemas, these historic venues evoke memories of a grandeur now faded and distant.

T HE SERENE GARDEN OUTSIDE
Mission Basilica San Diego
de Alcalá is an ideal place for quiet
reflection or an after-church gathering. With an inspirational statue
as a constant companion, visitors
find solace and friendship in the
peaceful surrounds.

FOUNDED IN 1769 AND MOVED to its current Mission Valley location five years later, Father Junípero Serra's Mission Basilica San Diego de Alcalá is today a Catholic parish church, as well as an attraction for history buffs (PAGES 130 AND 131).

As Father Serra moved northward through California, he established his second—and largest—mission at San Luis Rey in Oceanside (LEFT). Recalling the original mission style of architecture, the Immaculate Conception Catholic Church was dedicated in 1919 in what is today Old Town State Historic Park (OPPOSITE).

THE VIEW FROM ATOP MOUNT Soledad in La Jolla offers an unobstructed panorama of San Diego, from the ocean to the mountains. Easter services are held annually at the bottom of the 43-foot-tall cross that crowns the peak.

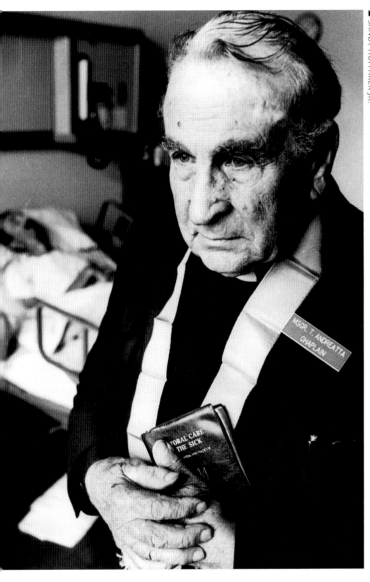

SAN DIEGO'S ETHNIC DIVERSITY blows full gale through the religious community. Solemnly reverential or energetically spiritual, worship services and ministries span the range of the many faiths celebrated in the city.

SIMPLE WHITE HEADSTONES
stand in quiet formation
at Fort Rosecrans National Cem-
etery, the final resting place for
more than 50,000 soldiers who
served their country honorably
(OPPOSITE). Echoing that stark
symmetry, the flower fields of
Carlsbad evoke a colorful har-
mony all their own (LEFT).

ITH SPIRES REACHING to the sky, the Gothic-modern Mormon temple in La Jolla stands as an object of wonder to those passing by on Interstate 5.

P ERCHED HIGH ON A HILL overlooking the ocean, the Immaculata Catholic Church and its distinctive blue dome are visible for miles. The interior of the Span- ish Renaissance cathedral, located on the campus of the University of San Diego, is a treasure of stained glass and artwork.

VIRTUALLY EVERY BUILDING ON the campus of the University of California at San Diego is an architectural wonder. A gathering place for students during the day, the distinctive Price Center wel- comes concerts and special events after dark (OPPOSITE), while the downright quirky outward ap- pearance of the engineering build- ing balances the serious subject matter taught within (ABOVE).

WITH THEIR ABUNDANCE OF angles, boxes, and curves, buildings in Southern California are designed to catch the sunshine and lure it inside. Opened in 1987, Regents Square I & II offers more than 300,000 square feet of multi-purpose space.

THE 90-DEGREE ANGLES AND wide planes of the Louis Kahn-designed Salk Institute for Biological Studies are softened by the perpetual motion of water (OPPOSITE). Elsewhere in the city, color and neon help temper otherwise sharp forms to eye-pleasing effect (LEFT).

S PRINGTIME COVERS THE CLIFFS
of La Jolla with vibrant
purples and yellows, providing a
picturesque backdrop for photographers. Similarly, a fairy-tale aura
surrounds John Cole's Book Shop
in La Jolla, framed by its vine of
lavender blossoms.

I N SAN DIEGO, A SHORT DRIVE from one neighborhood to another becomes an impromptu tour of local architectural styles. From a cozy house in La Jolla (TOP) to a colorful row of cottages in Oceanside (BOTTOM) to the tile roofed homes in North Park (OPPOSITE), each can be said to fully represent the San Diego lifestyle.

WORLD-CLASS CITY

A DRIVING FORCE IN THE CITY for decades, San Diego's military heritage is celebrated at the annual Grand Military Encampment, held at the Embarcadero Marina Park (OPPOSITE). The pomp and circumstance of life in the armed forces also makes its mark in civilian circles, from local theater productions (TOP) to marching bands on parade (BOTTOM).

▼ SANDY HUFFAKER JR.

MILITARY DEPLOYMENT MAY be a sad routine for San Diego families, but seeing loved ones return home is oh, so sweet (OPPOSITE). As if their rigorous training routines weren't enough, soldiers often blow off steam while awaiting their orders by challenging one another to contests of physical prowess (ABOVE).

NAMED FOR HEROIC AVIATOR Charles Lindbergh, the San Diego International Airport/ Lindbergh Field is one of the world's few airports situated in the heart of a city. As planes descend, they must carefully pick their way through a maze of high-rise buildings before reaching the harborside runway.

LONG IMMERSED IN MILITARY trappings, San Diegans are unabashedly proud and thrilled by displays of naval air power. Whether the occasion calls for an F-14D Tomcat (OPPOSITE TOP), the ever popular Blue Angels (TOP), or a Navy Seals display team (OPPOSITE BOTTOM), locals never tire of the exciting maneuvers and daring stunts.

H ANG GLIDING ALONG THE cliffs at Torrey Pines State Reserve is about as close to flying as you can get. Perhaps emulating the area's snowy white seagulls, gliders take in a bird's-eye view of sunbathers on "clothing optional" Black's Beach.

L INKING DOWNTOWN WITH
the island of Coronado, the
San Diego-Coronado Bay Bridge
makes a graceful, two-mile sweep
across the water. When fog rolls in,
boats passing beneath the span
see only a suspended apparition,
the two endpoints obscured in
the damp haze.

A S THE SINKING SUN CASTS A golden glow over Belmont Park's Giant Dipper, the enormous wooden roller coaster awaits its next group of fearless riders.

BY DAY, THE SAN DIEGO-Coronado Bay Bridge offers views of Mexico, the downtown skyline, Coronado, the naval sta-tion, and the bay. After dark, the span itself is the main attraction, creating a mystical light show against the nighttime sky.

BUILT IN 1925, THE GIANT Dipper has taken its rightful place on the National Register of Historic Places. With more than 2,600 feet of track, the venerable wooden roller coaster is the centerpiece of Belmont Park, which lures all manner of fun-seekers with its rides, indoor swimming pool, and countless other diversions.

M ISSION BAY WELCOMES hordes of swimmers, boaters, skiers, windsurfers, crew teams, and kayakers. And that's just in the water. On sunny weekends, paths around the bay are alive with joggers, skateboarders, bicyclers, and plain old folks just out for a stroll (PAGES 170-173).

JUST IN CASE THE SUN AND SKY don't provide enough color, San Diegans bring their own. Bright banners make for an eye-catching spectacle along Shelter Island (TOP), and the inside of a sky-surfing balloon reveals a dazzling display of geometrics (BOTTOM).

LINED UP ALONG MISSION BAY, sailboats adorned in pinks, blues, and yellows seem eager to be on the water, perhaps to greet the dipping, twirling kites that will soon fill the sky above them.

SERIOUS SURF

GRAHAM BLAIR

S URFING IS ALWAYS SERIOUS business in San Diego, where nearly everyone gets in on the act. But when the Bud Surf Tour comes to town, wave riders of the highest caliber display eye-popping form and technique as they challenge Mother Nature head-on.

SOME SAY THAT ONCE SURFING gets in your blood, it never leaves. Plenty of seniors demonstrate their still-agile form on San Diego's beaches, where form of a different kind is also on display.

LOCALS DON'T ABANDON THE ocean just because the sun goes down. Midnight contests put a different spin on hanging 10, as surfers work the waves in the moonlight.

IN 1990, TWIN BROTHERS MARK and Brian Simo founded Carlsbad-based No Fear, fueling the new "attitude wear" segment of the apparel industry. Their popular line of sportswear, which includes T-shirts emblazoned with catchy phrases, captures the mystique surrounding surfing and other extreme sports.

S AN DIEGO ARCHITECT STUART Resor knows how to combine his passions for wood-paneled cars and tasty waves. Founder of the Wavecrest Woodie Meet and cofounder of the California Surf Museum, he poses proudly atop his classic 1940s Mercury Woodie, with a trusty surfboard close at hand.

Locked up after a long day of rescues, jellyfish stings, and sunburns, the lifeguard station at Mission Beach patiently awaits another round of swimmers, surfers, and sunbathers (PAGES 184 AND 185).

186

SUNSET MAY SIGNAL DAY'S END for some beachgoers, but plenty of others are just getting started. One evening ritual finds locals patiently scanning the sky for the legendary "green flash," which occurs during the split second after the sun dips below the horizon.

CHILDREN FIND MUCH TO SATisfy their endless curiosity along the San Diego coast. Building sand castles, searching for sea treasures, and maneuvering among the myriad wide, flat rocks can make for hours of fascinating adventure.

I N 1997, TO KICK OFF THE FIRST annual International Sandfest on Fiesta Island, 80 sculptors from 18 countries collaborated on the Lost City of Atlantis. The largest and tallest sand castle ever built, the six-story work of art required 74,000 cubic yards of sand (LEFT AND TOP RIGHT). No less impressive is the annual U.S. Open Sandcastle Competition on Imperial Beach, which draws artists from around the world to create spectacular sculptures that tickle the fancy of onlookers (BOTTOM RIGHT AND OPPOSITE).

Life's a Beach San Diego

SAN DIEGANS ARE A COMPETI-tive sort. From the La Jolla Rough-Water Swim (OPPOSITE) to a traditional lifeguard competition (CENTER) to the aquatic leg of a triathlon (RIGHT), locals work overtime inventing different ways to test their mettle in and out of the water.

ONE WAY TO FIND THE AREA'S best views is to hop on your bicycle. Even casual riders are rewarded with easily accessible cliff-top vistas of the ocean. For those with a little more stamina, a grueling adventure in the mountains promises unparalleled panoramas of the valleys below.

MUCH MORE THAN JUST A mode of transportation, bicycles give their riders an opportunity to challenge the elements. A little bit of hiking may be involved, but payoff in the form of a downhill or airborne rush makes it all worthwhile.

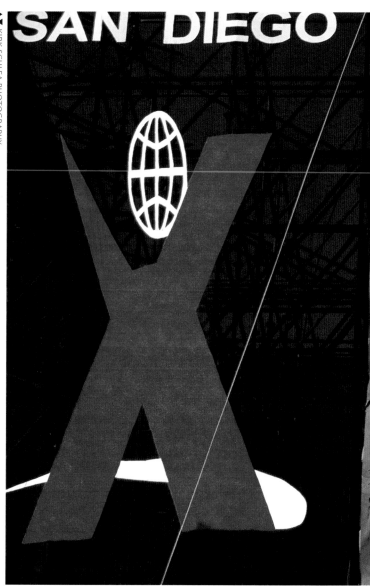

SAN DIEGO

FOR THOSE WHO FIND TRADI-tional recreation too tame, the X Games are heaven-sent. Mariners Point in Mission Bay challenges rock climbers to defy gravity, while the street luge competition takes participants to the outer reaches of the county, where steep hills are the ideal venue for the death-defying downhill plunge.

J UMPING TO AVOID AN UNTIMELY collision, an in-line skater is oblivious to the watchful eye of a downtown wall painting (OPPOSITE). Not so for these leisurely pedestrians, who boldly return the mural's piercing stare (ABOVE).

204

W HETHER ENJOYING THE
simplicity of a pickup
game or dreaming of greater glory
in the NBA, San Diego's teenagers
comb the inner-city streets and
playgrounds in search of an
empty court.

ACHIEVING EXCELLENCE CAN BE a lonely pursuit. Long after most athletes have called it a day, you'll find a few tenacious souls working hard to refine their skills on the courts, courses, and fields of San Diego County.

P ATIENTLY AWAITING THEIR next call to action, these baseball helmets seem ready to jump from their well-ordered nests (OPPOSITE). Forming a symmetry all their own, rows of concrete cylinders steadfastly defy motion (ABOVE).

SINCE MOVING UP TO THE Majors in 1969, the San Diego Padres have made it to the World Series only once—in 1984. But whether the club's riding high in the championship hunt or languishing in last place, hometown heroes like third baseman Ken Caminiti (TOP), center fielder Steve Finley (BOTTOM LEFT), pitcher Sterling Hitchcock (OPPOSITE), and right fielder Tony Gwynn (BOTTOM RIGHT) inspire rabid devotion in fans.

▲ KIRK SCHLEA PHOTOGRAPHY

IKE THE PADRES, THE SAN Diego Chargers have made it to the big show only one time. Nevertheless, every year brings fresh dreams of a shot at the Super Bowl, and the talent and drive of such players as linebacker Junior Seau (LEFT) draw thousands of hopeful onlookers to Qualcomm Stadium (OPPOSITE TOP).

PERHAPS NOT AS HIGH-PROFILE as football heroes or baseball stars, other San Diego athletes make indelible marks of achievement on their respective sports. Here, boxer Terry Norris proudly drapes himself with his championship belts (OPPOSITE), and bowling legend Joe Norris cradles the ball that he has repeatedly rolled to victory (ABOVE).

S AN DIEGANS ARE KNOWN TO be especially zealous when it comes to hitting the links, but with countless first-rate courses and the ability to play year-round, who wouldn't be? Torrey Pines, a municipal course positioned on a bluff overlooking the ocean, is the site of the Buick Invitational of California (OPPOSITE). That tournament—along with the annual Mercedes Championships, held in La Costa from 1969 to 1998—always draws the best of the pros, including the inimitable Tiger Woods (TOP).

FROM THE POSH GROUNDS OF the Rancho Santa Fe Polo Club in affluent North County (OPPOSITE) to the Lakeside Rodeo in laid-back East County (ABOVE), the speed and skill of horses and their riders are always good for thrills and spills.

A ND AWAY THEY GO! AS STEEDS fly around the oval at the Del Mar Race Track, grandstand spectators anxiously clutch their tickets, dreaming of a big payoff at the finish line.

B UILT WITH WPA FUNDS IN 1937, the seaside Del Mar Thoroughbred Club was co-founded by Bing Crosby and Pat O'Brien. Recently remodeled, the summertime equestrian venue is a favorite haunt of Tinseltown celebrities looking for action "where the surf meets the turf."

A T NIGHT, ORDINARY THINGS sometimes take on an extraordinary appearance. It's all work and no play as an industrious crane creates a dazzling display on the harbor (ABOVE). Producing its own spectacular light show is a twirling ride at the Del Mar Fair, where fun is always the first order of business (OPPOSITE).

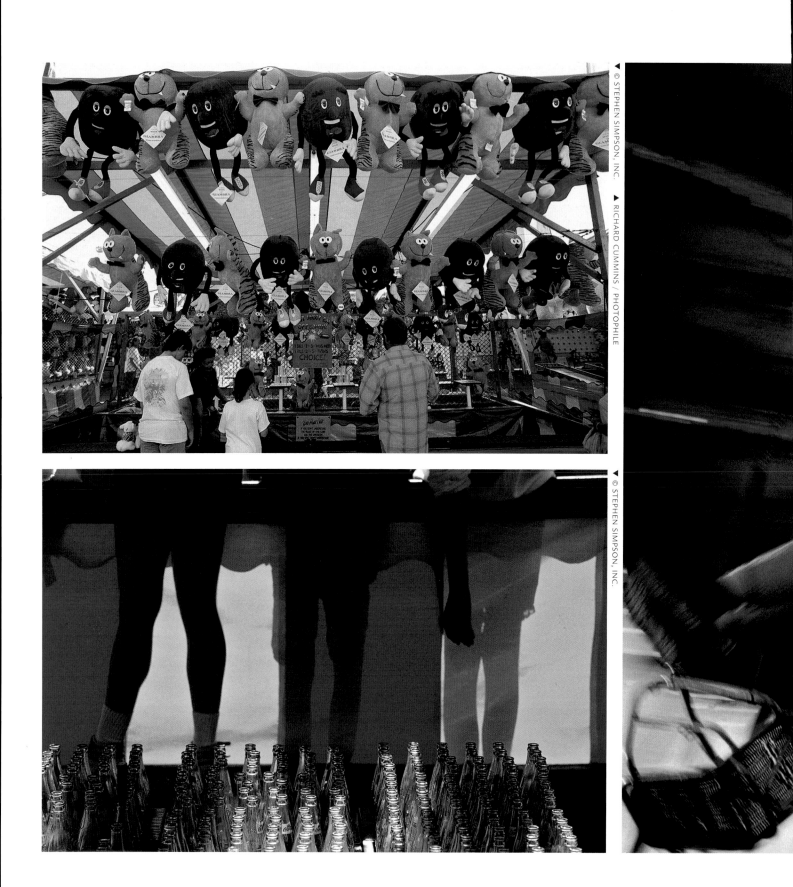

EACH YEAR, WHEN THE COUNTY fair descends on Del Mar, thousands of revelers flock to the midway fun zone to savor legend- ary cinnamon rolls, take the ride of a lifetime, and try their luck at games of chance and skill.

AUTUMN SIGNALS THE START OF apple festival time in Julian, an old gold-mining town located approximately 60 miles northeast of San Diego. Hungry folks invade the mountain village to sample one of Mom's famous apple pies (THIS PAGE) or a jar of homemade honey from one of many roadside stands (OPPOSITE).

S AN DIEGO'S ETHNIC GROUPS come together each year to celebrate their diversity at the International Friendship Festival in El Cajon. Begun in 1990, the event draws enthusiastic participants who don traditional costumes, perform native songs and dances, and share delicacies from their homeland.

232

THANKS TO A TEMPERATE climate and plenty of TLC, the region's crop of fresh produce keeps San Diegans smilin' year-round. Often, the fruits of the earth find their way to a local farmer's market, but when fall arrives, they also lend their color to festive seasonal displays.

Ramona Historical Society

Take a drive east of San Diego to the bedroom community of Ramona, where life is simpler and hardy folks still like to survey their spread in the glow of a new day. There, in the Valley of the Sun, you'll find the Guy B. Woodward Museum, which displays the tools and other artifacts once used by settlers to tend their fields and manage their livestock (BOTTOM).

S AND DUNES IN THE IMPERIAL Valley create an ever shifting landscape of ridges and valleys (OPPOSITE), while the peaks sur-rounding the El Capitan Reservoir remain comfortably static as the waters rise and fall around them (ABOVE).

S PRINGTIME BRINGS AN EXPLO- sion of wildflowers to the Anza-Borrego Desert, blanketing the stark region with brilliant color (OPPOSITE). To the south, stately cacti in the arid surrounds of Baja California give company to the coyotes and jackrabbits that comb the terrain looking for sustenance (ABOVE).

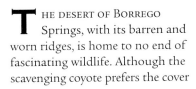

THE DESERT OF BORREGO Springs, with its barren and worn ridges, is home to no end of fascinating wildlife. Although the scavenging coyote prefers the cover of darkness to hide his nefarious deeds, lounging lizards seek only a warm spot in the sun to snooze the day away. Some reptilian residents are content to spend their days and nights at the world-famous San Diego Zoo, noted for its wide range of rare and exotic creatures (RIGHT).

STRANGE CRITTERS POINT THE way to the Children's Museum, a former electrical warehouse in downtown San Diego. Designed to enlighten and entertain young minds, exhibits like this dino-car are both created and admired by ingenious visitors to the interactive facility.

B ALBOA PARK HAS MORE THAN
its share of museums that
celebrate technological ingenuity,
from the San Diego Aerospace
Museum, which offers an over-
view of the country's history off
the ground (OPPOSITE TOP), to the
San Diego Automotive Museum,
which brings visitors back down
to earth with its antique cars and
motorcycles (BOTTOM). Also in the
park are the Hall of Champions
Sports Museum, which pays tribute to homegrown athletic prowess (OPPOSITE BOTTOM), and the
Natural History Museum, which
showcases all creatures great and
small (TOP).

246

AT SEA WORLD, VISITORS CAN get up close and personal with the likes of Shamu the Killer Whale and his somewhat smaller, but no less impressive, friends. The 150-acre marine-life entertainment park on Mission Bay features daily shows and more than 20 exhibits to delight both young and old.

WHILE SOME SEALS INDULGE in the cushy, well-fed life that only Sea World can provide (ABOVE), others opt for a more vagabond existence, popping up occasionally on Seal Beach in La Jolla and plaintively seeking a handout (OPPOSITE).

SCRIPPS INSTITUTION OF Oceanography is world renowned for its dedication to marine science. Opened in 1992 as the public education center for Scripps, the Birch Aquarium displays more than 3,000 types of marine life and is a favorite field trip destination for students (PAGES 250 AND 251).

JOAN EMBERY, GOODWILL AM-bassador for the San Diego Zoo since 1970, was a regular guest on *The Tonight Show Starring Johnny Carson*, where she entertained audiences with a parade of exotic animals. On or off the air, the zoo's cuddly cast of characters always manage to put on a great show.

ACCUSTOMED TO THE MANY animal lovers that visit the San Diego Zoo each year, this curious giraffe noses around, perhaps looking for an afternoon treat.

S TRUTTING HIS STUFF AT THE San Diego Zoo, this zebra proudly shows off his striped togs (RIGHT). Elsewhere, a creature of a different sort borrows the look to make her own fashion statement while sunbathing on South Mission Beach (LEFT).

A LEAP OF FAITH: IT'S ARGUABLE whether the better show is to be found at the zoo, where agile chimps fly from limb to limb (ABOVE), or on the set, during the filming of the motion picture *Raven* (OPPOSITE).

KEN JACQUES

ROBERT T. NOBLE

HOLLYWOOD HAS LONG BEEN attracted to San Diego, even as far back as 1959, when *Some Like It Hot*, starring Jack Lemmon in fetching drag and the ever glamorous Marilyn Monroe, was shot at the Hotel del Coronado (OPPOSITE LEFT). Today, it's not uncommon to see the likes of Burt Reynolds (LEFT) and other stars, in town to film movies and TV shows.

S AN DIEGO'S PERFORMING ARTS scene offers something for everyone, including remarkable revues starring female impersonators (OPPOSITE). These talented divas go to great lengths—and plenty of beauty supply stores—to achieve that perfect look. And sometimes, the effect is even better than the real thing.

EVERY ONCE IN A WHILE, SAN Diegans don their best sandals and dress shorts to savor the city's full measure of theatrical and musical performances. Not just for seniors are the snappy productions staged at the Lawrence Welk Village retirement community in Escondido (TOP LEFT). Other crowd pleasers include the San Diego Repertory Theatre, which features plays like Luis Valdez's *Zoot Suit* (TOP RIGHT) and *Buddy . . . The Buddy Holly Story* (BOTTOM LEFT), and the La Jolla Chamber Music Society, which makes its mark with such celebrated guests as cellist Yo-Yo Ma (BOTTOM RIGHT).

THE PERFORMING ARTS ARE growing in stature in San Diego, thanks to extraordinary local and visiting talent. Leading such memorable performances as *La Traviata*, renowned conductor Richard Bonynge is a frequent guest of the San Diego Opera (TOP). Keeping on their toes are local favorites Sylvia Poolos and Max Tchernychev, pictured here during the California Ballet Company's production of *Swan Lake* (BOTTOM).

KEN JACQUES

EVERY YEAR, THE GREATER SAN Diego Chamber of Commerce presents the INSIGHTS World Conference, which invites world leaders and role models to teach and inspire. In 1996, political potentates Mikhail Gorbachev (RIGHT) and Jimmy Carter (LEFT) enthralled crowds at the Convention Center. Poet Maya Angelou (OPPOSITE LEFT) and former British Prime Minister Margaret Thatcher (OPPOSITE RIGHT) graced the stage the following year.

AMID A DARKENING SKY, CLOUDS part briefly to form a sunny halo over the Wild Animal Park (ABOVE). Similarly, a small, solitary sandbar assumes its own circular shape as it peeks through the waves at Silver Strand State Beach (OPPOSITE).

OBLIVIOUS TO THE BEAUTY
of a twilight sky, obsessed
golfers hustle to complete one
more hole before that last light
fades and darkness obscures the
course (PAGES 268 AND 269).

BIDDING FAREWELL TO YET AN-
other glorious day, colorful
kites and a lone hot-air balloon
float in a golden sky, as if to reach
up and grab the precious remaining moments of daylight.

T HOSE WHO REJUVENATE BODY
and soul on the waters of
San Diego regretfully head for
safe harbor and dry land as the
day takes its leave, pausing for
a moment to reflect on an afternoon well spent.

AT THE ENTRANCE TO SAN Diego Bay, the Point Loma peninsula welcomes the last of the stragglers as fog envelops the coastline in a damp blanket of gray (LEFT). Guiding home the day's voyagers is the Cabrillo Lighthouse, situated at the tip of the harbor (PAGES 276 AND 277). It's only fitting that the historic beacon was named for the first Spanish explorer to set foot on these fair shores, thereby uncovering what San Diegans now know is a treasure more precious than gold.

PROFILES IN EXCELLENCE

A LOOK AT THE CORPORATIONS, BUSINESSES, PROFESSIONAL GROUPS, AND COMMUNITY SERVICE ORGANIZATIONS THAT HAVE MADE THIS BOOK POSSIBLE. THEIR STORIES—OFFERING AN INFORMAL CHRONICLE OF THE LOCAL BUSINESS COMMUNITY—ARE ARRANGED ACCORDING TO THE DATE THEY WERE ESTABLISHED IN SAN DIEGO.

AGOURON PHARMACEUTICALS, INC. ■ ALLIANCE PHARMACEUTICAL CORP. ■ AMERICAN MANUFACTURING CONCEPTS, INC. ■ AMERICAN RED CROSS ■ AMERICAN SPECIALTY HEALTH PLANS ■ THE ARROWHEAD GROUP OF COMPANIES ■ AUROR BIOSCIENCES CORPORATION ■ BANNISTER STEEL, INC. ■ BARONA CASINO/BARONA BAND OF MISSION INDIANS ■ THE BE & BREAKFAST INN AT LA JOLLA ■ BF GOODRICH AEROSPACE/AEROSTRUCTURES GROUP ■ BRAUN THERMOSCAN ■ BROW MARTIN HALLER & MCCLAIN, LLP ■ CHILDREN'S HOSPITAL AND HEALTH CENTER ■ THE CITY OF SAN DIEGO ECONOMI DEVELOPMENT DIVISION ■ COMSTREAM ■ COX COMMUNICATIONS ■ CYMER INC. ■ DOUGLAS E. BARNHART, INC. ■ DP CONSTRUCTION, INC. ■ DUCKOR SPRADLING & METZGER ■ THE EASTLAKE COMPANY ■ EMBASSY SUITES SAN DIEGO BAY AN LA JOLLA ■ ENOVA CORPORATION ■ FPA MEDICAL MANAGEMENT ■ GENETRONICS, INC. ■ GOLDEN EAGLE INSURANC CORPORATION ■ GOODWILL INDUSTRIES OF SAN DIEGO COUNTY, INC. ■ GRAY CARY WARE & FREIDENRICH LLP ■ GREATE SAN DIEGO CHAMBER OF COMMERCE ■ HEWLETT-PACKARD ■ HIGH TECHNOLOGY SOLUTIONS, INC. ■ INVITROGEI CORPORATION ■ JACOR COMMUNICATIONS, INC. ■ JENNY CRAIG, INC. ■ KERCHEVAL ENGINEERS/PBS&J ■ KSWB-TV ■ TH LIGHTSPAN PARTNERSHIP, INC. ■ LUCE, FORWARD, HAMILTON & SCRIPPS LLP ■ MARDX DIAGNOSTICS INC. ■ MCM ARCHITECTS & PLANNERS ■ MCMILLIN COMPANIES ■ MERRILL LYNCH ■ MONTGOMERY WATSON AMERICAS ■ MORGAN RUM RESORT & CLUB ■ NATIONAL UNIVERSITY ■ NBC 7/39 ■ NCR CORPORATION ■ NOKIA MOBILE PHONES AMERICA ■ NORTH ISLAND FEDERAL CREDIT UNION ■ ODGEN ENVIRONMENTAL AND ENERGY SERVICES ■ OVERLAND DATA ■ PACIFIC BELL ■ PARADISE VALLEY HOSPITAL ■ QUALCOMM INCORPORATED ■ QUINTILES CNS THERAPEUTICS ■ R&B REALTY GROUP OAKWOOD CORPORATE HOUSING ■ RESIDENCE INN BY MARRIOTT-LA JOLLA ■ SAFESKIN CORPORATION ■ SAN DIEGO COMMUNITY COLLEGE DISTRICT ■ SAN DIEGO CONVENTION & VISITORS BUREAU ■ SAN DIEGO CONVENTION CENTER CORPORATION ■ SAN DIEGO DATA PROCESSING CORPORATION ■ SAN DIEGO HOSPICE CORPORATION ■ SAN DIEGO NATIONAL BANK ■ SAN DIEGO STATE UNIVERSITY ■ SAN DIEGO UNIFIED PORT DISTRICT ■ SANYO NORTH AMERICA CORPORATION ■ SCRIPPSHEALTH ■ SHARP HEALTHCARE ■ SIERRA OPTICAL ■ SOLAR TURBINES INCORPORATED ■ SONY TECHNOLOGY CENTER-SAN DIEGO ■ SOURCE SERVICES CORPORATION ■ SOUTHWEST AIRLINES ■ SUNDSTRAND POWER SYSTEMS ■ SUNRISE MEDICAL INC. ■ SYMPHONY TOWERS ■ TOPS STAFFING SERVICES, INC. ■ U.S. GRANT HOTEL ■ UNIDEN SAN DIEGO RESEARCH AND DEVELOPMENT CENTER ■ UNIVERSITY OF CALIFORNIA, SAN DIEGO ■ UNIVERSITY OF SAN DIEGO ■ WAXIE SANITARY SUPPLY ■ WELLS FARGO & CO.

1852-1960

1852
WELLS FARGO & CO.

1870
GREATER SAN DIEGO CHAMBER OF COMMERCE

1873
LUCE, FORWARD, HAMILTON & SCRIPPS LLP

1880
PACIFIC BELL

1887
SAN DIEGO STATE UNIVERSITY

1898
AMERICAN RED CROSS

1904
PARADISE VALLEY HOSPITAL

1910
U.S. GRANT HOTEL

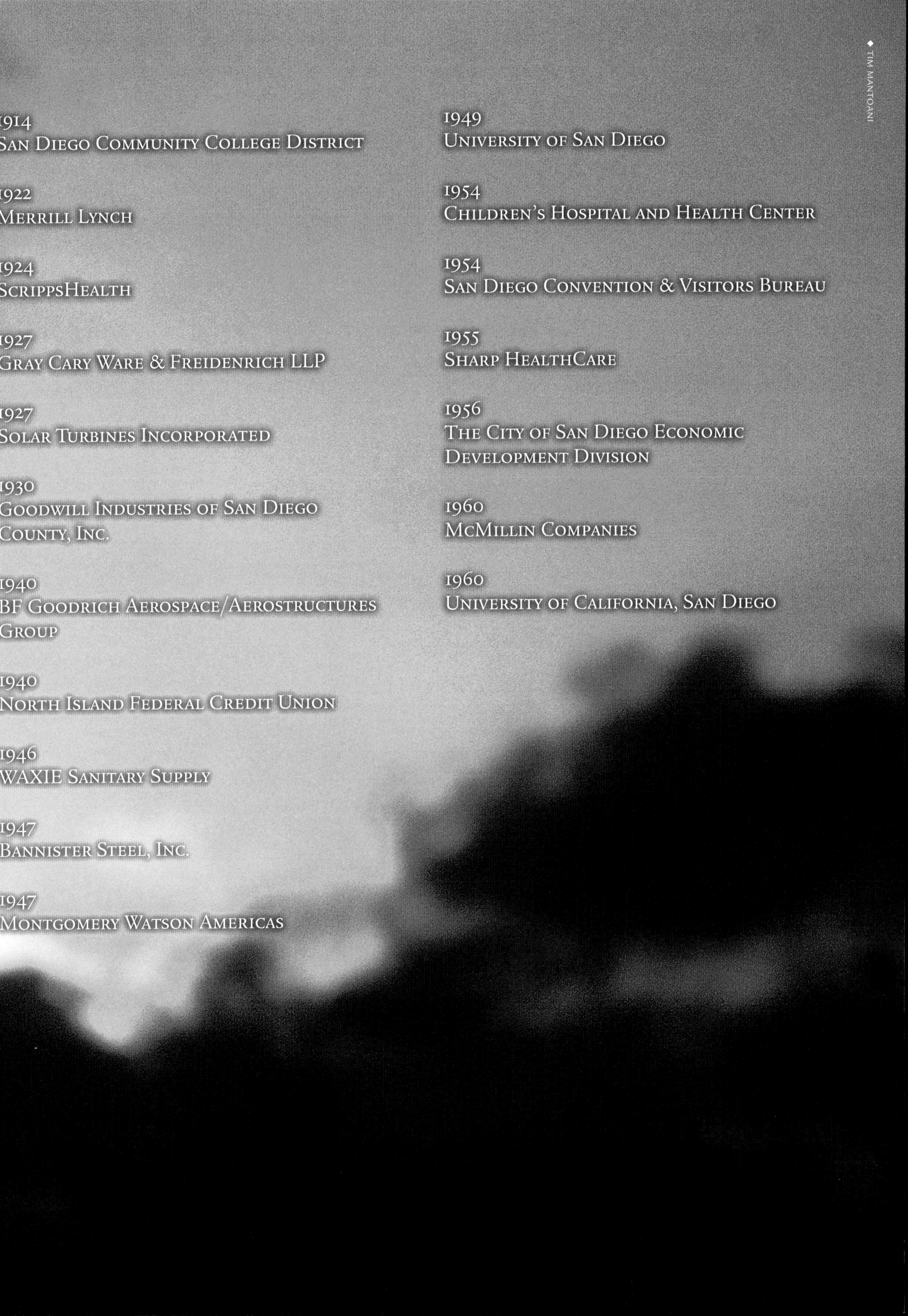

1914
SAN DIEGO COMMUNITY COLLEGE DISTRICT

1922
MERRILL LYNCH

1924
SCRIPPSHEALTH

1927
GRAY CARY WARE & FREIDENRICH LLP

1927
SOLAR TURBINES INCORPORATED

1930
GOODWILL INDUSTRIES OF SAN DIEGO
COUNTY, INC.

1940
BF GOODRICH AEROSPACE/AEROSTRUCTURES
GROUP

1940
NORTH ISLAND FEDERAL CREDIT UNION

1946
WAXIE SANITARY SUPPLY

1947
BANNISTER STEEL, INC.

1947
MONTGOMERY WATSON AMERICAS

1949
UNIVERSITY OF SAN DIEGO

1954
CHILDREN'S HOSPITAL AND HEALTH CENTER

1954
SAN DIEGO CONVENTION & VISITORS BUREAU

1955
SHARP HEALTHCARE

1956
THE CITY OF SAN DIEGO ECONOMIC
DEVELOPMENT DIVISION

1960
MCMILLIN COMPANIES

1960
UNIVERSITY OF CALIFORNIA, SAN DIEGO

WELLS FARGO & CO.

FOUNDED IN 1852 TO SERVE WESTERN PIONEERS, WELLS FARGO & C• soon opened in San Diego's Old Town and immediately began pr• viding vital banking and express services. Today, in San Dieg• County, Wells Fargo operates a network of 122 outlets with more tha• 200 automatic teller machines (ATMs), and provides local bankin• services through 1,500 employees and resident senior managemen•

Wells Fargo is the eighth-largest bank holding company in the United States, with nearly 2,000 outlets and more than 4,000 ATMs in 10 western states.

"In San Diego, Wells Fargo customers enjoy specialized services from a cadre of professional bankers. Our expertise covers the needs of both businesses and individuals," says Sam Brown, senior vice president. "With decision makers that live in San Diego, we understand the needs of the San Diego community and, as one of the community's leading banks, we take pride in being an innovator in product development, delivery, and service."

SERVING SAN DIEGO'S INDIVIDUALS

Wells Fargo's Retail Banking group offers a complete line of financial products and services featuring both traditional branches and in-store supermarket locations. In-store branches and banking centers feature a full line of bank services seven days a week and are conveniently located in most Vons stores, with additional outlets in Ralph's and Albertson's locations.

Wells Fargo's Premier Banking service delivers highly personalized service. An ability to meet client needs regarding questions on investments, financial planning, and money management has created a new level of personal service in the finance industry. In addition, Private Client Services provides investment management, trust, full-service brokerage, credit, custody, and private banking to a select group of clients whose financial situations require a customized management approach. Local portfolio managers, brokers, trust officers, and credit specialists provide sophisticated services for these high-net-worth clients.

SERVING THE COMPLETE NEEDS OF BUSINESS

Wells Fargo's services aren't limited to just retail clients. Via its Business Banking group, Wells Fargo is th• nation's number one small-business lender. The bank's 12-person San Diego team delivers lines of credit, equipment financing, and real estate loans to businesses wit• annual revenues below $10 millio•

The Commercial Banking grou• serves companies above $10 millio• in annual revenues. Formed in th• late 1970s, the San Diego Region• Commercial Banking Office provides knowledge of local industrie• and significant decision-making authority to the San Diego marketplace. The staff of 25 provides a full complement of banking se• vices to business customers.

To augment Wells Fargo's ful• complement of corporate service• Wells Capital Management provides a wide range of investment management services to institutional clients in San Diego and throughout the United States. This 100 percent-bank-owned subsidiary manages $37 billion in assets for corporations, foun-

tured Finance. Asset Origination provides acquisition, bridge, and mezzanine financing to highly leveraged or nontraditional real estate transactions. Commercial Mortgage Origination is the permanent commercial real estate loan arm of the bank. Structured Finance provides financing to companies undergoing a change in capital structure as a result of an acquisition or a change in ownership.

...tions and endowments, pension ...ans, hospitals, and the bank's ...ternal mutual fund families ...tagecoach and Overland Express). ...ells Capital Management has ...pertise in both fixed-income ...quidity, intermediate, and mu-...cipal) and equity (value, growth, ...all-cap, and international) ...anagement.

Wells Fargo also provides San ...iego companies a full range of ...ofessional employee benefit ...rvices. As trustee, the bank's ...stitutional Trust establishes ...d administers qualified plans ...ch as 401(k)s, profit sharing, ...d defined benefit pensions. ...ells Fargo presently has more ...an 2,000 client relationships ...d administers more than $30 ...llion in employee benefit trust ...sets.

DIVERSITY OF
USINESS SERVICES

...eal estate project financing is ...ovided through the San Diego ...fice of the Real Estate Group. ...ne of the largest construction ...nders in the United States, Wells ...argo is committed to gaining a ...orough understanding of a bor-...wer's company, projects, and ...perations. Wells Fargo has a ...ommitment to real estate clients ...ationwide through a network of ... offices.

The Wells Fargo HSBC Trade ...ank serves businesses with inter-

national activities. The Trade Bank is a joint venture between Wells Fargo and Hong Kong Shanghai Bancorp Holdings, plc. Customers benefit from a full range of trade services, trade finance, foreign exchange, and international payments and cash management products, plus access to the HSBC network of more than 5,000 offices worldwide.

Another example of this versatility is Wells Fargo's Capital Markets Group, which offers a broad line of traditional and non-traditional financial products through three operating divisions: Asset Origination, Commercial Mortgage Origination, and Struc-

Wells Fargo rounds out its commitment to the community through its Corporate Community Development Group, which is responsible for coordinating Wells Fargo's $45 billion, 10-year Community Reinvestment Act (CRA) loan program. The program ensures that the credit needs of low-income families and small businesses served by Wells Fargo are properly addressed.

Wells Fargo has certainly become a leader in its field. Its success can be attributed to a vast array of services, delivered locally through specialized departments. "By segmenting the market and providing appropriate and value-added services to each market, we've demonstrated the ability to meet the community's needs," says Brown. "We're really providers of anytime, anywhere banking."

AS AN ADVOCATE FOR BUSINESSES LARGE AND SMALL, THE GREATE San Diego Chamber of Commerce exists to create and captu regional economic prosperity. Established in 1870, the Chamb is one of the oldest entities in San Diego and now one of th largest such organizations in the country, with more than 4,20 members. ■ Chamber members comprise more than one-thir

of the San Diego region's employment base, says Lynelle Berkey, executive vice president and chief operating officer of the organization. "These are exciting times for us, especially 1998," says Berkey. "We've consistently been able to show our members that there is real value to being a member of the Chamber."

CHAMBER FACTS

The Greater San Diego Chamber of Commerce is actually the sixth-largest chamber in the United States. The Chamber's board of directors is composed of 72 executives, representing businesses of all sizes. Forty percent of Chamber

member businesses are minority owned.

The Chamber also has 80 full-time employees to service its member organizations. Programs developed and presented by the Chamber include Public Policy; INSIGHTS, the Chamber's annual speaking symposium; Member Services; Information/Economic Research; Sales; Marketing; and the Small Business Development Center.

In an effort to include a wide variety of businesses in the Chamber, membership dues in the bureau start at $400 per year, and increase to $1,000 per year for the Circle of Influence level of membership.

With more than 4,200 members, it's impossible to pinpoint a specific demographic for Chamber members. "We've got representatives of nearly every industry," says Berkey, "from manufacturing to high-tech and everything in between."

MEMBERSHIP BRINGS PRIVILEGES

Today, the Greater San Diego Chamber of Commerce has evolve into an extremely influential bus ness organization, providing a powerful voice for members at the local, state, and national levels. "The Chamber has a long track record of winning victories at all levels that make San Diego a bet ter place to live and work," says Berkey. "We are committed and focused on government efficienc education, infrastructure, region alization, military, and other issue that affect the economic base of San Diego."

Other direct benefits of being a part of the Chamber include networking, marketing/exposure bottom-line discounts, and profes sional services/information service

Networking is aided by the more than 200 annual events presented by the Chamber. These events include special speakers and seminars that draw attendance from 50 to 5,000, offering excellent opportunities to make influential contacts among other chamber members.

Membership in the Chamber carries with it a wide range of privileges. As Chamber members, businesses have direct access to a variety of marketing vehicles. Each member receives four listings in the *Business Referral Directory*, a

AS AN ADVOCATE FOR BUSINESSES LARGE AND SMALL, THE GREATER SAN DIEGO CHAMBER OF COMMERCE EXISTS TO CREATE AND CAPTURE OPPORTUNITY TO LEAD THE REGION TO PROSPERITY.

THOMAS MAGNO

al resource circulated through-
t the region. Members also have
e opportunity to sponsor other
blications and events, which
ovide additional exposure to
e overall business community.
Chamber members reap more
ngible benefits in the form of
centives and discounts. A Blue
ield Health Services Plan is
ailable to members. Other such
nefits include substantial dis-
unts on Golden Eagle Workers'
mpensation insurance, AT&T
ng-distance service and toll-free
one numbers, Paychex payroll
vices, and GTE Mobilnet corpo-
te and employee cellular benefit
ogram. Other member-to-member
scount programs offer addi-
nal savings and opportunities.
"There really are so many value-
ded benefits that we offer," says
rkey. "One achievement from
97 that we're especially proud
is our San Diego Chamber of
mmerce benefits package. That's
product that we took statewide.
offers an exceptional product to
e business community, and as
goes statewide, it will give us
en higher buying power."
Annually, more than 100,000
ople worldwide contact the orga-
zation for referrals to local busi-
sses, and Chamber members
rtainly top the list of recom-
endations. But far more than
mply a vehicle for exposure, the
namber functions as a valuable
source for the information busi-
sses need to succeed. Small
isiness Development seminars
d free business counseling, for
ample, are just a couple of ways
e Chamber helps members stay
rrent with economic and busi-
ss environment developments.

ISIGHTS

ch year, the Chamber produces
ore than 200 events for the San
ego community and beyond.
nose events include the Busi-
ss to Business Expo, an annual
eeting of Chamber members, the
dres Luncheon, the Congressional

THE MISSION BASILICA DE ALCALA,
WHICH WAS ESTABLISHED IN
1776, WAS THE FIRST MISSION
IN GREATER SAN DIEGO (TOP).

WITH SAN DIEGO BAY AND POINT
LOMA IN THE BACKGROUND, THOU-
SANDS OF GREATER SAN DIEGO
RESIDENTS ENJOY THE CORONADO
ISLAND PUBLIC GOLF COURSE
EACH YEAR (BOTTOM).

Luncheon, the Distinguished
Leadership Luncheon, the Spotlight on San Diego Business, and
the Women's Forum.

But the biggest profile event
each year is the INSIGHTS Symposium. "It's an event the Chamber
and the whole community can
be proud of," says Berkey. Each
October, INSIGHTS brings prominent politicians, entertainers, writ-
ers, and inspirational speakers to
the San Diego Convention Center
to address the important issues

of the day. Recent speakers have
included Margaret Thatcher,
Mikhail Gorbachev, Tom Peters,
Maya Angelou, and Larry King.

In addition to the speaking
symposium, INSIGHTS includes
the Student Leadership Program;
the Tour of Technology, a two-day
exhibit in the convention center;
and a golf tournament. "INSIGHTS
is really about globalization," adds
Berkey. "It's about bringing the
world together. And what better
place than San Diego?"

THE LAW FIRM OF LUCE, FORWARD, HAMILTON & SCRIPPS LL was founded in 1873, and has experienced steady growth sinc then due to its ability to adapt to the ever changing needs clients. Luce Forward takes a service-oriented approach to i practice, regularly surveying clients on their level of satisfactio and taking responsibility for staying informed about client business and industry trends.

Luce Forward's philosophy of service also extends to the community. The firm has a healthy tradition of providing community service, leadership, and pro bono services. Those services have been extended to the San Diego Opera, Old Globe Theater, University of San Diego, Children's Hospital, Holiday Bowl, Boy Scouts, Girl Scouts, YMCA, Burn Institute of San Diego, and many other community groups.

"We pride ourselves on hiring lawyers who are the best of the best," says Luce Forward partner and executive committee member Charles A. Bird, "and these lawyers quite often take on leadership positions in many of these community organizations."

FROM THE BEGINNING

The firm's founder, Moses A. Luce, a Civil War hero and Medal of Honor recipient, set the tone for service in the community. Luce drafted San Diego's first city charter, and the organizational meeting for the first San Diego Public Library was held in his law office. The Luce legacy was carried on by his son and grandson, Edgar A. Luce Sr. and Edgar A. Luce Jr.

Charles H. Forward was admitted to the California bar in 1911, and a merger with his practice in 1929 created the firm Stearns, Luce & Forward. F. Tudor Scripps joine the firm as a Stanford graduate in 1934. Another Stanford graduate, Thomas M. Hamilton, signed on in 1959. Since then, the law firm's name has stood as Luce, Forward, Hamilton & Scripps. The addition of 45 lawyers in February 1994 made it possible for Luce Forward to open offices in Los Angeles, San Francisco, and New York.

Headquartered in downtown San Diego, Luce Forward maintains an office in La Jolla; the firm also opened an office in Chicago in October 1996. Of Luce Forward's 173 lawyers across the country, 127 are based in San Diego.

TAKING CARE OF BUSINESS

Luce Forward draws upon the talent and experience of its practice groups and six offices to respond to the various needs of its clients, regardless of the size or complexity of the legal issue.

San Diego-based clients of Luce Forward might be individuals who need help with estate planning, representatives of start-up companies, or local companies with Nasdaq listings. Or a client might be the City of San Diego, which was the case in early 1997, when local activists challenged the expansion and financing of Jack Murphy Stadium (now known as Qualcomm Stadium).

The firm's major areas of practice include litigation, general business, securities, employment and labor law, real estate, tax, bankruptcy, finance, products liability and warranty, international, technology, environmental, white-collar

THE LAW FIRM OF LUCE, FORWARD, HAMILTON & SCRIPPS LLP WAS FOUNDED IN 1873 BY MOSES A. LUCE, A CIVIL WAR HERO AND MEDAL OF HONOR RECIPIENT (LEFT).

LUCE, FORWARD, HAMILTON & SCRIPPS LLP IS HEADQUARTERED IN DOWNTOWN SAN DIEGO AT ONE AMERICA PLAZA (RIGHT).

G. SILVERSTEIN

WASHINGTON STOCK PHOTO, MICHAEL HOWELL

me, and trusts and estates. Luce orward's San Francisco and Los ngeles practices include a wide nge of litigation, real estate, d commercial matters. Luce rward also represents clients roughout the nation on all as- cts of litigation, insurance cov- ge, and reinsurance, and is a ember of the Pacific Rim Advisory uncil, a network of major inter- tional law firms in more than important commercial centers ound the world.

A unique aspect of Luce rward's practice is the firm's ience Advisory Group. The oup's expertise and knowledge ver a wide spectrum of technical d scientific areas, which makes it

an invaluable resource for legal cases involving real property trans- actions, regulatory compliance, business liabilities, environmental assessments, feasibility studies and remediation, forensic scientific analyses, and site assessment. These scientists are available to attorneys in all of Luce Forward's practice areas, and offer advice, answer questions, and conduct research on everything from complex regu- latory problems to reviewing and conducting cost analyses on work done by outside consultants.

A SPECIAL MISSION

The mission statement of Luce Forward says that the firm aims to provide quality, efficient solu-

tions to its clients' legal needs in order to enable clients to achieve their goals and objectives. "Mission statements may sound alike, but what's behind them is what really counts," says Bird. "In all our prac- tices, we are creative, aggressive problem solvers. There's no typical way to resolve a dispute or develop a project. We have searched for creative solutions for our clients for more than 125 years, and that's what we'll continue to do."

After more than a century, Luce, Forward, Hamilton & Scripps LLP continues the tradition begun by its founder, serving both clients' needs and the San Diego commu- nity with the firm's talents and expertise.

FROM ITS OFFICES IN (CLOCKWISE FROM TOP LEFT) LOS ANGELES, NEW YORK, CHICAGO, AND SAN FRANCISCO, AS WELL AS THE SAN DIEGO AND LA JOLLA OFFICES, THE LUCE FORWARD MISSION STATEMENT REMAINS THE SAME: TO PROVIDE QUALITY, EFFICIENT SOLUTIONS TO CLIENTS' LEGAL NEEDS IN ORDER TO ENABLE CLIENTS TO ACHIEVE THEIR GOALS AND OBJECTIVES.

ASK ANY OF CALIFORNIA'S 32 MILLION RESIDENTS WHOM THEY RE on for their telecommunications needs and an overwhelming majority will give the same answer: Pacific Bell. The compar that provides cutting-edge telecommunications and da services throughout San Diego and the rest of the state—fro standard telephone services to high-speed Internet dial-u

CLOCKWISE FROM TOP:
FROM STANDARD TELEPHONE SER-
VICES TO HIGH-SPEED INTERNET
DIAL-UP ACCESS TO DIGITAL WIRE-
LINE AND WIRELESS SERVICES,
PACIFIC BELL IS A DAILY PRES-
ENCE IN THE BUSINESS AND PER-
SONAL LIVES OF THE PEOPLE IT
SERVES.

TODAY, PACIFIC BELL EMPLOYS
50,000 CALIFORNIANS AND TAL-
LIES AN ANNUAL PAYROLL OF
$2.7 BILLION.

IN SAN DIEGO COUNTY ALONE,
PACIFIC BELL SPENDS MORE THAN
$300 MILLION ANNUALLY TO IM-
PROVE ITS TELECOMMUNICATIONS
NETWORK INFRASTRUCTURE TO
BETTER SERVE CUSTOMERS.

access to digital wireline and wire-less services—is a daily presence in the business and personal lives of the people it serves.

HISTORY OF INNOVATION
Established more than 120 years ago as the American Speaking Telephone Company (ASTC), the firm has enjoyed a history of in-novation. In 1878, for example, it introduced the first telephone exchange in the state—and the third in the world—in San Francisco. Two years later, it merged with National Bell Telephone Company (now AT&T) to create the Pacific Bell Telephone Company, an im-mediate leader in the industry. That same year, Pacific Bell helped place the first long-distance call in the West—between San Francisco and San Jose.

More than a century later, Pacific Bell is still setting the stan-dard in telecommunications. In 1983, AT&T formed Pacific Telesis Group—a holding company for Pacific Bell and other telecommu-

nications ventures—which spun off as an independent, publicly traded organization a year later. And in 1996, Pacific Telesis agreed to become part of SBC Communi-cations Inc., an international leader in the telecommunications indus-try with more than 31 million access lines and 4 million U.S. wireless customers, as well as investments in the telecommunications busi-ness in eight foreign countries.

Today, Pacific Bell employs 50,000 Californians and tallies an annual payroll of $2.7 billion. More than 4,700 of these employ-ees reside in San Diego County, putting more than $208 million worth of salaries into the local economy.

MORE THAN JUST TELEPHONE SERVICE
Pacific Bell provides local tele-phone service to 77 percent of Californians, who make more than 60 million calls annually on its network. To maintain its service quality, Pacific Bell spends more

than $1 billion a year on its net-work infrastructure, including $300 million spent in San Diego County alone.

But as California approaches the millennium, Pacific Bell has gone well beyond its original tel phone services, embracing the di tal era with its own Internet servic Pacific Bell Internet; high-speed ISDN service; and dedicated dig tal lines. In addition, through Pacific Bell Mobile Services, the company offers digital wireless communications that include pa ing, messaging, and other advance services.

In the future, Pacific Bell pla to take advantage of industry de regulation, which has opened up the $7.3 billion long-distance ma ket and $2.9 billion video marke "The growth potential for our business is staggering," says Robe E. Ferguson, regional president. "There is exploding demand for Internet access and high-speed data services, not to mention th increased use of wire-line and wir less phones. We will continue to invest and be a leader in these area

With all these services, it's no surprising that the company has received wide recognition and ac claim. Recently, Pacific Bell and its parent company were ranked as Most Admired Telecommuni-cations Company in the World by *Fortune* magazine. And as the awards and the services keep mu tiplying, Pacific Bell sees nothin but opportunity in its future. "Customers tell us they want to be able to buy all their telecom-munications services from one company," says Ferguson. "Pacif Bell is focused on being that one company."

F ROM ITS ORIGINS MORE THAN 100 YEARS AGO AS A COLLEGE FOR TRAIN-
ing elementary school teachers, San Diego State University (SDSU)
has grown to become one of the country's finest institutions of
higher learning. It has also made enormous contributions to the
quality of education—and the quality of life—in the San Diego region.
SDSU's goals are simple: teaching, scholarship, and service. And in

striving to reach them, the university helps to prepare its students
to lead society toward a promising
future.

In scholarship and research,
SDSU has clearly distinguished
itself. It offers bachelor's and
master's degrees in more than
140 majors and 10 joint doctoral
degree programs. Its commitment
to graduate education and its broad
range of baccalaureate programs
prompted the Carnegie Foundation
for the Advancement of Teaching
to classify SDSU as a Doctoral II
university.

The primary reason for the
school's success is the caliber of
its faculty, who compete nationally
for research and educational grants
and contracts. Their success rate
is significantly above the national
average: During the 1995-1996 fiscal year, they garnered an unprec-
ented $74 million in new funding.

ROOTED IN SAN DIEGO
Although it's more than a century
old, the university has not forgot-
ten its roots. It produces nearly
80 percent of the teachers in San
Diego schools, says Stephen L.
Weber, SDSU president. But the
teaching profession is not the only
sector to benefit from SDSU graduates. "Half of the engineers working in San Diego are our alumni,
as are a large portion of city and
county government employees,"
says Weber. "We are dominant
in the business community."

The university strives to do
more than produce top-quality
graduates; it also contributes more
than $750 million to the local
economy each year. More than
half of that figure—$455 million—
is spent directly by the university.

In fact, if SDSU were described
in industry terms, it would be
a $455 million corporation with
3,900 employees and a record of
steady growth during its century
of operation. In addition, the university creates an estimated 12,204
regional jobs, which, in turn, produce $407 million in related wages.

Weber says SDSU's impact on
the region is also unique in that
78 percent of its alumni live in San
Diego. "We're one of the few universities in the nation that can make
that claim," he says. "A very large
proportion of our students come

from and return to San Diego. We
essentially produce the workforce
here. The reason we describe ourselves as San Diego's university is
because of our relationship with
the region.

"This region is really poised
on the edge of the future—because
of its concentration of emerging
technology businesses and its location on the Pacific Rim and the
Latin American border," says Weber.
In light of that, SDSU will continue
to immerse itself in the issues, problems, and opportunities facing the
San Diego area.

CLOCKWISE FROM TOP:
SAN DIEGO STATE UNIVERSITY'S
GOALS ARE SIMPLE: TEACHING,
SCHOLARSHIP, AND SERVICE. AND
IN STRIVING TO REACH THEM, THE
UNIVERSITY HELPS TO PREPARE
ITS STUDENTS TO LEAD SOCIETY
TOWARD A PROMISING FUTURE.

STEPHEN L. WEBER SERVES AS
PRESIDENT OF SAN DIEGO STATE
UNIVERSITY.

IN SCHOLARSHIP AND RESEARCH,
SDSU HAS CLEARLY DISTIN-
GUISHED ITSELF. IT OFFERS BACH-
ELOR'S AND MASTER'S DEGREES
IN MORE THAN 140 MAJORS AND
10 JOINT DOCTORAL DEGREE
PROGRAMS.

ALAN DECKER PHOTO

JIM BRADY PHOTO

DAVE FRIEND PHOTO

A CROSS THE NATION, ACROSS THE STREET, AND THROUGHOUT TH world, the Red Cross is the first to respond with help and hope. I addition to being an international symbol of humanitarianisr since 1863, the Red Cross has also been an integral part of Sa Diego County for a century. In 1998, the Red Cross celebrat 100 years of service to San Diego: providing relief to victims c

disasters, large and small, and helping families prevent, prepare for, and cope with emergencies 24 hours a day, 365 days a year.

People often mistake the American Red Cross for a government agency because of its ties to the military and its duty to provide for the American people during times of disaster. On the contrary, the Red Cross receives no government funding for these services. It is an independent, community-based, not-for-profit organization that relies on the generous contributions of time and money from individuals, businesses, and foundations in San Diego County. Their support ensures that the Red Cross is ready to respond when help can't wait.

A CENTURY OF SERVICE
The Red Cross movement grew out of a desire to "bring assistance without discrimination to the wounded of the battlefield; alleviate human suffering; protect life and health; ensure respect for human beings; and promote mutual understanding, friendship, cooperation, and lasting peace." Governed by international principles of impartiality, humanitarianism, and neutrality, the American Red Cross serves every community.

In San Diego, the Red Cross emerged as a result of assistance efforts during the Spanish-American War. In February 1898, President William McKinley sent American Red Cross founder Clara Barton to Cuba. Her mission was to distribute supplies to Cubans held in camps by the ruling Spanish government. On May 26 of that year, the founding members of the San Diego Red Cross met for

the first time and organized a drive to send lemons and dried fruits to support the relief effort.

Since that time, the San Diego Red Cross has been at work everyday, helping people keep their families and communities safer. In 1911, the San Diego Red Cross sent two nurses to Tecate to provide aid to refugees of the Mexican Revolution. During the following years, the local Red Cross helped more than 1,000 refugees and even served on the battlefield, becoming the only chapter in the United States to have actually served on a battlefield.

During the height of the poli epidemic in 1957, Red Cross volur teers in San Diego helped with what was called the world's first mass anti-polio inoculation of adults, sponsored by the San Dieg Medical Society and Departmen of Public Health. And in 1978, th Red Cross assisted emergency officials during the aftermath of the Pacific Southwest Airlines ai line crash by providing canteen service, helping at the temporary morgue, and providing assistance to families of the victims.

LOCAL ORGANIZATION
Although the mission of the Rec Cross has served well the past 10 years, the range of services and the structure of the organizatior have changed to meet the needs of the community. The San Dieg and El Centro chapters merged in 1983 to form the San Diego/ Imperial Counties Chapter. The organization's headquarters is located in Hillcrest, and there ar 19 office sites throughout the tw counties and on military bases to deliver services locally.

The volunteer board of directc governs the chapter and is made up of community leaders who

...re about and are interested in ...rving their community. A major ...rength of the organization is its ...gion of 5,000 local volunteers— ...any of whom are on call to re...ond to disasters within moments ...f receiving notice. Each year, vol...nteers support their communities ...rough the American Red Cross ...y donating an average of 500,000 ...ours of service.

Everyone benefits from the ...tivities of the Red Cross, accord...g to Dodie Rotherham, chief ...ecutive officer of the San Diego/ ...mperial Counties Chapter. "At ...ome time or in some way, every ...mily in San Diego will be touched ...y the Red Cross," she says. "It may ...e preventive, such as giving your ...mily the tools you need to better ...repare for disasters; or it may be ...sponsive, such as giving your ...mily a place to stay when access ...o your home is cut off due to a ...ging brush fire. The Red Cross ...an integral part of keeping ...milies safe in San Diego."

...ROAD RANGE OF ...ERVICES

...ed Cross chapters across the ...ation provide basic programs ...ch as relief to victims of disas...rs and a means for members of ...he armed forces to communicate ...ith family members during an ...mergency. Beyond those two ...ommon threads, each Red Cross

chapter actively assesses the needs of its community and offers other programs that fall within the mission of helping people prepare for, respond to, and cope with emergency situations. In San Diego, the Red Cross focuses on five major programs: Disaster Services; Armed Forces Emergency Services; Health and Safety; Transportation, for senior citizens and people with disabilities; and the Women, Infants, and Children (WIC) supplemental food program.

Disasters take on many shapes and sizes. The Red Cross in San Diego responds to a residential fire every day, helping families with their immediate, emergency needs such as temporary housing and the means to purchase groceries and new clothing. Red Cross

volunteers meet with disaster victims to assess their situation and then offer additional services that assist through the recovery process. This can often mean help with purchasing household items such as beds and cooking utensils, or replacing prescription medications or even occupational supplies.

The Red Cross tries to minimize the impact of disasters on families, businesses, and communities over time by educating San Diegans on how to better prepare for disasters. Volunteers are busy throughout the year providing free community education classes for individuals, civic organizations, and neighborhood groups. In addition, these classes are taught to the employees of businesses throughout San Diego.

FROM LEFT:
EVEN THOUGH TECHNOLOGICAL ADVANCES MAKE COMMUNICATION BETWEEN FAMILIES MORE AVAILABLE, THE MILITARY RELIES ON THE RED CROSS NETWORK THROUGHOUT THE WORLD TO VERIFY EACH EMERGENCY REQUEST.

GOVERNED BY INTERNATIONAL PRINCIPLES OF IMPARTIALITY, HUMANITARIANISM, AND NEUTRALITY, THE AMERICAN RED CROSS SERVES EVERY COMMUNITY.

WORKING TOGETHER, SOME BOY SCOUTS PROVIDE NEIGHBORS IN NEED WITH COMFORT KITS.

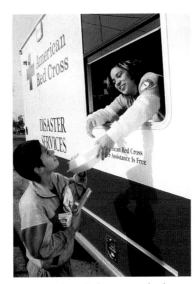

San Diego is home to the largest military complex in the United States, and the Red Cross works with military members and their families on a daily basis. The Red Cross helps thousands of families each year stay connected during a crisis. For example, when a young boy was hospitalized while his father was out at sea, the Red Cross was able to contact the father and help arrange for emergency leave so he could be at his son's side. Even though technological advances make communication be-tween families more available, the military relies on the Red Cross network throughout the world to verify each emergency request. The San Diego County Red Cross has established such expertise in the area of emergency communication that the chapter recently began providing emergency communications services to families throughout the western United States.

Keeping families safe and prepared is a theme that weaves through all of the services that the local Red Cross provides, but it is the Red Cross Health and Safety programs that vividly turn those words into action. The national Red Cross movement to train communities through health and safety programs actually has its roots in San Diego. In the early 1900s, longtime volunteer and San Diegan Mrs. Sam Brust outlined an idea that won nationwide support to provide a series of lectures on first aid and simple hygiene to the public. Those early classes covered such topics as "Bruises,

RED CROSS CHAPTERS ACROSS THE NATION PROVIDE BASIC PROGRAMS SUCH AS RELIEF TO VICTIMS OF DISASTERS.

292

SAN DIEG

ounds, and Bleeding" and Mother and Baby." Today, the cope encompasses a range of first d, CPR, and safety classes that eet the needs of businesses, mergency response personnel, d families alike. The Red Cross aches young adults how to become ore responsible baby-sitters and ains people of all ages in water fety. The Red Cross provides w-cost certification training for ursing assistants, and provides ee child-safety seats and safety aining to low-income families.

The WHEELS transportation rogram continues to grow, serving an increasing number of clients n San Diego County. Whether is a visit to the doctor's office the grocery store, Red Cross HEELS drivers provide San iegans unable to use the regular ansit system the security and onvenience of curb-to-curb transortation, thereby greatly increasing eir independence and mobility. he Red Cross also contracts with gencies to provide for their speific needs, such as transporting ersons living with AIDS to medial appointments.

The San Diego/Imperial Counties Chapter of the Red Cross is the only Red Cross in the nation to administer a Women, Infants, and Children (WIC) program, and is San Diego County's largest provider of WIC services. WIC gives children a healthy start by providing vouchers for nutritious foods. WIC Works is more than a slogan; it is a reality. Red Cross WIC staff work hard to ensure that the communities it serves have all the tools they need to choose a healthy lifestyle. That

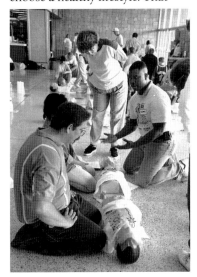

dedication has won the Red Cross WIC program numerous awards for its innovative outreach programs, and for making a significant contribution to the diverse cultural and ethnic communities in its service areas.

GOOD NEIGHBORS

The American Red Cross is personal. It touches individuals and families in different ways. For some people, the Red Cross is the CPR class they took last month at their workplace. For others, it's the WHEELS van that took them grocery shopping. For young people, it is the swim class they took last summer or the volunteer who taught them what action to take in case of an earthquake. No matter what the Red Cross means on an individual basis, one thing is clear: The Red Cross is more than an agency that just appears during times of disaster. For the past 100 years, it has been here in the community, touching the lives of families and friends. And no matter what the situation, the Red Cross will be there to help when help can't wait.

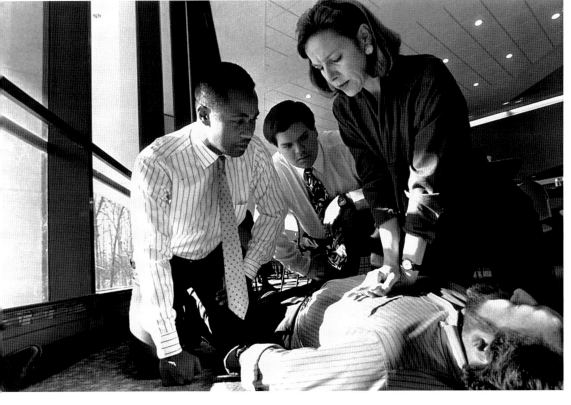

KEEPING FAMILIES SAFE AND PREPARED IS A THEME THAT WEAVES THROUGH ALL OF THE SERVICES THAT THE LOCAL RED CROSS PROVIDES, BUT IT IS THE RED CROSS HEALTH AND SAFETY PROGRAMS THAT VIVIDLY TURN THOSE WORDS INTO ACTION, OFFERING A RANGE OF FIRST AID, CPR, AND SAFETY CLASSES THAT MEET THE NEEDS OF BUSINESSES, EMERGENCY RESPONSE PERSONNEL, AND FAMILIES ALIKE.

WHEN ELLEN G. WHITE HELPED TO PURCHASE THE EMPT Potts Sanitarium and an adjacent tract of land in 1904 her purpose was to begin an Adventist health care insti tution. With guidance and support from White, wor began on restoring the facility—from wiring the buildin₃ for electricity to creating a new roof made of tin can

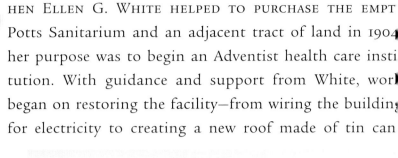

to drilling a much-needed well for water.

In the subsequent 94 years, the original 50-room building has grown into a 238-bed, acute care hospital, providing numerous programs and services to meet the changing needs of the San Diego community. Some of its newer lifestyle programs focus on such modern-day issues as weight reduction and stress management.

A PROUD HISTORY

Without the vision, determination, and personal sacrifice of White, the purchase and establishment of Paradise Valley Hospital would not have been possible. Dr. T.S. Whitelock, an Adventist physician practicing in San Diego, was the one who brought the Potts Sanitarium to White's attention. When Whitelock discovered the property could be purchased at a fraction of its original asking price, White and a close friend, Josephine Gotzian, put up the required $4,000. The rural setting appealed to Gotzian, who had a firm belief in the healing properties of nature.

Because of immediate interest in the surrounding community, patients began arriving before the hospital was officially open. At first, housing hadn't even been prepared for staff nurses, who initially lived in tents. By 1909, a school of nursing had been established to train nurses to care for patients throughout the growing facility.

During the first two decades of its existence, the sanitarium was under constant construction. In the early 1920s, Burden Hall was

erected, providing 50 additional rooms, including operating rooms Prestige came not long afterward. In 1940, Paradise Valley received the American Hospital Association' Hospital of the Year award for th fourth consecutive year.

Though growth continued through the 1950s, it was in 1966 that a new hospital building was completed. In March of that year, the first patient, a pregnant woman was admitted. Within hours, the patient population doubled—with the successful delivery of her baby.

Programs and facilities continued to be added to the Paradise Valley facility in the 1980s and 1990s, such as a 12-bed chemical dependency unit, a transitional care unit, the Premier 65 Seniors program, the Center for Health Promotion, a 10-bed neonatal intensive care unit, and a four-story Outpatient Pavilion.

CONTINUING THE FOUNDING MISSION

At Paradise Valley Hospital there is a strong belief that health en-

CLOCKWISE FROM TOP:
THE FRONT ENTRANCE OF PARADISE VALLEY HOSPITAL FEATURES A COMMISSIONED SCULPTURE, TITLED *CHRIST, OUR HEALER*. THE SCULPTURE FEATURES CHRIST ASSISTING A MOTHER IN GIVING MEDICINE TO HER YOUNG CHILD, WITH AN OLDER SIBLING STANDING CLOSE BY.

A BUSY MATERNITY WARD IN THE 1930S CREATED A BUSY NURSERY. HERE STUDENT NURSES ATTEND TO THE BATHING AND CHANGING NEEDS OF SEVERAL NEWBORN INFANTS.

THE ARCHWAY OVER THE ENTRANCE ROAD TO PARADISE VALLEY SANITARIUM WAS REBUILT IN 1994 AND IS A HISTORICAL LANDMARK ON THE CAMPUS OF PARADISE VALLEY HOSPITAL.

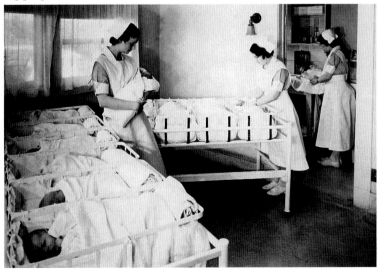

ompasses more than just the absence of sickness. This belief is reflected in its mission, which states, "Paradise Valley Hospital is a diverse family of caring professionals committed to continuing our Seventh-Day Adventist heritage of quality services. We work to enhance our patients' total well-being, and to improve the health of our diverse communities."

The mission represents not only the heritage of the facility, but also its focus for the future. This solid commitment to the community is what drives the programs and services provided by Paradise Valley Hospital.

With the health care industry shifting focus from inpatient services to outpatient services, Paradise Valley provides a full continuum of programs that promote a holistic approach to health care. Health education and prevention services, healthier community initiatives, and parish nursing services are available. Key outpatient services located in the Outpatient Pavilion include cardiology, clinical laboratory, radiology, and full rehabilitation services. Radiology is a West Coast showcase site for Shimadzu, the manufacturers of the latest scientific developments in radiological technology, and provides radio-fluoroscopy rooms, as well as magnetic resonance imaging (MRI), mammography, and ultrasound services.

The South Bay Rehabilitation Center offers physical, occupational, and speech therapies. Specialists in rehabilitative medicine manage patients recovering from head, spinal, or orthopedic injuries, as well as stroke victims. Specialized services, such as occupational medicine, include a hand therapy program—with an emphasis on helping individuals return to work.

Paradise Valley is actively involved in numerous community programs, including the nationally recognized collaborative Partners for Prevention. The hospital's thorough involvement and commitment to the community is the same mission that drives Partners for Prevention's efforts.

Partners for Prevention is a diverse group of community stakeholders who believe that a healthier community becomes a reality through partnerships with community groups, civic grassroots leaders, and other community coalitions and agencies. Partners has been actively involved with numerous initiatives and prevention strategies for the last four years, especially as they relate to youth and youth violence in developing seamless approaches for all healthier community initiatives.

Paradise Valley also is involved in the National City Christmas in July program, and provides other community-based activities, including an immunization program, behavioral health services, guest van service, CLUB Walk mall walking program, and Thanksgiving food drives, just to name a few.

Throughout its many years of continued service to the community, Paradise Valley Hospital has continued to fulfill its mission of providing quality health care services to those in the surrounding community. It's more than just a statement on the wall. It is a way of life for this institution and its employees, volunteers, and medical staff members.

CLOCKWISE FROM TOP LEFT: PARADISE VALLEY HOSPITAL PROVIDES BEAUTIFULLY DECORATED BIRTHING SUITES FOR EXPECTANT MOMS. EACH SUITE IS DESIGNED TO BE ALL-ENCOMPASSING, INCLUDING LABOR, DELIVERY, RECOVERY, AND POST-PARTEM (LDRP) CARE IN ONE ROOM DURING THE HOSPITAL STAY.

QUALITY NURSING CARE IS A PRIORITY AT PARADISE VALLEY HOSPITAL.

THERAPISTS WITH THE SOUTH BAY REHABILITATION CENTER AT PARADISE VALLEY HOSPITAL WORK WITH PATIENTS TO HELP THEM REGAIN MOBILITY AND LEARN ADAPTIVE TECHNIQUES THAT WILL ASSIST THEM IN THEIR RECOVERY FROM ILLNESS OR INJURY.

CHEFS AT PARADISE VALLEY HOSPITAL PREPARE NUTRITIONAL, BALANCED MEALS FOR PATIENTS. VEGETARIAN ENTRÉES ARE OFFERED FOR PATIENTS WHO PREFER THAT OPTION.

▲ MARK DASTRUP

U.S. GRANT HOTEL

COMPLETED IN 1910, THE U.S. GRANT HOTEL IS KNOWN AS TH Jewel of Downtown San Diego. A Grand Heritage Hotel, the fou star, four-diamond property has been listed on the Nationa Register of Historic Places since 1979. The U.S. Grant Hotel wa built by Ulysses S. Grant Jr. in honor of his father, who was Civil War hero and the 18th president of the United State

A GRAND HERITAGE HOTEL, THE FOUR-STAR, FOUR-DIAMOND PROPERTY HAS BEEN LISTED ON THE NATIONAL REGISTER OF HIS-TORIC PLACES SINCE 1979. THE U.S. GRANT HOTEL WAS BUILT BY ULYSSES S. GRANT JR. IN HONOR OF HIS FATHER, WHO WAS A CIVIL WAR HERO AND THE 18TH PRESIDENT OF THE UNITED STATES (TOP).

COMPLETED IN 1910, THE U.S. GRANT HOTEL IS KNOWN AS THE "JEWEL OF DOWNTOWN SAN DI-EGO." THROUGH ITS COMMITMENT TO DELIVERING CONSISTENTLY HIGH LEVELS OF SERVICE TO TRAV-ELERS, THE HOTEL SHOULD RETAIN THIS PRESTIGIOUS MONIKER FOR MANY YEARS TO COME (BOTTOM).

"We've always played a major role in the community," says U.S. Grant Hotel General Manager Joe Duncalfe. "We're very much a social center for the city, and we've always had close ties with the military. Thirteen presidents have stayed here."

The U.S. Grant Hotel contains 280 rooms—including 60 suites—and offers 18 meeting rooms and thousands of square feet of meeting space. Depending on the season, up to 60 percent of the hotel's business consists of meeting and convention groups. The hotel has full convention services, including state-of-the-art audiovisual and telecommunications capabilities.

CURRENT AMENITIES
On December 15, 1985, an $80 million renovation of the hotel was completed. "We used to have 437 rooms," says Duncalfe. "But we reduced that when we remodeled. We maintained the historic aspects of the property, but we updated many other things, in-

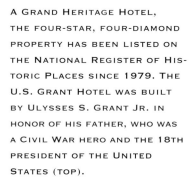

cluding a retrofitting that meets the standards of the ADA [Americans with Disabilities Act]."

Rooms contain traditional, reproduction mahogany furnishings, including two-poster beds, Queen Anne-style armoires, and wingback chairs. Bathrooms contain travertine marble and ceramic tile baths, and each room has a remote-control television, complete with cable and movie services. In addition, many suites feature built-in bars, fireplaces, chandeliers, and Jacuzzi bathtubs.

With 33,000 square feet of luxurious meeting space, the U.S. Grant can accommodate meetings as small as four, or receptions as large as 1,000. Facilities include the 8,100-square-foot Grand Ballroom, 2,033-square-foot Ballroom Foyer, 5,590-square-foot Pavilion Room, and 1,152-square-foot Pavilion Foyer. Also available are the mid-size Crystal and Horton rooms, which are each approximately 2,600 square feet.

FINE DINING
In 1997, the San Diego Restaurant Association chose the U.S. Grant

as the best for hotel dining. It wa the sixth time in eight years that the hotel's Grant Grill had been selected for the Gold Medallion Award. The Grill is set in rich wood, shining brass, and warm fabrics, and is a downtown favorite for express lunches, late-night dining, cocktails, and live jazz on Friday and Saturday evenings. Other dining options within the hotel include the Sidewalk Café and the Grant Grill Lounge.

A piece of history that lives on at the hotel is afternoon tea. Five days a week, approximately 50 people take a break for traditional afternoon tea in the hotel. With a classical harpist and pianist playing in the background, scones and crumpets are served on fine china, along with petits fours and finger sandwiches.

Reflecting the rich heritage of its name, the U.S. Grant Hotel is proud to be called the Jewel of Downtown San Diego. Through its commitment to delivering con sistently high levels of service to travelers, the hotel should retain this prestigious moniker for man years to come.

ith more than 100 years of experience, Merrill Lynch is a leading global financial management and advisory company with a presence in 43 countries across six continents and approximately 54,200 employees worldwide. In San Diego, Merrill Lynch has been in business since 1922. ■ The downtown office,

cated in the Imperial Bank Building in San Diego, is the headquarters for the Rancho California district. The 12 San Diego-area offices not only employ more than 00 financial consultants and support staff, but also include offices of the Merrill Lynch Trust Company of California, Business Financial Services, Mortgage and Credit, and Merrill Lynch Life Agency.

ONG HISTORY

Since its beginning, Merrill Lynch, founded by Charles E. Merrill, has operated on the belief that the opportunities of the markets should be accessible to everyone. It was Merrill's lifework to bring Wall Street to Main Street. Now, with total client assets of more than $1 illion, Merrill Lynch is the leader planning-based financial advice and management for individuals and small businesses.

As an investment bank, the company has been the top global underwriter of debt and equity securities eight years running, and leading strategic adviser to corporations, governments, institutions, and individuals worldwide. Through Merrill Lynch Asset Management, the firm operates one of the world's largest mutual fund groups.

Another focus of Merrill Lynch that originated with its founder putting the interest of the customer first. Today, that customerst philosophy is expressed in ve principles that define the way Merrill Lynch does business: client focus, respect for the individual, teamwork, responsible citizenship, and integrity. These principles are the standards used by

employees of the firm to measure decisions made daily.

DEFINING FINANCIAL GOALS

Merrill Lynch's financial consultants stress planning that considers a broad range of financial needs. The firm's consultants help clients define their financial goals, determine the amount of time they have to reach those goals, and establish their performance expectations.

A wide range of services work to tailor comprehensive strategies for managing clients' total portfolios. Merrill Lynch continues to enhance and develop products to accommodate client needs. In 1977, the Cash Management Account was introduced, and has proved to be a powerful personal asset management tool for investing, saving, borrowing, and spending.

In 1997, Merrill Lynch On Line began providing a Web-based service that gives clients electronic access to account information, portfolio information, specialized research, and bill payment. In addition to financial consulting services, the client has access to specialists in areas such as mortgages, personal credit, insurance, estate planning, trusts, and small-business and employee benefit services.

Whether assisting with mergers and acquisitions for large corporations or consulting with a young couple just beginning a financial portfolio, Merrill Lynch leads the way in providing trusted advice based on financial expertise, global perspective, and long-term view. The principles of client commitment that originated with Charles Merrill himself are effectively guiding the firm towards a successful future.

THE SAN DIEGO-AREA OFFICES, THE FIRST OF WHICH WAS ESTABLISHED IN 1922, CONTINUE MERRILL LYNCH'S 111-YEAR-OLD COMMITMENT TO EXCELLENCE. THE SAN DIEGO-AREA MANAGERS AND SPECIALISTS SUPPORT MORE THAN 200 FINANCIAL CONSULTANTS WITH MORTGAGE, TRUST, CREDIT, INSURANCE, FINANCIAL PLANNING, AND BUSINESS FINANCIAL SERVICES.

THE SAN DIEGO COMMUNITY COLLEGE DISTRICT (SDCCD) SERVE close to 100,000 students at hundreds of locations every semeste Its tradition of quality education dates back to 1914, when Sa Diego Junior College first opened its doors to 35 students. SDCCD's three community colleges (the word "junior" was replace in 1968 to highlight close ties with surrounding communitie:

continue to provide affordable, quality postsecondary education. Course fees are only $12 a credit unit, and financial aid is available to those in need. The average cost for a full-time student is less than $1,000 per year for tuition and books—the most affordable educational buy in the country.

Today, in addition to the district's three colleges, there are six major Continuing Education Centers. The SDCCD, which operates under an annual budget of more than $250 million, is one of the largest employers in San Diego County. Its 5,000 employees, with annual salaries and benefits of $98.5 million, pay taxes and spend locally. Not only does the district serve the community as a source for employment and an educational access point for everyone, but it also buys goods and services totaling $30 million a year.

SDCCD policy, enacted by a five-member, locally elected board of trustees and one student board member, is carried out by Chance lor Augustine Gallego.

THREE COMMUNITY COLLEGE CAMPUSES

The district's three colleges—City Mesa, and Miramar—are open to anyone 18 years old or older, with or without a high school diplom. Although they all offer the traditional community college curricul including general education, prepa ration for transfer, and vocationa training, the complexions of the colleges are different.

Established in 1914, City Colleg was the first community college in San Diego. The campus is located in the heart of downtown and reflects the diversity of its surrounding community. The multiethnic institution offers a strong world cultures program and an honors core curriculum from which students transfer to such prestigious institutions as Harvard, Princeton, Stanford, and the University of Chicago. It is also the home of a technology incubator for new businesses and a Center for Applied Competitive Technologies, one of eight region: advanced technology centers des ignated by the State of California to assist manufacturers in modernizing their management and production capabilities. In addition, the college's radio station, KSDS-FM, was named the best jazz station in the nation.

As one of the nation's largest community colleges, Mesa offers an enormous variety of programs and collegiate experiences, incluc ing 96 associate degree programs and 56 vocational certificate programs. The Humanities Institute hosts annual festivals celebrating

FRIENDSHIPS MADE AT ANY OF THE SAN DIEGO COMMUNITY COLLEGE DISTRICT'S COLLEGES CAN LAST A LIFETIME.

MELANIE CARR

MELANIE CARR

SAN DIEGO'S PLEASANT, MEDITERRANEAN CLIMATE ALLOWS OUTDOOR STUDY MUCH OF THE YEAR.

rldwide cultures and has brought
tionally renowned speakers
ch as musician Yo-Yo Ma and
il rights activist Rosa Parks to
e region. According to the Cali-
rnia Postsecondary Education
mmission, Mesa ranks first in
n Diego County and 12th among
tewide community colleges for
e number of students who trans-
to the University of California
d California State University.

Miramar, SDCCD's fastest-
owing college, uses collaborative
orts with public and private sec-
rs to spend tax dollars efficiently
meeting student and commu-
y needs. A joint project with
e City of San Diego and Pardee
nstruction, for example, has
ulted in Hourglass Field Com-
inity Park, a 32-acre athletic
mplex that provides Miramar
dents and area residents with
creational facilities. While still
important part of Miramar's
aracter, the campus' original
cus on public service training
olice and fire) is enhanced by
ong vocational programs built
th private industry linkages,
cluding advanced transportaon, mortgage brokerage and
nking, and biotechnology.

LIANCES WITH
IE COMMUNITY
ie district helps maintain a
mbiotic relationship with the
mmunities it serves by offering
eral additional services that
ich beyond the student popula-
on to benefit the community at
ge.

At more than 380 sites through-
t the city, SDCCD's Continuing
lucation Centers offer noncredit
isses for adults in job training
well as life skills and enrich-
ent topics. Among the diverse
ferings are courses to prepare
idents for entry-level jobs in
tomotive, electronic, and manu-
cturing companies; training in
fice skills and computer opera-
ns; and classes in vocational
iglish and English as a second

language, citizenship programs,
parenting, child development,
and programs for older adults.

The district's Employee Training Institute (ETi) in Point Loma
is a training organization for business, government, and industry
that offers customized training to
improve local businesses. Clients
have included Qualcomm Inc.,
IBM Corporation, SAIC, and
Sony.

SDCCD maintains direct links
with area businesses in the form
of advisory committees. Composed
of local businesspeople and educators, these committees help keep

the district abreast of training
needs and job opportunities within
the business community.

Through these programs and
others, the San Diego Community
College District has evolved in
direct response to the increasing
needs of its surrounding communities, resulting in continuous
growth and change. Over the years,
however, the organization's goal
has remained the same: to provide
an educational experience that
enables each individual to realize
his or her potential, and become
a productive and successful member of the community.

MELANIE CARR

MELANIE CARR

CLOCKWISE FROM TOP LEFT:
SDCCD PROFESSORS, MANY OF
WHOM HAVE DOCTORATES AND
COULD TEACH AT THE UNIVERSITY
LEVEL, PREFER THE LEARNING
ENVIRONMENT OF THE COMMUNITY
COLLEGE.

SDCCD STUDENTS MAY USE ANY
OF THE DISTRICT'S MANY LIBRAR-
IES AND LEARNING RESOURCE
CENTERS. INCREASINGLY, THE
DISTRICT IS GOING ON-LINE WITH
ELECTRONIC ACCESS TO TEACHING
AND LEARNING MATERIALS.

AN ASSOCIATE DEGREE PROVIDES
A SOLID FOUNDATION FOR THE
FUTURE. STUDIES SHOW THAT
COMMUNITY COLLEGE GRADUATES
WHO TRANSFER TO A UNIVERSITY
DO AS WELL AS OR BETTER THAN
STUDENTS WHO STARTED AT
THE UNIVERSITY.

WITH ITS EXTENSIVE AND RENOWNED NETWORK OF HO▪ pitals, physicians, nurses, and home health service▪ Scripps is a world leader in the diagnosis, treatment, ar▪ management of disease, and is at the forefront of medic▪ innovation and clinical research. This not-for-profi▪ community-based health care delivery network includ▪

six acute care hospitals, two skilled nursing facilities, more than 2,000 affiliated physicians, numerous outpatient offices (including an affiliation with Mercy Health Centers), and county-wide home health services.

A HISTORY OF CARING

The Scripps network began in La Jolla in 1924 when Ellen Browning Scripps founded both Scripps Memorial Hospital and Scripps Metabolic Clinic. The two operated together for several years, then separated in 1946. ScrippsHealth was formed in 1991 by the reunification of Scripps Memorial Hospitals with Scripps Clinic and Research Foundation. In 1995, ScrippsHealth and the Scripps Clinic Medical Group signed an agreement that

restructured their relationship, but retained the affiliation. Also in 1995, Mercy Hospital (San Diego's oldest hospital, founded in 1890) joined ScrippsHealth. Mercy was formerly a part of Catholic Healthcare West, which acquired an interest in Scripps.

With more than 7,000 employees, ScrippsHealth is the health care entity within the parent organization Scripps Institutions of Medicine and Science (SIMS). Other SIMS entities are The Scripps Research Institute (TSRI), which conducts scientific research, and the Scripps Foundation for Medicine and Science, which raises funds for ScrippsHealth and TSRI.

Scripps' stated mission is to make a measurable, positive difference in the health of individu-

als in the communities it serves. The organization is dedicated to providing quality, cost-effective, and socially responsible progra▪ that deliver all levels of acute an▪ convalescent care, promote wellnes▪ and improve the quality of life f▪ those with chronic illness.

PROJECT SCRIPPS

Part of being a leader in health car▪ involves leading its reform. As Scripps prepares for the new mille▪ nium, hospital staff and physicia▪ are participating in an exciting, visionary process called Project Scripps. Simply put, Project Scripp▪ is about returning patient care decisions to patients and their doctors, improving patient acces▪ to health care services, and chan▪ ing the way these services are pai▪

SCRIPPS MEMORIAL HOSPITAL-
LA JOLLA WAS THE FIRST SCRIPPS
HOSPITAL.

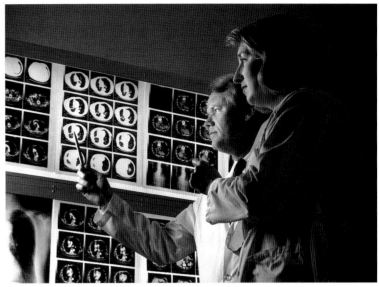

, so that more of each health care ·llar goes to helping patients.

Scripps' leaders note that the ·ason for Project Scripps is the ·tion's tumultuous health care ·rket, which has undergone tre·ndous change in recent years. ·hough the United States has ·en known for its excellent sys·m of health care, it has also been ·own for high costs, too many ·pensive tests, excess hospital ·ds, and too many doctors. The ·sponse of insurance companies ·s been managed care, a system ·signed to lower costs by elimi·ting the incentive for overtreat·ent by closely "managing" which ·edical treatment and services ·ll be paid for by health plans. ·nfortunately, managed care also ·eans less money available to ·ysicians and hospitals to care ·r patients. And, many health ·re decisions have been taken ·vay from patients and physi·ns. Among the many benefits ·Project Scripps are the reestab·hment of care-givers and patients ·health care decision makers, and ·e preservation of a community·lued, nonprofit, locally governed ·d -based health care system in ·n Diego County.

Project Scripps is a bold, inno·tive, unprecedented action plan ·make the patient, once again, ·e focus of health care. Through ·is initiative, Scripps is forming

strategic partnerships and redesigning its health care delivery system to reduce redundancies and promote patient-friendly and efficient, world-class systems of excellence.

Scripps is establishing partnerships with physicians, telecommunications and information technology companies, health plans, and other health care providers. No strategy is more important than the equal partnership between ScrippsHealth (the hospital and home health provider) and ScrippsHealth Physicians, a countywide organization composed of independent physicians and members of medical groups. Together with information technology companies, Scripps is building the kind of state-of-the-art,

integrated information systems that are mandatory for the new millennium. And, in creating alliances with health plans and health benefits purchasers, Scripps is creating its own special brands of coverage that emphasize physicianpatient decision making.

Through Project Scripps, Scripps is developing the ideal health care network for the year 2002, providing the right care, in the right place, at the right time.

With quality care, firm roots in the past, and a strong plan for the future, ScrippsHealth will continue its excellent track record of service to the community as it continues to be a vital part of the health care field for many years to come.

MERCY HOSPITAL AND MEDICAL CENTER JOINED THE SCRIPPSHEALTH NETWORK OF HOSPITALS IN 1995. SAN DIEGO'S OLDEST HOSPITAL, MERCY WAS FOUNDED IN 1890 (LEFT).

WITH ITS EXTENSIVE AND RENOWNED NETWORK OF HOSPITALS, PHYSICIANS, NURSES, AND HOME HEALTH SERVICES, SCRIPPS IS A WORLD LEADER IN THE DIAGNOSIS, TREATMENT, AND MANAGEMENT OF DISEASE, AND IS AT THE FOREFRONT OF MEDICAL INNOVATION AND CLINICAL RESEARCH (RIGHT).

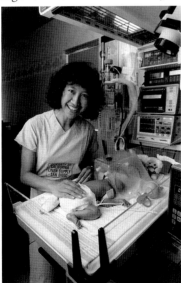

SCRIPPS' STATED MISSION IS TO MAKE A MEASURABLE, POSITIVE DIFFERENCE IN THE HEALTH OF INDIVIDUALS IN THE COMMUNITIES IT SERVES.

I N 1993, PALO ALTO-BASED WARE & FREIDENRICH WANTED TO WIN A GREAT share of the lucrative Silicon Valley securities and intellectual proper litigation market. San Diego-based Gray Cary Ames & Frye desired a high corporate securities and intellectual property licensing profile among th entrepreneurs turning the city into a high-technology and biotech nology center. Today, both goals are being met, thanks to the 1994 merg

of the two firms. Now a California powerhouse, Gray Cary Ware & Freidenrich LLP is San Diego's largest law firm.

"The purpose of the merger was to marry the special expertise in technology that Ware & Freidenrich had in Silicon Valley with the long-standing market leadership we have here in San Diego," says Chairman and CEO J. Terence O'Malley.

A HAPPY MARRIAGE

Today, more than 280 lawyers work for Gray Cary Ware & Freidenrich LLP in the firm's Northern California, San Diego-area, and Austin, Texas, offices. The San Diego offices consist of a location in the downtown area, one in the Golden Triangle, one in La Jolla, and one in the Imperial Valley. The team of lawyers is supported by a 400-person staff of administrators, legal analysts, paralegals, information specialists, consultants, and secretaries.

A full-service law firm, Gray Cary Ware & Freidenrich LLP boasts the largest noninstitutional law library in San Diego County, with more than 60,000 volumes. Each of the firm's offices is linked to a computerized legal research system that is connected to government, regulatory, legal, and corporate data banks. Furthermore, every attorney has a laptop computer that is part of a companywide network with access to both the firm's intranet and the World Wide Web.

Gray Cary Ware & Freidenrich LLP offers clients a wide spectrum of services. Major areas of practice include corporate securities, litigation, employment services, intellectual property, general business, finance, tax, real estate, bankruptcy,

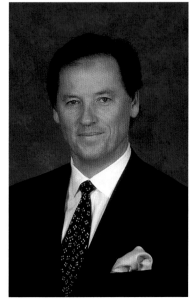

and trusts and estates. Attorneys work at solving clients' problems through teams of lawyers that combine specialized expertise with an in-depth understanding of the client's industry. In addition to industry-based practice groups focusing on real estate development, information technology, life sciences, and financial services, legal specialties include environmental, international, patent, appellate, and product liability law.

But it was the high-tech and biotech business sector that was the major impetus for the merger, and it's paying off dividends. In 1997, Gray Cary Ware & Freidenrich LLP represented clients effecting mergers and acquisitions (M&A) exceeding $15 billion. Since 1994, the organization has helped oversee more than 100 public securities offerings.

Three leading components of the firm's 1997 M&A activity came through assisting 3Com's $8.8 billion acquisition of U.S. Robotics, as well as Ascend's $3.7 billion

acquisition of Cascade, and the $1 billion Network Associates merge Other companies represented in M&A deals by Gray Cary Ware & Freidenrich include Synopsis, Firefox, Maxtor, Digidesign, Garre Aviation, and Bay Networks.

PROUD LOCAL HISTORY

The roots of the San Diego firm go back to 1910 when Gordon Gr. opened his law practice. Early on Gray initiated the firm's tradition of community service by helping found the city's first Rotary Clul

Adding to that spirit was Walte Ames, who also became a prominent figure in San Diego. He helpe organize the California Pacific International Exposition, which ultimately was responsible for developing Balboa Park—the con tinuing crown jewel of the city. Additionally, Ames conceived an led the construction of the nation ally recognized Timken Art Museu in Balboa Park. He also assisted founding the San Diego Taxpaye Association and San Diegans Inc both of which are now major dow town leadership groups.

The firm was established as Gray Cary Ames & Frye in 1927. Since then, it has represented cli ents in every segment of the city' economy. Clients have included the San Diego Zoo, Sea World, Salk Institute, University of San Diego, University of California, and many other civic institution

Following in the footsteps of the firm's founders, Gray Cary War & Freidenrich LLP lawyers have played roles in almost every cultura business, social, and nonprofit orga nization in the county. This reco of community service includes rol as policy makers and advisers to th d Globe Theater, the San Diego Opera, and various universities, useums, hospitals, and libraries, d many Gray Cary lawyers have ne on to become members of e state and federal judiciary.

Pointing out that community rvice is still a major part of the lture at Gray Cary Ware & eidenrich LLP, O'Malley notes at the firm has been recognized the local Pro Bono Law Firm of e Year for three out of the past years. In addition, a recent ghlight for the firm came in 98 when the Board of the San iego County Bar Association ted to award Gray Cary the an- al Community Service Award the firm's Partnership in Edu-

cation Program. It was the first time a law firm had received the award.

Gray Cary Ware & Freidenrich LLP is in its 5th year as partner to the John Muir Alternative School, a K-12 magnet school, and contributes hundreds of hours each year and substantial material benefits toward improving the education of Muir students. Some of the highlights of the partnership include Gray Cary attorneys teaching classes on constitutional rights, gender issues and personal law; reading and arithmetic tutoring; an annual food drive to provide Thanksgiving dinners to families of Muir students who might otherwise go without; a month dedica-

tion to Women in Business issues; and a one-on-one job mentoring program that pairs every senior at the school with an attorney mentor.

Another highlight for the firm came in 1995, when David Monahan was named the California Trial Lawyer of the Year by the American Board of Trial Advocates. It was the first time in 25 years that the award had gone to an attorney outside of Los Angeles or San Francisco.

With outstanding lawyers, a commitment to community service, and a heightened presence in the high-tech and biotech arenas, Gray Cary Ware & Freidenrich LLP will proudly continue its long-standing presence in the region.

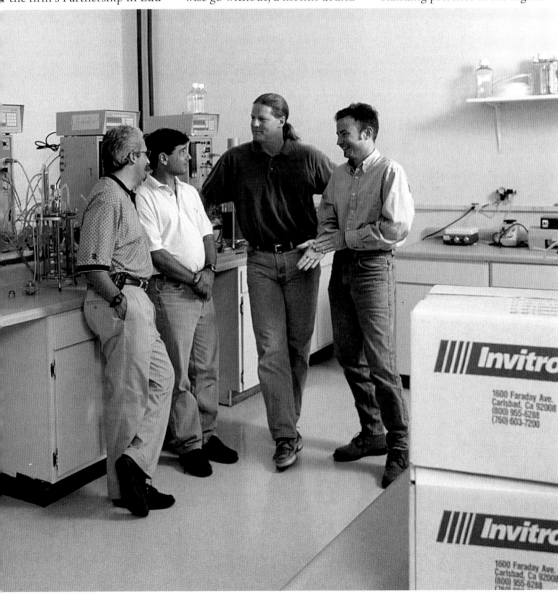

INVITROGEN, A LEADING BIOTECHNOLOGY COMPANY AND A GRAY CARY WARE & FREIDENRICH LLP CLIENT, DEVELOPS, MANUFACTURES, AND MARKETS MOLECULAR BIOLOGY RESEARCH TOOLS AND SERVICES. ALONG WITH GRAY CARY ATTORNEY PAUL HURDLOW (FROM LEFT) ARE INVITROGEN VICE PRESIDENT JOSEPH M. FERNANDEZ, PRESIDENT LYLE C. TURNER, AND GENERAL COUNSEL WARNER BROADDUS.

SOLAR TURBINES INCORPORATED, HEADQUARTERED ON THE CITY downtown waterfront, is a significant element of San Diego economic backbone. As one of California's largest exporters of manufactured goods, Solar Turbines is also one of the large such exporters in San Diego and one of the city's largest employer Solar employees—numbering 3,300 locally in two manufacturin

plants and several office buildings, plus 2,400 international employees in 40 offices and plants worldwide— are continuing a heritage of sophisticated production that began in 1927.

The company builds a family of powerful gas turbine engines, natural gas compressors, and electricity-producing generator sets that primarily serve industrial needs. In fact, Solar is the world's leading manufacturer of industrial gas turbines ranging up to 18,000 horsepower, with more than 10,000 currently in service in 85 nations. Year in and year out, Solar exports more than 70 percent of its products.

"Solar Turbines has been a steadfast contributor to the success of San Diego's economy," says Greater San Diego Chamber of Commerce President Gilbert A. Partida. "San Diego is fueled by manufacturing exports, and Solar is one of the largest—making its contribution invaluable."

"Great organizations start at the top, and Solar President Don

Ings sets a high standard for community involvement," says Julie Wright, president and chief executive officer of the San Diego Economic Development Corporation. "As one of San Diego's leading manufacturers, Solar and its employees are woven into the fabric of this wonderful community, helping it to grow and prosper."

Over the past several years, Solar and its employees, combined with the Caterpillar Foundation, have contributed millions of dollars to support more than 150 San Diego community service organizations. In addition to financial contributions, Solar employees volunteer about 16,500 hours per year on community service projects ranging from literacy programs to helping the homeless through the Solar Turbines Employees' Volunteer Club.

In terms of taxes, payroll, and local purchase of goods and services, Solar employees have an impact on the community of roughly $500 million a year—a long way from the handful of engineers and mechanics who, in 1927, had the courage, imagi-

nation, and skills to build one of the world's first metal airplanes.

OWNED BY A LEADER

Solar is owned by Caterpillar Inc of Peoria, Illinois, the world's larg est manufacturer of earthmoving construction, mining, and mater als handling equipment, and a major manufacturer of diesel an natural gas engines. Caterpillar h approximately 60,000 employee worldwide.

In the early 1990s, Caterpillar invested $190 million in capital improvements at Solar's San Dieg operation, and the company plar to spend another $300 million to upgrade San Diego facilities in the late 1990s. This degree of com mitment strengthens Solar's impac upon the San Diego economy, while creating the foundation for increased business.

Caterpillar has also made a substantial investment in Solar's manufacturing process. For example, the company's computer controlled machinery produces precision, quality metal compo nents. Solar's computer-aided design equipment has helped

SOLAR TURBINES INCORPORATED, HEADQUARTERED ON THE CITY'S DOWNTOWN WATERFRONT, IS A MAJOR ELEMENT OF SAN DIEGO'S ECONOMIC BACKBONE. AS ONE OF CALIFORNIA'S LARGEST EXPORTERS OF MANUFACTURED GOODS, SOLAR TURBINES IS ALSO ONE OF THE LARGEST SUCH EXPORTERS IN SAN DIEGO AND ONE OF THE CITY'S LARGEST EMPLOYERS (TOP).

SOLAR HAS INSTALLED MORE THAN 10,000 GAS TURBINE SYSTEMS IN 85 NATIONS (BOTTOM).

ost the company's position
an innovator in minimizing
haust emissions from its engines
d in designing advanced heat
changers to conserve energy.

VARIETY OF
INOVATIVE PRODUCTS

lar's key products are industrial
s turbine engines from 1,590 to
800 horsepower; natural gas
mpressors; gas-turbine-driven
mpressor sets and mechanical
ive packages; and generator sets
th electrical outputs ranging
om one to 13 megawatts. The
mpany also makes a variety
advanced steam generators
oilers).

Solar pioneered the concept of
tory-packaged small industrial
s turbines in 1960, when it intro-
ced the 1,000-horsepower Saturn
gine in generator sets and gas
mpressor sets. By 1998, the com-
ny had manufactured more than
,000 industrial turbomachinery
ckages, which is nearly double
e total from any other manufac-
rer. The units have logged 350
llion operating hours—a level
experience equivalent to almost
,000 years.

Most of Solar's products are
ed in the oil and gas industry
production, processing, and
peline transmission of natural
s and crude oil. A growing num-
r of customers, however, are using

Solar equipment to produce energy
for their own plants and processes—
simultaneously generating electricity while using the turbine's
exhaust heat for processing applications in the production of pharmaceuticals, chemicals, and food
products. Another major portion
of its client base uses Solar generator sets that supply fixed-base electrical power or emergency backup
power for vital telecommunications complexes and computer
centers.

Solar's research and development takes place in-house. With
an international sales organization,
local manufacturing and shipping,
worldwide on-site installation,
follow-up customer service operations, and a global parts distribution network, Solar is a fully
integrated operation.

Solar's San Diego facilities
consist of three main sites. The
700,000-square-foot world headquarters facility sits alongside
San Diego Harbor, adjacent to
Lindbergh Field. Bounded by
Harbor Drive, Pacific Highway,
and Laurel and Hawthorne streets,
Solar's waterfront buildings house
research, engineering, development
testing, component manufacturing,
and executive and administrative
functions.

The 400,000-square-foot
Kearny Mesa plant houses the gas
compressor manufacturing unit,

gas turbine assembly, assembly
of complete gas compressor sets,
generator sets and mechanical-
drive packages, and final product
testing and shipping. And the
160,000-square-foot Sky Park
Court and Customer Services
facilities contain application engineering, package engineering,
project engineering, and construction services offices.

Other major operations include
divisions producing modules for
the oil and gas industry in Texas;
several large overhaul centers in
Texas, Canada, Belgium, Indonesia,
Malaysia, Australia, and Mexico;
and a component remanufactur-
ing plant in Mexico. Sales and
service offices are located throughout the world.

SKILLED, DEDICATED EMPLOYEES
AT SOLAR TURBINES ARE A KEY
FACTOR CONTRIBUTING TO THE
COMPANY'S LEADERSHIP AND
SUCCESS.

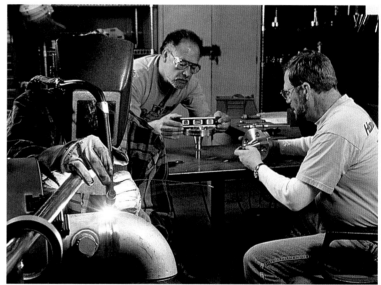

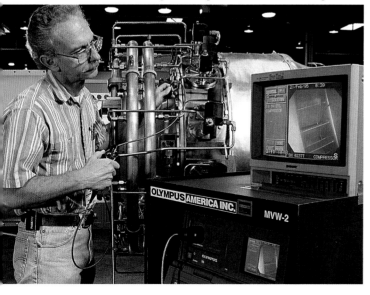

ORIGINS IN AIRCRAFT MANUFACTURING

Solar began as an aircraft manufacturing company inspired by the excitement in the aviation and metal industries after Charles Lindbergh's successful transatlantic flight in May 1927. In fact, Lindbergh's plane was built in what is today part of Solar's waterfront plant.

Though Solar built only three airplanes, the new technology and skills that evolved put the company at the forefront of a new industry, making specialty metal products for the fledgling aviation industry. After many variations and numerous market and economic changes, Solar's expertise led the company toward its current specialty—making sophisticated turbines to supply the world with energy.

The aircraft company was housed in a 10,000-square-foot shop in a vacant fish cannery, where Juniper Street abruptly ends at the harbor. Next door was the aircraft company that built Lindbergh's *Spirit of St. Louis*.

Over the years, components produced for the U.S. military in the ever expanding plant helped America in many wars—cold and hot. There were stainless steel exhaust manifolds and other parts for fighter planes and bombers, water desalting equipment for ships, and portable electrical generator sets to operate military radar equipment and missile controls.

Solar's troubleshooting research also helped avoid problems commonly developed during battle. For example, Solar engineers—working without fee—solved high-altitude metal fatigue problems on engine parts of the World War II P-38 fighter. They later did similar research for the U.S. War Department on other aircraft. The engineering know-how and design techniques developed by Solar research laboratories contributed to the company's leadership role in manufacturing durable, specialty high-temperature metal structures. Solar's expertise also prepared the company for its prosperous future in turbines.

STABILITY THROUGH DIVERSITY AND EMPLOYEE COMMITMENT

Over the years, through economic downturns, the Great Depression, and occasional recessions, the company turned out such items as metal frying pans, bookends, popsicle trays, kitchen sinks, midget race car bodies, coffee brewers, stainless steel caskets, and—for a short time—redwood lawn chairs. Because of this versatility, Solar was able to make a postwar transition from military to industrial product lines.

Edmund T. Price, Solar's president from shortly after the company's inception until his 1956 retirement, once told a newspaper reporter a depression-era story that continues to epitomize the spirit of the company's employees: In 1932, during the darkest days of the depression, "we had no money to meet the payroll. We owed money to the banks. I walked out into the shop and told the men I was sorry, but it was the end of the line. We were closing up.

"Ironically, that morning we had received an order for 126 exhaust manifolds for the Boeing 247 transport. It was a $26,000 order, but we had no money to meet the payroll, so we had to close.

"The men listened with serious faces. There was silence for a minute after I had finished speaking. The

A 14,100-HORSEPOWER MARS MECHANICAL DRIVE UNIT POWERS A CENTRIFUGAL GAS COMPRESSOR ON THIS SOLAR-ENGINEERED PACKAGE AT A GAS PROCESSING PLANT.

ll James spoke up. 'What the
ll are we waiting for?' he asked.
e took off his coat and walked
er to his bench. The other men
lowed. We were still in business."

For several weeks, every man
orked without pay to preserve
e company. Those workers are
ll remembered today. Solar's
imployee-built, all-faith chapel
the grounds of Harbor Drive
int is open at all times. Some-
e is often inside, reading a Bible,
ving a prayer, or just sitting in
intemplation. There are weekly,
indenominational services dur-
g lunch or work breaks.

Outside, there's an open-air
iing area where a bronze plaque
immemorates James, who led
fellow employees back to work:
memory of W.A. James, drop
mmer operator in 1932, who
d faith in his team."

Solar attributes its success over
e years to the dedication of its
iployees. The company is com-
tted to providing a workplace
at is safe and pleasant, one that
omotes growth, opportunity,
imwork, and reward.

Today, self-directed work teams
currently striving to solve prob-
ns and bring new ideas to the
refront at Solar. These teams
e encouraged to take an active
le in the management of the
mpany's business by identifying
illenges and implementing their
n innovative plans. They are

provided the resources necessary
to meet their challenges, along
with the authority to make decisions and follow through.

Efforts of Solar employees
are rewarded through a generous
performance incentive plan and
other incentives that encourage
attention to quality. Solar's benefits package is considered highly
competitive within the industry.
A comprehensive Solar training
program provides opportunities
for employees to grow in both
leadership and technical areas;
higher education is encouraged
through company reimbursement
of tuition and books. Solar believes
this level of commitment to its
workforce is valuable insurance
for the company's future.

TOUCHING LIVES
ACROSS THE GLOBE

Today, the big "made in San Diego"
gas turbine engines turned out by
Solar employees can be found in
more than 85 countries around
the world. They're on oil rigs in
the North Sea, compressing natural gas as it comes from beneath
the ocean, and pumping oil through
pipelines in the Middle East, Brazil,
Indonesia, Texas, and virtually
anywhere else that oil and natural gas are produced.

Tourists arriving in Bermuda
and Hawaii at the height of the
season enjoy air-conditioning and
light produced by Solar-manufac-

tured electricity "peaking" generator sets. Solar units produce steam
and electrical power for processing kelp into valuable chemicals
at San Diego's Kelco, Inc. and at
industrial sites around the world.
Nearly 100 Solar gas turbines are
compressing natural gas or generating electricity for pipelines in
the Soviet Union, and many U.S.
telephone centers rely on Solar
generators for emergency backup
power.

Indeed, the company's employees and products contribute to the
lives of people all over the world
in many ways. From its beginnings
in 1927, Solar Turbines Incorporated
has continued to strive for innovation, adapting to—and creating—
new technology and growing with
San Diego.

SOLAR TURBINES' EMPLOYEES—
NUMBERING 3,300 LOCALLY IN
TWO MANUFACTURING PLANTS AND
SEVERAL OFFICE BUILDINGS, PLUS
2,400 EMPLOYEES IN 40 OFFICES
AND PLANTS WORLDWIDE—ARE
CONTINUING A HERITAGE OF SO-
PHISTICATED PRODUCTION THAT
BEGAN IN 1927.

S OME PEOPLE THINK OF GOODWILL INDUSTRIES AS A PLACE TO DISCAI unwanted items or buy knickknacks at a fair price. But there more to Goodwill than collecting and selling. Goodwill's goal h not wavered in the 95 years of its national existence—improvin the employability of people with disabilities. ■ Goodwill's defir tion of disability is not limited to the physical, but includes ar

barrier to employment. Recipients of the organization's goodwill include dislocated workers, the illiterate, welfare recipients, the elderly, teenage parents, the homeless, and immigrants.

A CENTURY OF CARING

In 1902, European immigrants made up the bulk of Pastor Edgar James Helms' Methodist Mission in Boston. Helms started what would become a national movement by collecting unwanted clothing and household goods from Boston's elite. Parishioners prepared the items for resale, and then sold them in the church basement. The win-win system provided jobs for the unemployed and affordable goods for the needy. Thus, Goodwill Industries was born. "A hand up, not a handout" was one of the phrases coined by Helms.

In 1930, Helms recruited Methodist Minister Myron Insko, fresh from doing missionary work in India, to start San Diego operations. The first location was on Imperial Avenue, and in 1933, the

organization moved to Fifth Avenue in the Gaslamp Quarter.

CLEAN AND FRIENDLY

Today, Goodwill Industries of San Diego County has 13 locations. "We are clean and friendly; that's what makes us different," says Executive Director Mike Rowan. Goodwill's stores and services provide employment for about 420 people in the San Diego area. "We sell a lot of clothing and household items, but the product is really the worker," says Rowan. The retail stores train and hire individuals to process donations and work on the sales floor. Nearly 83 percent of the revenue earned from the Goodwill stores, along with the money raised from providing contract services to community-based businesses, is channeled into job training, placement programs, and other community services.

The Apprenticeship Program, one such vehicle Goodwill has developed to provide jobs, gives people six months of on-the-job, paid training in a realistic work environment. The goal is to teach trainees the skills necessary in

finding competitive jobs. Goodw boasts a 70 percent success rate for those who complete the cours And success equates to jobs.

A new job maker for Goodwi is the contract work it can perfor for the business community. Ap plicants awaiting openings in th Apprenticeship Program provid Goodwill with a workforce to off local companies. This eager grou of people can perform tasks suc as subassembly, packaging, and off-load work, which isn't alway cost effective for a company to p form with its own staff. Goodwi welcomes the opportunity to su ply workers for both temporary and long-term contract work.

Goodwill Industries of San Diego County began building it reputation for success by creatin job opportunities for disabled workers more than 60 years ago "Improving employability is ou goal," says Rowan. The individu als whom Goodwill helps can ga more than just a new job and ar economic advantage. Through their work, they are able to buil self-confidence, friendships, ind pendence, creativity, trust, and empowerment—the work ethic.

THE APPRENTICESHIP PROGRAM, A VEHICLE GOODWILL INDUSTRIES HAS DEVELOPED TO PROVIDE JOBS, GIVES PEOPLE SIX MONTHS OF ON-THE-JOB, PAID TRAINING IN A REALISTIC WORK ENVIRONMENT. THE GOAL IS TO TEACH TRAINEES THE SKILLS—INCLUDING COMPUTER LITERACY—NECESSARY IN FINDING AND RETAINING COMPETITIVE JOBS (TOP).

GOODWILL'S CAFETERIA PROVIDES FOOD SERVICE TRAINING, BANQUET SERVICES FOR COMMUNITY GROUPS, AND MODERATELY PRICED NUTRITIOUS MEALS FOR EMPLOYEES. IN THIS ENVIRONMENT, APPRENTICES CAN EARN A PAYCHECK WHILE LEARNING TRANSFERABLE SKILLS (BOTTOM).

JOE BUTTS

S URVEY AFTER SURVEY HAS SHOWN THAT NORTH ISLAND FEDERAL Credit Union's (NIFCU) members like doing business with their credit union. A member-owned, employee-focused financial cooperative, NIFCU is committed to providing overall value to its members by continually improving quality service and customized products. ■ One of some 12,000 credit unions in the United

ates, NIFCU ranks 45th in size the nation and 10th in California. currently serves nearly 130,000 embers at nine branch locations roughout San Diego County d through its TeleService Call nter, which handles 50,000 ls each month.

"NIFCU is successful because hallmark is its focus on supe-or service for members," says 3O Michael Maslak. "Our ap-oach to achieving service excel-nce is to create a culture that lues our employees as our key set. When our employees are ated with caring and respect, ey in turn will treat our mem-rs with the same service spirit. ie results of member surveys, cret shoppers, focus groups, d frontline employee input ve given NIFCU an accurate d positive picture of where it nds with its members."

Because of this customer focus, FCU ranks above other financial stitutions in objective compari-ns. Some 94 percent of NIFCU's embers rated positive satisfac-n with the credit union in the t two surveys conducted. NIFCU's

independently administered employee opinion survey results are also extremely high.

HISTORY OF SERVICE
NIFCU's membership charter was first approved in September 1940. This original credit union served civil service employees of North Island Naval Air Station and their families. NIFCU's charter was expanded to include naval personnel throughout San Diego. After deregulation in 1982, the credit union further expanded its charter and has added a number of select employee groups to its field of membership.

Founded on the belief that working people could govern their own financial institutions cooperatively, NIFCU is much different from a regular bank. For example, the credit union's earnings are returned to its members in the form of affordable financial services, rather than in the form of profit for a limited group of shareholders. NIFCU's board of directors is composed of individuals elected from its membership who volunteer their time to the credit union.

And the members' earnings are paying for quite a variety of services. NIFCU offers a full complement of financial products, including savings and checking accounts, certificates of deposit, money market accounts, auto and consumer loans, credit cards, and real estate loans, among others. In addition to its branch offices and TeleService Call Center, the credit union maintains a computerized, 24-hour telephone teller, as well as a wide network of ATMs. In addition, NIFCU established a subsidiary in 1991—North Island Financial and Insurance Services—to provide insurance and investment products.

Fueled by high marks on member surveys—not to mention four California Eureka Awards for Quality and Service Excellence—NIFCU is steadily rising to the top of the credit union industry. In 1997, NIFCU earned the Gold Level, Best-in-Class Eureka designation, which uses the rigorous Malcolm Baldrige award criteria. As the company enters the new millennium, it is poised to truly become a leader in both services and customer satisfaction.

NORTH ISLAND FEDERAL CREDIT UNION (NIFCU), HEADQUARTERED IN CHULA VISTA, IS STEADILY RISING TO THE TOP OF THE CREDIT UNION INDUSTRY. IN 1997, NIFCU EARNED THE GOLD LEVEL, BEST-IN-CLASS EUREKA DESIGNATION, WHICH USES THE RIGOROUS MALCOLM BALDRIGE AWARD CRITERIA (TOP).

POLYMORPHOUS PARADISE, BY ARTIST DAVID SCHWEITZER, WAS COMMISSIONED BY NIFCU TO CELEBRATE ITS HOME AND ITS MOTTO "SAN DIEGO'S OWN" (BOTTOM).

THE FIRST GREAT CITY OF THE 21ST CENTURY IS MORE THAN slogan to San Diego Mayor Susan Golding: It is San Diego destiny. ■ Today's San Diego is on the leading edge of econom and social change—boldly redefining the role of government an its relationship to the people it serves. Leading the charge is th city's Economic Development Division (EDD). The division

charged with improving the quality of life for San Diego and its neighborhoods. To do this, EDD works to create a healthy atmosphere for business.

"We don't hire the people who work in local business," says Michael Montgomery, economic development manager for the city, "but we do create a positive atmosphere for the businesses that make those jobs a reality."

DIVERSIFYING THE ECONOMY

For many years, San Diego's economy depended on federal defense spending. When government spending declined and major defense employers laid off workers in the late 1980s, the local economy fell into recession. From 1990 through 1994, the San Diego region lost nearly 40,000 defense manufacturing jobs.

While defense spending declined drastically—and with it San Diego's employment base—aerospace technology spilled over into advances in communications, software, and electronic instruments. These, plus bioscience advances developed at the Salk Institute, other prestigious research institutions, and the University of California-San Diego, led to struggling clusters of high-tech firms founded on intellectual properties and researc and development. But start-up companies, even high-tech ones, have a difficult time competing in a global economy.

In 1991, as San Diego's econom continued its downward spiral, a economic development task forc recommended ways that the city could help diversify the economy Unlike reports that collect dust on a shelf, nearly every recommen dation in the six-volume report issued in December 1991 was impl mented by April 1992.

Most critical, according to th report, was the goal to help stru gling biotech companies throug the complicated permit process. Otherwise, the report noted, the companies would soon leave for other states. A biotech ombudsm was immediately appointed. Thi concept was soon applied to oth high-tech companies, leading to the creation of the Business Expansion and Retention, or BEAR, Team. The BEAR Team helps high-tech companies and major employers through the permit process and offers incentives to minimize facility costs.

San Diego's leaders took othe steps to create a business-friend atmosphere. They cut the busine. tax, which is now the lowest of any major city in the nation. Fee for manufacturing industries we drastically reduced. And, in addi tion to the BEAR Team's assistanc the development permit process was reinvented from top to botto

With the help of a modest federal grant, San Diego created new institutions to assist busine

SAN DIEGO IS PERFECTLY SITUATED TO BE THE FIRST GREAT CITY OF THE 21ST CENTURY.

growth. The San Diego World Trade Center started to help local companies learn how to export. The High Technology Resource Center—now the San Diego Manufacturing Extension Center—was created to provide technical assistance to high-tech firms. The Technology Incubator was formed to grow high-tech start-ups. And San Diego State University instituted the Defense Adjustment Training Center, to train laid-off defense workers in the new technologies.

To address the high-tech businesses' capital access needs, the Emerging Technology—EmTek—Loan Program was created from federal and local funds. Administered by EDD's Business Finance section, this loan program rounds out the usual array of tax-exempt bond financing, SBA-guaranteed funding, and other niche lending programs.

The city council also created the Office of Small Business (OSB) in 1992, to assist the 50,000 small businesses in San Diego, which account for 90 percent of the businesses and half the job growth since 1991. OSB provides business assistance, advocacy for a business-friendly climate, and information resources, plus marketing and business retention support through the city's 16 Business Improvement Districts (BIDs).

Finally, EDD's Neighborhood Revitalization Team manages capital improvement projects in San Diego's oldest neighborhoods. Projects may include tree plantings, neighborhood identification signs, and public art, along with traditional street and sidewalk projects, new lighting, and other capital needs. The Revitalization Team's hallmark is its partnerships with neighborhood groups and the BIDs.

"Our division relies on community partnerships," says Montgomery. "In cooperation with neighborhood groups, industry groups, the nonprofit section, small businesses, and even other cities in the

region, we work to improve the quality of life for all San Diegans."

NATIONAL RECOGNITION

EDD has been recognized across the nation for its efforts. In 1996, it won the top award from the National Council of Development Finance Agencies for writing the first Enterprise Zone bond financing. In 1997, EDD won the Silver Award from the National Council for Urban Economic Development for its defense conversion program, and the California Association for Local Economic Development grand prize for its high-technology resource center.

The city's initiatives and the mayor's vision for the 21st century blend into a comprehensive economic development strategy. "Mayor Golding has identified the top business clusters for growth," Montgomery says. "It's our responsibility to maintain that growth in a balanced manner." The key business clusters are telecommunications, software,

electronics, defense manufacturing, business services and finance, and biotechnology.

"San Diego is where technology is moving," says Montgomery. "We're a magnet area. We work with the local schools and universities to maintain our high-quality workforce. With an outstanding climate, high quality of life, high-tech growth, and quality workforce, our economic prospects are unlimited."

ONE OF THE 16 BUSINESS IM-PROVEMENT DISTRICTS THROUGH-OUT THE CITY, THE GASLAMP QUARTER IS THE HISTORIC HEART OF SAN DIEGO (TOP).

IDEALLY SITUATED FOR TRADE WITH MEXICO, SAN DIEGO IS ALSO AN INTERNATIONAL HUB DUE TO ITS PROXIMITY AND AC-CESS TO THE PACIFIC RIM AND LATIN AMERICA (BOTTOM).

ROHR, INC.—OPERATING AS THE AEROSTRUCTURES GROUP, ONE O four BFGoodrich Aerospace business groups—has been a Sa Diego mainstay for nearly six decades. The Aerostructure Group's reputation as a highly respected supplier of engine related components and structures to the aerospace industr has its roots in the military aircraft boom of 1940. Compan

founder Fred Rohr, the "artist with metals" who fabricated the fuel tanks for Charles Lindbergh's fabled *Spirit of St. Louis,* had a vision perfectly timed for the massive surge in military plane production prompted by World War II. As the aircraft industry exploded from an era of limited, largely experimental production into a tenfold buildup, Rohr saw a clear role for a manufacturing subcontractor that could provide the prime aircraft builders with major structural assemblies. Rohr's vision became a reality on August 6, 1940.

The company Rohr formed with four associates in a San Diego law office that day has continued to gain renown as a supplier of engine-related components and structures ever since. Today, the Aerostructures Group is the leading independent supplier of nacelle and pylon systems to the world's major commercial airframe and engine manufacturers. Approxi-

mately 90 percent of the aircraft in the world's commercial aircraft fleet, excluding aircraft manufactured in the former USSR, contain one or more of the company's products as part of their nacelle, thrust reverser, or pylon systems.

CRITICAL COMPONENTS

Nacelles are the aerodynamic structures that surround engines. Pylons—sometimes called struts— attach the engine to the wing or

fuselage and link its systems to the rest of the aircraft. Thrust reversers redirect engine flow forward on landing to slow the aircraft. Nacelle and pylon system are highly engineered structures that embody all of the key interfaces between the jet engine and the airframe. Their design is critical to an aircraft's weight, fuel efficiency, and compliance with airport noise regulations.

More than a manufacturer, th Aerostructures Group is a system integrator—managing the design, tooling, manufacture, certificatior and delivery of complete nacelle systems in partnership with its customers. In addition to these core products, the company's capabilities include flight control surfaces, hot engine components, advanced metallic thermal protec tion systems, reengining programs. pulsation/surge control devices, and other aircraft structures.

The Aerostructures Group als offers regional aftermarket suppor to more than 150 airline operators

The story of the Aerostructure Group's transition from a set of drawing tables in the founder's garage to one of the world's leading aerospace manufacturers span

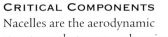

e war years, the jet age, and the
ternational expansion of the
rospace industry. It's the story
f a small subcontractor's trans-
rmation into a world-class sys-
ms integrator.

WO AND A HALF WEEKS
N A GARAGE

We started out in Rohr's back-
rd, in a garage, and at that time
e began designing drop hammers
nd heat treat tanks," recalled one
f the original five employees on
e company payroll. "We were in
e garage about two and a half
eeks before we found a three-
cory building at Eighth and J
creets in San Diego."

"The building was in San Diego's
holesale district, a location that
ade everything easier because
hen we needed tools and metal
upplies to fill our first orders, we
imply walked over to Western
Aetals Co., bought what we needed,
nd carried our purchases back to
he plant," according to another
arly employee.

Those first orders—which in-
olved the manufacture of special
lips for Consolidated Aircraft
Corp.—provided Rohr with its
irst major contract in 1940: the
lesign and installation of Sperry
ombsights on the Consolidated
LB-30 aircraft (the British version
of the B-24 bomber). Later that
ear, Lockheed boosted Rohr's
usiness with an order for cowl-
ngs for its Hudson A-28 bombers.

Needing more space for its
Irop hammers and heat-treating
quipment, Rohr negotiated the
ourchase of 10 acres of land on
he shore of lower San Diego Bay
n Chula Vista, the site the company still occupies today.

NTO THE TOP
RANK OF AIRCRAFT
SUBCONTRACTORS

After the successful completion of
he Sperry bombsight installation,
Rohr was awarded a contract by
Consolidated that moved the company into the top rank of aircraft

subcontractors. The contract was
for the manufacture of ready-to-
install power packages (the motor
mounts, cowl panels and structure,
cowl flaps, plumbing, electrical
harness, and other accessories assembled around a bare engine) for
the PB2Y3 flying boat, the first time
an airframe manufacturer had subcontracted this particular unit.

Before the PB2Y3 even reached
the delivery stage, Consolidated
added another aircraft to Rohr's
growing program roster: the B-24
Liberator bomber. Production of
power packages for these two
aircraft would eventually reach
38,000 units.

When World War II ended,
so did Rohr's period of heady
growth. In 1947, Rohr received its
first order from Boeing Aircraft
Company and first its commercial
aircraft contract: cowlings for
Boeing's Stratocruiser airliner.

The 1950s saw Rohr expand
to Riverside, California; Winder,
Georgia; and Auburn, Washington.
By 1955, Rohr was building power
packages for the Douglas DC-7
and producing jet pods for Boeing's
B-52 bomber, KC-135 tanker, and
707 airliner. As the decade closed,
Rohr was well on its way to becoming a technological leader in
the use of numerically controlled
machine tools, aluminum honey-
comb structures, and the new
wonder metal, titanium.

THE 1960S ENDED
ON A HIGH NOTE

The 1960s ushered in the jet age
and a host of changes in aircraft
manufacturing. Because commercial jets were bigger and faster
than their piston-powered prede-
cessors, fewer aircraft were needed
to meet airline requirements. This
prompted a lull in commercial aircraft orders that lasted until the
mid-1960s.

Late in 1966, Rohr received a
contract to provide nacelles, struts,
and thrust reversers for the initial
version of the 747, the largest aircraft ever designed for commercial
use up to that point. This was the
first of what came to be known
as the wide-bodies. Shortly after
the 747 business was awarded to
Rohr, the company received one
of its largest initial orders to date:

THE ROHR AIRCRAFT CORPORA-
TION'S EXPERIENCE WITH NACELLES
FIRST BEGAN IN THIS LEASED,
THREE-STORY BUILDING IN SAN
DIEGO'S WHOLESALE DISTRICT
IN 1940 WITH THE PRODUCTION
OF COWLINGS FOR LOCKHEED'S
HUDSON BOMBER. THE BUILDING
STILL STANDS AT EIGHTH AND J
STREETS IN DOWNTOWN SAN DIEGO
(TOP).

IN RESPONSE TO PRESIDENT
FRANKLIN ROOSEVELT'S CALL IN
1940 FOR A TENFOLD INCREASE
IN THE PRODUCTION RATE OF MILI-
TARY PLANES, ROHR'S ASSEMBLY
LINES TURNED OUT AS MANY AS
56 POWER PACKAGES A DAY FOR
CONSOLIDATED'S B-24 BOMBER
DURING THE LAST THREE YEARS
OF WORLD WAR II (BOTTOM).

a $40 million contract to build the nacelles and pylons for Lockheed's gigantic C-5A heavy logistics transport for the U.S. Air Force. Bolstered by the C-5A, 747, and other new orders, the 1960s ended on a high note.

The Aerostructures Group took its first steps in the growing international market in the 1970s. In 1972, Airbus Industrie—a then virtually unknown consortium of British, French, German, and Spanish aerospace companies—awarded the company a contract to provide nacelle systems for the very first Airbus aircraft ever built: the twin-engine A300B. Not long after, the company established a French subsidiary in Toulouse to meet the challenge of the growing international market.

During the early 1980s, several key programs were added to Rohr's business base. These programs included the Boeing 737-300, the GE CF6-80C, the Rolls-Royce RB211-535E4, and the KC-135 reengining program. Further business expansion saw the initial deliveries of the McDonnell Douglas MD-80 ship sets and a subcontract award from Lockheed for pylons and nacelles for the C-5B heavy airlift airplane.

CENTERS OF MANUFACTURING EXCELLENCE

Winning the C-5B contract brought about a need for additional assembly space and helped launch the company's Centers of Manufacturing Excellence concept. These centers improve productivity and product quality by focusing on either the assembly or the manufacture of like hardware at a single plant location. This eliminates inefficiencies that can result from

mixing diverse product types at one site by giving these single site a sharper focus. Each of these Centers of Manufacturing Excellence specializes in one or more of the leading-edge capabilities that have made the Aerostructures Group a front-runner in aerospace manufacturing technology.

Today, the company has Centers of Manufacturing Excellence in Riverside, California; Heber Springs and Sheridan, Arkansas; Foley, Alabama; Hagerstown, Maryland; and San Marcos, Texas.

The company entered the 1990s with $1 billion in sales, a backlog of $2.2 billion, and a reputation as a world leader in nacelle systems and pylons—quite an accomplishment for a company that had its humble beginnings in a garage full of drawing tables back in August 1940.

In a development that signals the start of a very positive and exciting new era in Rohr's distinguished history, the company announced plans to merge with BFGoodrich Company in September 1997. The merger was finalized in December 1997. By melding the proud aerospace traditions of Rohr, Inc. and BFGoodrich into a new, stronger organization, this merger creates an even more capable competitor in the fast-changing aerospace industry—the BFGoodrich Aerospace/Aerostructures Group.

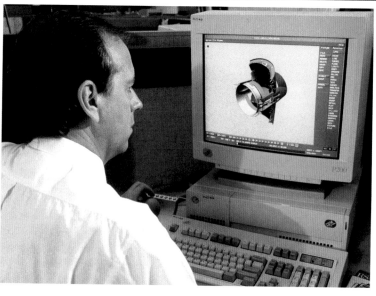

THE UNIVERSITY OF SAN DIEGO (USD) IS A COMMUNITY OF SCHOLars committed to the pursuit of truth, academic excellence, and advancement of knowledge. Chartered as a Roman Catholic institution, the school is preparing to celebrate its 50th anniversary as one of the most prominent educational institutions in Southern California. ■ USD may have been founded in 1949, but the

university as it is known today is the result of a 1972 merger of two schools. The San Diego College for Women—the first unit of the university at Alcalá Park—began classes in 1952. It was erected, financed, and equipped by the Society of Sacred Heart under the leadership of Reverend Mother Rosalie Hill, RSCJ. The second unit of the university, the College for Men and the School of Law, opened in 1954. Sponsored by the Diocese of San Diego, its founder was Bishop Charles F. Buddy, the first Catholic bishop of San Diego.

Independent and comprehensive, USD is dedicated to providing a value-based education to all students. "USD is a place you can call home," says Darcy Agatep, alumna of the university. "The feel is very much one of a close family orientation. Students come here from all over the world. One of the first things they find is people who are here to help them."

Students at the university have a wide variety of fields of study to choose from. The university offers 42 undergraduate degrees, 39 minorstudy programs, 18 master's degrees, and three doctoral programs. USD also hosts summer programs in a variety of nations around the world, including Spain, Italy, Mexico, and Japan.

MORE THAN JUST A GOOD EDUCATION

While the university is renowned for the quality of its educational programs, it has also received attention for the prominent speakers it has hosted. USD gained the national spotlight during the 1996 presidential campaign, when it played host to President Bill Clinton

and Senator Bob Dole for the final presidential debate. In addition to the televised debate, USD leaders sponsored several activities connected to the event that included the school's trustees, sponsors, and some of the 27,000 alumni.

The university has become accustomed to having visitors of wide acclaim: The official portrait of Mother Teresa was taken on the USD campus by photographer Pablo Mason during her visit in 1988.

USD draws a good deal of attention for such a "small" school. In fact, the total number of graduate and undergraduate students in 1997 was only 6,600. Still, there are no plans to increase the number of undergraduate admissions. Dr. Alice B. Hayes, president of the university, states, "The university is committed to small classes and close mentoring of students by faculty and staff. We want to continue to attract students with strong potential."

Instead, USD has a master plan for controlled growth. One major part of that growth will be a new sports facility. It will be funded in part by $7 million of a $10 million

gift from Sid and Jenny Craig, founders of Jenny Craig, Inc. The Jenny Craig Pavilion will contain an official college basketball court which converts to a multipurpose arena, and interscholastic/intramural sports support areas.

From its founding to today, USD has maintained the highest of standards for faculty and students. "USD has generated superior student values and work ethics," says Agatep. "Highly qualified students leave here. Companies often tell us we are producing strong individuals who are the leaders of tomorrow."

USD IS LOCATED ATOP ALCALÁ PARK WHERE THE VIEW CAPTURES BEAUTIFUL SAN DIEGO MISSION BAY (TOP).

COLACHIS PLAZA, WITH ITS SHUMWAY FOUNTAIN, IS A POPULAR MEETING POINT FOR STUDENTS TO STUDY, RELAX, AND SOCIALIZE (BOTTOM).

W

AXIE SANITARY SUPPLY, AMERICA'S LARGEST FAMILY owned distributor of sanitary maintenance supplies, ha been providing its customers with the best products an most reliable service in the industry for more than 5 years. ■ Founded in 1946 by brothers Harry and Morri Wax, WAXIE sells a complete line of more than 3,00

items, including chemicals, disposable paper products, equipment, and cleaning and building accessories. And it sells quite a bit. In fact, all the rolls of toilet paper it sells in a year would wrap around the world 54 times if they were tied together. Customers represent many different business sectors, including health care, commercial, food service, military, contract cleaners, hospitality, education, industrial, and retail.

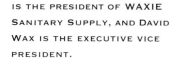

From its humble start in San Diego, the company soon grew rapidly as Morris and Harry assertively pursued new business and secured new clients. In the early 1970s, Morris' sons, Charles and David Wax, came to work for the company. Today, Charles is the company's president and David is the executive vice president.

Due to its increasing market presence, WAXIE has continued to expand, building a new facility in 1996 on 14 acres of land adjacent to its existing facility. The old building has been expanded into a new 111,000-square-foot facility, which houses the company's administrative offices, training room, and fully stocked, 4,500-square-foot showroom.

The WAXIE family now consists of 500 dedicated professionals working in 13 inventory centers throughout the West and Southwest, including San Francisco, Santa Ana, Los Angeles, San Bernardino, Palm Springs, Bakersfield, El Centro, Tempe, Tucson, Yuma, Salt Lake City, and Las Vegas.

The company works with man vendor partners to distribute its products, including Fort James and Rubbermaid.

SERVING THE CUSTOMER

WAXIE maintains a single-minded commitment to reducing its customers' total sanitary maintenanc costs. The company achieves this by offering the most knowledgeable sales consultants in the business, who are trained to solve problems and teach customers how to cut costs and improve performance. Another way WAXIE helps reduce a customer's total sanitary maintenance costs is by helping to eliminate those subtle, but substantial, procurement expenses.

WAXIE also offers computerized inventory tracking. Daily deliveries mean that customers get what they need when they need it, whether the customer is a small company or a multiple-branch operation. By not having to maintain large, expensive inventories, customers can eliminate the associated storage, shrinkage, and waste costs.

Charles Wax boasts that 97 percent of WAXIE's stock items are delivered in metropolitan areas the day after they are ordered. "On time, with no errors—that's our goal," he says.

SERVICE AFTER THE SALE

It is the service after the sale that sets WAXIE apart. More than 50 years in the industry have taught the company that every customer's needs are unique, and that the unexpected can always be counted on to happen. Whether it's crisis

tuations that demand last-minute deliveries, all-night training, special orders, or even a WAXIE consultant going along to lend a hand, WAXIE's legendary customer service proves the extent of its dedication to its customers by going far above what most people would expect, to see that its customers' needs re met.

ONGOING CUSTOMER SUPPORT AND EDUCATION

Being a WAXIE customer means unlimited access to the most cost-effective, cutting-edge solutions to sanitary maintenance problems and concerns. WAXIE provides regular seminars for customers, covering not only the basics, but "hot topics" vital to the successful operation of a business—topics such as workplace safety, floor care, washroom care, carpet care, skin care, OSHA requirements, and more.

WAXIE's subdividable training room can hold approximately 200 people, and has many high-tech educational tools. "We do a tremendous amount of training for people who use our products—how to take care of buildings, how to use our equipment, how to use our products," says Charles. With some of the larger pieces of equipment, such as automatic scrubbers and carpet cleaning machines, WAXIE's

dedicated machine specialists will even go to the customer's site and train maintenance workers to use proper techniques. WAXIE also has a service and repair department to work on the machines it sells as well as other machinery.

WAXIE recently introduced a facility maintenance analysis software program called Custodial Solutions™ to its customers. This program creates a database to analyze manpower allocation, labor costs, tasks and frequencies, inventory control, and employee management for a facility. "The program essentially tells the maintenance supervisor the best way to clean the facility," says Charles.

"We help our customers come up with ways to keep their building looking first-rate," he adds. "We also have personnel to install towel cabinets as well as tissue, soap, and seat-cover dispensers for our clients."

Charles says he sees many opportunities for growth down the road. "I feel optimistic because, geographically, the western U.S. has a healthy economy and a promising future. We try to create a positive impression on the customer with each interaction." That attitude, combined with 50 years of service, is sure to keep WAXIE successful for the next 50 years and beyond.

PRIVATELY OWNED BANNISTER STEEL, INC. IS THE OLDEST AN[D] largest steel fabricator in the San Diego area. The National City based company was founded in 1947 by Ralph Bannister, an[d] today continues to be run by his principle: a quality product [at] a good price, and on time. ■ Bannister founded the compan[y] that bears his name with little more than a pickup truck and [a]

portable welder. From there, things grew at a steady, even pace, gradually growing as Bannister's reputation for quality work grew. Today, the company employs 85 people, including 10 office personnel and 75 shop workers, not to mention

hundreds of subcontracted fieldwork positions. When Bannister died in 1995, the company was purchased by six longtime employees.

"Ralph was a teacher, as well as a great businessman," says Ted Rossin, president of the company.

"The principles he instilled in his employees of hard work and good judgment have allowed Bannister Steel to remain financially sound[.] In 1996, sales increased to $15 mil[-] lion and have been projected at $22 million in 1997."

CUSTOMER ORIENTED

Bannister Steel is responsible for several high-profile buildings and facilities in San Diego, most notably the downtown San Diego Horton Plaza shopping center and the grandstands at the Del Mar Racetrack. These high-profile customers come to Bannister for its excellent reputation.

"We're completely customer oriented," says Rossin. "When we make a promise to get our steel on a site, we do everything possibl[e] to get it there on time and on bud[-] get. We always work with customers to get them a quality product at a good price."

BANNISTER STEEL, INC. IS THE OLDEST AND LARGEST STEEL FABRICATOR IN THE SAN DIEGO AREA.

CENTRALLY LOCATED WITH A RAIL SERVICE IN ITS YARD, BANNISTER STEEL CAN GET TO JOBS QUICKLY, SAVING THE CUSTOMER TIME AND MONEY.

On average, the company fabricates more than 1,200 tons of steel per month. Because it is a relatively small company, Bannister limits its projects to 20-story-and-under buildings. The projects completed by the company include schools, office buildings, hospitals, and shopping centers.

CONQUERING CHALLENGES

Bannister Steel has stayed competitive because of its ability to identify and reduce high-cost areas in production. For example, Bannister has upgraded its W.A. Whitney Beamline with hydraulic lifters and conveyors to cut handling cost.

"The Beamline has been a workhorse for us—a very dependable workhorse," Rossin says. "This acquisition also helped us to design and improve our flow of material through the shop."

That competitive advantage has come in handy over the years, especially when Bannister Steel came face-to-face with its biggest challenge: building the grandstands for the venerable Del Mar Racetrack. Bannister workers had just 24 weeks to fabricate the project, and another eight weeks to erect it. It was a big job—the first phase alone called for 3,000 tons of steel.

Rossin says the project was a two-phase assignment, and one that had to be done at a very specific time. "No doubt, this was our biggest challenge," he says.

The girders for the grandstands are 70 feet long and each one weighs 16 tons. The welds holding the girders together had to be 100 percent ultrasonic tested. "Our welds were fantastic," says Rossin. "There were 12,000 ultrasonic tests done, and we had less than a 1.5 percent rejection rate. That's outstanding. For the second phase, again, each and every weld had to be tested. This time the rejection rate was less than 1 percent."

In all, the Del Mar job called for eight man-hours per ton, or 40,000 man-hours for the two phases of work. It took 80 hours to do one girder, not including the necessary welding. "The results are quite gratifying," says Rossin. "Every season when the gates open for the racing season, hundreds of thousands of people flock to the racetrack to watch the ponies thunder around the track."

SUPPORTING SAN DIEGO

The Del Mar Racetrack isn't Bannister Steel's only claim to fame. In 1984, the company began construction on the phantasmagoric Horton Plaza. "With all the different levels and the way things skew together, that was another challenge," says Rossin. "But we came in right on schedule. You

definitely can't hold up a retail property."

Bannister has also done work for most of San Diego's largest general contractors. Its work includes the Hahn Tower in the Golden Triangle, five San Diego trolley bridges for the Metropolitan Transit Development Board, the sound-system supports at Qualcomm Stadium, four buildings for Qualcomm in Sorrento Mesa, four buildings for NCR in Rancho Bernardo, and the airport tower at Lindbergh Field.

Occasionally, Bannister takes on projects in nearby areas like Palm Springs or Santa Barbara, although it prefers to stay in San Diego. "As long as the work is here, we'll continue to concentrate on San Diego," says Rossin. "We're centrally located, and we have a rail service directly into our yard. We can get out to the jobs very quickly, saving our customers time and money. And most important, we enjoy being a local company."

With an eye for quality and a desire to make every customer happy, Bannister has put itself at the forefront of the steel fabrication industry. Staying ever mindful of its founder's principles—and its customers' needs—Bannister Steel will enter the next century doing what it does best, supporting San Diego.

M
ONTGOMERY WATSON AMERICAS IS ONE OF THE FASTEST growing environmental consulting firms in the country listed among *Forbes* magazine's Top 500 Private Firms. As a full-service environmental engineering, planning, design, construction management, and program management consulting firm, Montgomery Watson provides its clients with a comprehensive range of environmental services.

One of the company's areas of specialization is industrial hazardous waste management services. "We serve the world's environmental needs," says Harold Glaser, vice president of Montgomery Watson in San Diego. "We provide a host of services in the environmental field for a variety of local, state, and federal agencies, as well as major private sector industrial and commercial companies."

SUPPORTING SAN DIEGO
Montgomery Watson has been providing engineering services to the San Diego market since 1947, and established a permanent office in the area in 1968. The company, which is headquartered in Pasadena, California, was founded by engineer James M. Montgomery, a graduate of Cal Tech. Montgomery Watson's first project in the San Diego area involved designing the Alvarado Water Filtration Plant for the City of San Diego. The company also acted as engineering planner and designer for the City's Metropolitan Wastewater System in the mid-to-late 1950s.

Montgomery Watson continued to support the City of San Diego and other local cities and water districts on various projects for the next 30 years. In 1988, the firm was selected to be the program manager for the $1.5 billion upgrade and expansion of the City's wastewater treatment and water reclamation programs. San Diego's reclamation program is especially vital in a region with limited water resources. The recently completed North City Water Reclamation Plant, a $190 million facility, is the first large-scale water reclamation plant in San Diego, and can recycle up to 30 million gallons of wastewater per day.

AWARD-WINNING STAFF
Montgomery Watson's main office downtown supports projects in San Diego and Imperial counties as well as Tijuana and northern Baja California, Mexico. A sepa-

THE CITY OF SAN DIEGO IMPORTS MORE THAN 90 PERCENT OF ITS WATER SUPPLY. THE NORTH CITY WATER RECLAMATION PLANT WILL PRODUCE RECLAIMED WATER FOR LANDSCAPE IRRIGATION AND PROVIDE AN ALTERNATIVE TO USING LIMITED, IMPORTED SUPPLIES.

THE MISSION TRAILS PIPELINE AND FLOW REGULATOR STRUCTURE WILL PROVIDE OPERATIONAL AND CONTINGENCY STORAGE FOR TREATED WATER (LEFT AND RIGHT).

te program management (PM) fice is colocated in the headarters of the City of San Diego's etropolitan Wastewater Department. In total, 35 people are emoyed locally by Montgomery atson. According to Bill Butler, Montgomery Watson vice president and program manager, the n Diego program management am is one of the company's best tributes. "We have great stability among our employees; people signed to a major program stick ith the assignment for a long me. Our people are extremely rofessional and dedicated," says utler. "Our San Diego consultants e experts in their field and lend pport to Montgomery Watson's her offices around the world." Iontgomery Watson has 125 offices roughout 30 countries.

Even with the firm's worldwide fluence, its work in San Diego as not gone unnoticed. In 1997, Iontgomery Watson won the merican Society of Civil Engineers (ASCE) Outstanding Civil ngineering Award for the design d construction of the Mission rails Pipeline and Flow Regulatory tructure project (an 18 million llon, buried concrete reservoir). hat same year, the company suported the city in winning the olden Watchdog Award, given the San Diego County Taxayers Association for a project Iontgomery Watson helped the ty to develop—the Miramar Coeneration Facility. This innovave facility produces power using ethane gas from the adjacent ndfill and from biosolids that me from the nearby water reclation facilities. The facility burns e gas in engines that produce ectricity, and then uses the elecicity to run the water reclamation nd biosolids processing facilities, ving money and natural resources t the same time.

Water repurification is a safe, fective way to supplement the gion's water supply. For more an a decade, Montgomery Watson

has assisted the City of San Diego in testing technologies that utilize advanced water treatment to repurify wastewater. With the use of state-of-the-art technology, reclaimed water will undergo further processing—a pretreatment process, reverse osmosis, disinfection, and nitrate removal—to produce repurified water. By blending this stringently treated repurified water with imported supplies in the San Vincente Reservoir, San Diego can diversify its water supply and maximize the use of local resources, reducing its reliance on imported water.

A COMMITMENT TO WORLD-CLASS SERVICES

As Montgomery Watson prepares to enter the 21st century, its plan

is to continue building a strong business by providing the best in environmental services through state-of-the-art technologies. The company is also dedicated to continuing its expansion in the water, air, and earth science markets for its private and public sector clients.

With a long history of service in San Diego and across the world, Montgomery Watson has seen enormous growth in the last 10 years. "The company has grown from 1,000 employees nationally in 1987 to 3,500 worldwide today," Butler says. "We expect to continue to grow locally by providing worldclass engineering and utility consulting support to both private and public clients throughout San Diego and Imperial counties, and in Mexico."

REVERSE OSMOSIS IS USED TO REMOVE DISSOLVED MINERALS— SUCH AS SALTS AND OTHER CONTAMINANTS—FROM WATER. IT WORKS BY PUMPING WATER THROUGH A SPECIAL MEMBRANE THAT FILTERS OUT ALL POLLUTANTS (LEFT).

IN SAN DIEGO, WATER REPURIFICATION HAS BEEN STUDIED FOR MORE THAN A DECADE. MONTGOMERY WATSON'S PROPOSED OZONE DISINFECTION PROCESS USES STATE-OF-THE-ART TECHNOLOGY TO MIMIC NATURE'S OWN WATER CYCLE (RIGHT).

THE METRO BIOSOLIDS CENTER/ COGENERATION FACILITY, AN INNOVATIVE, NEW FACILITY, WILL USE A PROCESS KNOWN AS COGENERATION TO PRODUCE ELECTRICITY FROM LANDFILL GAS AND BIOGAS.

SINCE CHILDREN'S HOSPITAL AND HEALTH CENTER FIRST OPENED IT doors in 1954, its mission has been to "restore, sustain, an enhance the health and developmental potential of children ■ Now the San Diego region's only designated pediatric traum center, and the only area hospital solely dedicated to pediatr care, Children's is helping San Diego prepare for the 21s century. "Our goal is to help create a region where all children go to school healthy and ready to learn how to be productive, responsible citizens," says Blair Sadler, Children's president and CEO. "Today's children are tomorrow's leaders."

CHILDREN'S HEALTH CARE NEEDS ARE DIFFERENT

From birth through adolescence, children have special health care needs that are different from those of adults. Their bodies respond differently to injury and illness. And most children do not understand—or know how to deal with— the experience of serious illness or hospitalization. Children's responds to these needs by providing expert pediatric care within a unique healing environment.

Quality pediatric care requires special training and a special sensitivity that is perfected through caring for children 100 percent of the time. From mild illness and injury to the most severe medical emergency, Children's Hospital's specially qualified clinical staff and affiliated physicians provide a full continuum of care designed especially with the young patient in mind. Children's also provides services in child development, mental health, speech and hearing, child abuse prevention, and other specific health care areas.

HEALING ENVIRONMENT

As health care has changed over the years, the community need for dedicated pediatric care has continued to increase. Children's has responded by creating a hospital environment just for kids that incorporates state-of-the-art technology with a climate of caring. Designed specifically to help kids get healthy and stay healthy, Children's Hospital promotes heal ing and reduces anxiety through a unique combination of design, light, color, and art. Within this environment of caring, both

▼ JERAN AERO-GRAPHICS, INC.

...ildren and their families become part of the healing process.

Children's Hospital's latest addition to its nationally acclaimed healing environment is the Leichtag Family Healing Garden. Designed by an award-winning landscape architect with the input of hospital staff, auxiliary members, children, and parents, the garden is a blend of interactive wonder and peaceful respite for both children and adults. All of the elements of nature are represented, as symbols of hope, beauty, and life, and as reminders of the ongoing process of growth and renewal.

SERVING ALL COMMUNITIES

From its numerous outpatient clinics to its state-of-the-art hospital in Kearny Mesa, Children's operates as an integrated pediatric health care system, in partnership with primary care physicians from throughout the region. Children's serves all communities throughout San Diego and Imperial counties, with satellite locations and affiliated providers in Oceanside, Vista, Escondido, Temecula, Rancho Bernardo, Chula Vista, La Mesa, El Cajon, and Alpine.

Today, Children's is active in numerous community outreach programs, including health education, early intervention and counseling, childhood immunizations, child abuse prevention, and child safety issues. In partnership with other community-based organizations—like the Greater San Diego Chamber of Commerce and the Safe Kids Coalition—Children's Center for Healthier Communities for Children is helping to link San Diego families with the educational tools and community services they need to raise healthy children. Children's also works with local schools, businesses, government, and law enforcement.

To help kids reach their full potential, Children's Board of Trustees recently committed $1 million per year to support these

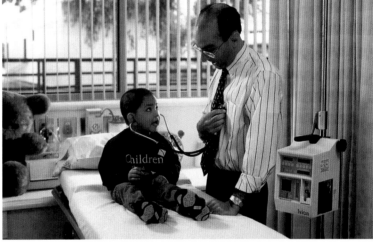

efforts. Children's has become a complete health system, caring for kids within their neighborhoods and helping them stay healthy and safe.

Children's has more than 700 physicians on staff at its Kearny Mesa hospital, with more than 2,000 employees, 400 volunteers, and 1,300 auxiliary members. More than half of Children's Hospital's physicians are specialists representing all branches of surgery, medicine, and psychiatry. Children's provides care to about 20,000 kids every year, serving about 10,000 inpatients and handling about 200,000 types of outpatient and specialty-clinic visits annually. Additionally, Children's Hospital's medical teams perform an average of 50 surgeries each day, including heart surgery, and care for more than 100 trauma patients each month.

Out of 292 licensed beds, 24 are designated as pediatric intensive care and 33 as neonatal intensive care. Additionally, there are eight ICU, 30 special care, and 69 surgical beds. The outpatient department has more than 35 pediatric subspecialties and 100 physicians to treat children who often require multiple services.

THE TASK AHEAD

"Children's Hospital's mission is reflected in the outstanding expertise and ability of our physicians, in the quality and character of our nurses and clinical specialists, in the selflessness and care of our auxiliary and volunteers, and in the vision and commitment of our trustees," says Sadler. "To know the history of this wonderful institution's 44 years is to know a process of constant renewal and rededication, of philanthropy and selflessness, and of compassionate medical excellence. Hundreds of thousands have benefited from this precious resource. Many are parents themselves now; some are grandparents."

It is this potent combination of strengths that will enable Children's to do even more for children's health now and in the future—in times which pose some of the most daunting challenges ever.

THE LEICHTAG FAMILY HEALING GARDEN AT CHILDREN'S HOSPITAL AND HEALTH CENTER IS A BLEND OF INTERACTIVE WONDER AND PEACEFUL RESPITE FOR BOTH CHILDREN AND PARENTS (TOP).

QUALITY PEDIATRIC CARE REQUIRES SPECIAL TRAINING AND A SPECIAL SENSITIVITY THAT IS PERFECTED THROUGH CARING FOR CHILDREN 100 PERCENT OF THE TIME (BOTTOM).

SHARP HEALTHCARE'S DRIVING MISSION IS TO IMPROVE THE HEALT of those it serves. The organization is committed to excellence i health care, and its goal is to offer quality care and services tha set community standards and exceed patients' expectations. Sharp HealthCare's roots go back to 1946, when the San Dieg Hospital Association (SDHA) was formed to raise funds fo

building a hospital in San Diego. In 1949, the P.L. Gildred family donated 12.5 acres in Kearny Mesa to SDHA as a proposed hospital site. The following year, Thomas E. Sharp—a rancher and radio communications pioneer—gave $500,000 to SDHA in memory of his son, Air Force Lieutenant Donald N. Sharp, who was killed in World War II. Ground was then broken in 1954, and the Donald

N. Sharp Memorial Community Hospital was opened in 1955.

Since the beginning of its operation, Sharp HealthCare has pioneered the use of new technologies and implemented new services. Among its long list of San Diego County firsts, Sharp conducted the first open-heart surgery, installed the first electronic pacemaker west of St. Louis, established the first driver-education program for disabled individuals, and performed the first heart transplant.

INTEGRATED, REGIONAL DELIVERY SYSTEM

Sharp HealthCare is an integrated, regional health care delivery system. With seven hospitals and 24 clinics located throughout San Diego County, the system serves all of the region's varied geographic, economic, and cultural communities. Acute care hospitals are located in Kearny Mesa, La Mesa, Coronado, Point Loma, and Chula Vista. Sharp HealthCare's medical groups—

Sharp Rees-Stealy, Sharp Mission Park, and Sharp Community— reach from Fallbrook to Imperia Beach to El Cajon. Serving a popu lation of approximately 3 million and operating 1,750 beds, the sys tem includes approximately 2,30(physicians on medical staffs with 1,100 of those in medical groups. Throughout its entire system, th health care organization has a total of 10,000 employees.

In addition to its acute care facilities, Sharp HealthCare oper ates the Sharp Mary Birch Hospita for Women, which opened its doo in 1992. Nationally recognized for outstanding hospital-based women's services, the facility serve women at all stages of life and pro vides a single location for comple care. It is the largest and most extensive freestanding center for women's health in Southern Cali fornia and is one of only five suc facilities in the entire country. More than 8,100 babies are deliv ered annually at Sharp Mary Birc Hospital for Women, making it

...e busiest maternity service in ...alifornia. Overall, one-third ...f all babies born in San Diego ...ounty are delivered at a Sharp ...ospital.

In 1997, Sharp completed a ...hree-year quality evaluation by ...he Joint Commission on Accredi-...ation of Healthcare Organizations ...ith the highest scores it's ever ...eceived—all six hospitals scored ...bove the 90th percentile.

...ARGEST PROVIDER ...F SERVICES

...ccording to Sharp HealthCare ...resident and CEO Michael W. ...urphy, being the largest pro-...ider of acute care in San Diego ...ounty sets Sharp apart. "From ...tate-of-the-art mechanical heart ...evices that help prolong the lives ...f patients awaiting a heart trans-...lant to offering low-cost flu shots ...o senior citizens, Sharp is com-...nitted to providing the best pos-...ible health care in San Diego," ...e says.

Murphy adds, "Sharp's rehabili-...ation centers at Sharp Memorial ...nd Grossmont hospitals get re-...errals from around the nation

because of their reputation for providing the most comprehensive rehabilitation services in Southern California." These centers treat more than 600 acute rehabilita-tion inpatients and more than 6,000 outpatients every year.

RESPONSIBILITY TO THE COMMUNITY

"Sharp HealthCare has a history of fulfilling its responsibilities as a not-for-profit health care system by providing community benefit activities that meet the needs of the communities served," says Murphy. The organization pro-vided $70.6 million in community benefit activities in 1997, and of that, $66 million went toward uncom-pensated and undercompensated care. "All Sharp HealthCare hospi-tals, except Mary Birch Hospital for Women, operate 24-hour emer-gency rooms that offer care to all patients regardless of their ability to pay," he says.

Also in 1997, Sharp gave major support to the Sidney Kimmel Cancer Research Center. Murphy says the remaining funds were committed to health promotion

and disease prevention, medical research and professional train-ing, and health care to vulnerable populations and the broader community.

"Our commitment to excellence runs across the organization, from the front desks of our hospitals and clinics to the operating rooms and intensive care units," says Murphy. "We are striving to re-spond to the ever changing health care environment by providing high-quality, compassionate, cost-effective care for all San Diegans."

FROM SALES OF LESS THAN $100,000 IN ITS FIRST YEAR, McMILLI
Companies has fashioned itself into a major force among Souther
California builders and developers. It was recently ranked by *Profe
sional Builder* magazine as one of the nation's housing giants.
Corky McMillin, founder and CEO of McMillin Companies, wa
born in Missouri in 1929. His family came west when he was

FROM SALES OF LESS THAN
$100,000 IN ITS FIRST YEAR,
MCMILLIN COMPANIES HAS FASH-
IONED ITSELF INTO A MAJOR FORCE
AMONG SOUTHERN CALIFORNIA'S
BUILDERS AND DEVELOPERS. IT
WAS RECENTLY RANKED BY PRO-
FESSIONAL BUILDER MAGAZINE
AS ONE OF THE NATION'S HOUS-
ING GIANTS (LEFT).

CORKY MCMILLIN IS THE FOUNDER
AND CEO OF MCMILLIN COMPA-
NIES, THE OLDEST BUILDING EN-
TERPRISE IN SAN DIEGO COUNTY
(RIGHT).

teenager, and at 16, he was working for his father, a small building contractor. This start at the
working end of a hammer led to
the founding of McMillin's own
company in National City in 1960.
McMillin Companies has since
expanded into small-tract development and into the development of multi-neighborhood
communities.

McMillin Companies is the
oldest building enterprise in San
Diego County. Its subsidiary,
McMillin Realty, ranks as the
county's largest independent real
estate firm. In addition to real
estate sales and mortgage financing, the family-run business spans
the complete land development
spectrum, including a fast-growing
commercial and industrial development division.

SUCCESSFUL MASTER PLANNING

"Years ago, when McMillin's first
modest ventures were started, we
established some basic guidelines
for ourselves," McMillin says. "Be
honest. Be fair. Work together. And
listen. From the very beginning,
we were determined that this was
going to be a company admired
not for the volume of its sales, but
rather for the quality of its work
and the integrity of its people."

Through tough years in a down
economy, McMillin Companies
maintained its staff—often at great
personal sacrifice for McMillin.
When the recession of the early
1990s ended, his employees—which
now number around 300—were
ready to move ahead.

As a result of their can-do attitude, the company currently has

two of the most successful master-
planned communities in San Dieg
County: Rancho del Rey in Chula
Vista, where nearly 3,000 of 4,00(
homes have been built; and Scripp
Ranch Villages in San Diego's
Scripps Ranch area, where about
1,000 of 3,000 homes have been
completed.

McMillin Companies also recently opened a new master-planne
community in Riverside County—
the 1,200-home Temeku Hills Go
and Country Club. A grand open
ing saw more than 3,000 anxious
home buyers and shoppers atten(
a balloon and golf festival in the
first of two neighborhoods that
will make up the community.

Another community in Riverside County, called Orangecrest
Hills, will contain more than 1,20
housing units when completed. I
all, McMillin controls some 4,00(
undeveloped acres in the adjacen
Riverside and San Diego counties
Such development has paid off:
The company was recently ranke(
as one of the leading sellers in the
nation of finished lots.

BEYOND HOUSING DEVELOPMENTS

McMillin Companies is also involved in projects beyond residential real estate. Its commercial and industrial division has become a major player in that arena, competing with larger and longer-established developers. McMillin's commercial and industrial projects include the 4S Business Park in Rancho Bernardo, the Wineridge Business Park in Escondido, the Parkway Business Centre in Poway, and Scripps Ranch Village Center in Scripps Ranch Villages.

Like no Southern California builder before it, McMillin has diversified into a broad-based family of independent—yet integrated—real estate companies. Buyers and sellers can benefit from a wide variety of professional services, including residential resale, mortgage banking, remodeling and custom home building, and corporate relocation services. In fact, McMillin's relocation division has been recognized as one of the best in the country; it helps families in all aspects of moving, including finding schools for children and employment for spouses.

FOCUS ON COMMUNITY

Even as the company grows, it never forgets that being a valuable member of the community is very important. Corky McMillin and his wife, Vonnie, are the parents

of two sons and a daughter, all of whom hold executive positions in the company.

Corky McMillin has been the recipient of a myriad of awards for his many accomplishments and for his contributions to the community. He won the Professional Achievement Award from *Professional Builder* magazine for the Scripps Ranch North community, cited as a national model for conscientious, large-scale land use back in the early 1980s. He received the City of Hope's Spirit of Life award and was named the Business Person of the Year by the National City Chamber of Commerce.

McMillin also was granted the Lee Hubbard Award, which recognizes individuals in San Diego who have made outstanding contributions to the building industry as well as to the community.

McMillin served as president of the San Diego Building Industry Association (BIA) and is a member of the BIA Hall of Fame. In 1998, his son, Mark, took the reins as BIA president.

McMillin Companies employees contribute time and resources to scores of charities—from youth sports to medical research organizations. McMillin and his wife are honorary chairpersons for the South Bay Family YMCA's capital campaign.

From its contributions to the real estate development industry, to the public service efforts of the McMillin family, McMillin Companies has carved a place for itself that reaches beyond its headquarters in National City and the entire San Diego County to make a mark throughout Southern California and beyond.

CLOCKWISE FROM TOP LEFT: BUYERS AND SELLERS CAN BENEFIT FROM A WIDE VARIETY OF PROFESSIONAL SERVICES MCMILLIN OFFERS, INCLUDING RESIDENTIAL RESALE, MORTGAGE BANKING, REMODELING AND CUSTOM HOME BUILDING, AND CORPORATE RELOCATION SERVICES.

MCMILLIN FOUNDED HIS OWN COMPANY IN NATIONAL CITY IN 1960. SINCE THEN, MCMILLIN COMPANIES HAS EXPANDED INTO SMALL-TRACT DEVELOPMENT AND INTO THE DEVELOPMENT OF MULTI-NEIGHBORHOOD COMMUNITIES.

"YEARS AGO, WHEN MCMILLIN'S FIRST MODEST VENTURES WERE STARTED, WE ESTABLISHED SOME BASIC GUIDELINES FOR OUR-SELVES: BE HONEST. BE FAIR. WORK TOGETHER. AND LISTEN," SAYS MCMILLIN, JOINED BY HIS SONS MARK AND SCOTT.

L OCATED ON 1,200 ACRES OF COASTAL WOODLAND, THE UNIVERSIT of California, San Diego (UCSD) is the southernmost campus o the world-renowned University of California system. Since it founding in 1960, UCSD has become one of the nation's premie teaching and research institutions. ■ "In a short time, UCSD ha. become a top-ranking educational institution respected worldwid.

for research, teaching, health care, and public service," says UCSD Chancellor Robert C. Dynes. "UCSD is an economic engine for the region, fueling the growth of biotech and high-tech industry. We also serve as a cultural and intellectual hub for a community that I believe will emerge as one of the great cities of the 21st century, particularly as the world arena shifts its focus to the Pacific Rim."

CAMPUS LIFE

More than 18,000 undergraduate, graduate, and medical students attend UCSD, learning in a stimulating environment where research excellence is at the heart of every program. The process of discovery and innovation is taught not only in the school's stellar science and engineering programs, but in its highly regarded liberal arts, performing arts, humanities, and social science divisions.

The National Research Council placed UCSD 10th in the nation in the quality of its graduate programs and faculty, which includes five Nobel laureates and a Pulitzer Prize-winning composer. *U.S. News & World Report* ranked the school's theater program third in the nation, with high rankings also awarded to the film program, the School of Medicine, and the School of Engineering.

With its theaters, galleries, concert halls, and the acclaimed Stuart Collection of outdoor sculpture, the campus is a major cultural center. The Geisel Library is the centerpiece of UCSD's extensive library system, serving as a regional resource, with 7,500 people entering UCSD libraries daily and 45,000 on-line information searches conducted each day from libraries, offices, and homes.

Through seminars, workshops, and classes offered by Extended Studies and Public Service and Continuing Medical Education programs, thousands of community members take advantage of the expertise available at UCSD, and teachers and students throughout the county are engaged in health and educational outreach activities directed by UCSD faculty and physicians.

Long before UCSD opened its doors, the University of California operated a marine biology station in San Diego that today is one of the largest and most important centers for marine science research and graduate training in the world: Scripps Institution of Oceanography. Now part of UCSD, the scientific scope of the institution encompasses studies of the oceans, atmospheric studies, and biological research, with projects ranging

THE GEISEL LIBRARY IS THE CENTERPIECE OF THE UNIVERSITY OF CALIFORNIA, SAN DIEGO'S (UCSD) EXTENSIVE LIBRARY SYSTEM, WHICH HOUSES 2.5 MILLION VOLUMES AND SERVES AS A RESOURCE FOR THE CAMPUS AND THE COMMUNITY ALIKE (LEFT).

UCSD'S THORNTON HOSPITAL PROVIDES A WARM, COMFORTING ENVIRONMENT FOR PATIENTS TO RECEIVE ADVANCED, STATE-OF-THE-ART CARE PROVIDED BY UCSD HEALTHCARE PHYSICIANS (RIGHT).

▲ ALAN DECKER PHOTO

om global warming to the development of pharmaceuticals from a life.

The popular Birch Aquarium Scripps, built in 1992 on an cean-view bluff adjacent to the CSD campus, is the newest in series of aquariums maintained Scripps. Each year 400,000 eople, including more than 60,000 hoolchildren, visit the aquarium enjoy the exhibits and learn ore about ocean science and e marine life of the Pacific.

N ECONOMIC FORCE

CSD ranks as the third-largest nployer in San Diego County. ith an annual operating budget ceeding $1 billion, UCSD's impact on the San Diego economy phenomenal. At last count, more an 120 companies, primarily in otech and high-tech industries, ere UCSD spin-offs, founded by CSD faculty, alumni, students, r staff, or based on UCSD technology. The UCSD Connect program actively promotes new nterprises that enrich the regional onomy. In order to provide more formation about the university, CSD maintains a Web site at tp://www.ucsd.edu.

CSD HEALTHCARE: 1EDICINE AT ITS BEST

he hallmark of academic medicine advancement of good health rough high-quality care, research, nd innovation. UCSD's School Medicine, which opened in 1968, as developed a system of hospitals nd patient services, called UCSD ealthcare, that rates among the ountry's best.

UCSD physicians and programs, rving patients of all ages, are constently featured in guides such the *U.S. News & World Report* nnual Best Hospitals in America urvey, the *Good Housekeeping* listgs of best specialists, and other onsumer guides to quality health re.

As the region's only universityased health care system, UCSD

Healthcare stands alone in its commitment to patient care, education, research, and service to the community. UCSD physicians provide a wide range of services, from primary care to highly specialized procedures, spanning infant and pediatric care to services for senior citizens.

"UCSD School of Medicine physicians and scientists are leaders in their fields, whether their emphasis is patient care or biomedical research," said Vice Chancellor for Health Sciences John F. Alksne, M.D. "The interaction of researchers with clinicians leads to advances in how we diagnose, treat, and even prevent disease, with new discoveries in medicine and technology benefiting not only our own patients, but patients everywhere."

UCSD's comprehensive system of patient care services is provided at state-of-the-art facilities, including UCSD Medical Center in Hillcrest, UCSD's Thornton Hospital in La Jolla, and several convenient outpatient centers, including the Shiley Eye Center adjacent to Thornton Hospital. UCSD-affiliated physicians also see patients at community-based practices throughout San Diego.

Besides providing family practice, internal medicine, pediatrics, OB-GYN, and seniors care, UCSD Healthcare offers an array of specialty services at the leading edge of

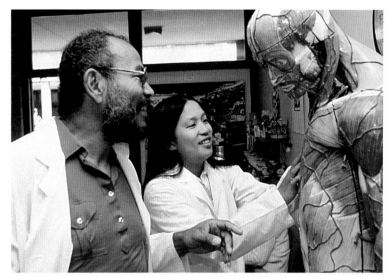

medicine. Cancer care is provided through the region's only National Cancer Institute-designated clinical and research cancer center. UCSD offers a comprehensive organ transplant program; high-risk pregnancy management and infant special care; and sophisticated emergency and trauma care that includes San Diego's Regional Burn Center and a hyperbaric medicine center.

UCSD physicians direct hundreds of clinical studies, providing access to promising new therapies for conditions ranging from asthma to headaches, heart failure to glaucoma. UCSD ranks in the top 10 medical schools nationally in numbers of clinical studies and research funding. Information about health care services and clinical studies is available through the UCSD Health Sciences Web site (http://health.ucsd.edu).

CLOCKWISE FROM TOP LEFT: THE BIRCH AQUARIUM AT SCRIPPS, FEATURING MARINE LIFE FROM THE PACIFIC NORTHWEST TO THE TROPICAL SOUTH PACIFIC, PROVIDES VISITORS WITH AN ENTERTAINING AND EDUCATIONAL EXPERIENCE.

UCSD IS RENOWNED AS A RESEARCH UNIVERSITY, WITH INNOVATION AT THE HEART OF THE STELLAR SCIENCE, ENGINEERING, AND MEDICAL PROGRAMS, AS WELL AS THE OUTSTANDING ARTS, HUMANITIES, AND SOCIAL SCIENCES DEPARTMENTS.

COMMENCEMENT SPEAKER PRESIDENT BILL CLINTON ADDRESSED THE UCSD GRADUATING CLASS OF 1997.

SINCE 1954, THE MAIN OBJECTIVE OF THE SAN DIEGO CONVENTION & Visitors Bureau (ConVis) has been to promote and market Greater San Diego as a vacation destination and a site for meetings and conventions. ■ "It's so important for a community like San Diego to have ConVis," says Reint Reinders, president and CEO of the organization. "We're the only agency that is marketing and

positioning the region to the outside world. We're an economic engine for San Diego because our goal is to bring outside money into the region."

Some major events that the bureau has brought to San Diego include the 1996 Republican National Convention and the 1998 Super Bowl. "These events help focus the eyes of the nation—and the world—on San Diego," says Reinders. "They give us the opportunity to show off our hospitality, and to show that we're a great place to visit or bring your business."

A Member Organization
ConVis is a private, nonprofit corporation comprised of approximately 1,600 organizations, businesses, local governments, and individuals seeking to build a better community through the visitor industry. Members include tourism-related entities such as hotels, restaurants, tour operators, caterers, retail stores, and transportation companies, as well as other businesses not directly linked to the visitor industry.

In terms of revenue generated, tourism is San Diego's third-largest industry—behind manufacturing and government/military spending. The visitor industry brought more than $4.3 billion into San Diego County in 1997 and provided approximately 125,000 jobs. More than 14.5 million visitors—from throughout the United States and around the world—came to San Diego in 1997.

The ConVis staff is comprised of 91 full-time and 180 part-time employees. Beyond San Diego, the bureau also maintains regional sales offices in Chicago and Washington, D.C. ConVis derives the majority of its funding from the local Transient Occupancy Tax (TOT) on hotel rooms. The TOT is levied on all hotel and motel rooms in the county and was established to support promotion of the region. As a membership organization, the bureau also receives financial support from membership dues.

Principal activities of ConVis include marketing, sales, and community relations. The bureau's marketing department focuses on advertising, national public relations, marketing promotions, cultural tourism, research, Internet business development, and the provision of an International Visitor Information Center. The sales department is charged with citywide convention center sales, convention sales for area hotels, convention services, and travel industry sales. ConVis' community relations team works on communications with local media, membership development, and member services.

"One of the best things about our business is that the tourism infrastructure is a great bonus to the people who live in San Diego," says Reinders. "We help make sure the beaches and the parks and the museums are kept up, and that is a contributor to the livability standard here."

THE SAN DIEGO CONVENTION AND VISITORS BUREAU (CONVIS) IS A PRIVATE, NONPROFIT CORPORATION COMPRISED OF APPROXIMATELY 1,600 ORGANIZATIONS, BUSINESSES, LOCAL GOVERNMENTS, AND INDIVIDUALS SEEKING TO BUILD A BETTER COMMUNITY THROUGH THE VISITOR INDUSTRY (TOP).

SINCE 1954, THE MAIN OBJECTIVE OF CONVIS HAS BEEN TO PROMOTE AND MARKET GREATER SAN DIEGO AS A VACATION DESTINATION AND A SITE FOR MEETINGS AND CONVENTIONS (BOTTOM).

1961-1984

1961
COX COMMUNICATIONS

1962
SAN DIEGO UNIFIED PORT DISTRICT

1965
NBC 7/39

1968
HEWLETT-PACKARD

1968
NCR CORPORATION

1969
BROWN MARTIN HALLER & McCLAIN, LLP

1971
NATIONAL UNIVERSITY

1971
R&B REALTY GROUP/OAKWOOD CORPORATE
HOUSING

1972
ODGEN ENVIRONMENTAL AND ENERGY SERVICES

1972
SONY TECHNOLOGY CENTER-SAN DIEGO

1974
TOPS STAFFING SERVICES, INC.

1977
DUCKOR SPRADLING & METZGER

1977
SAN DIEGO HOSPICE CORPORATION

1978
KERCHEVAL ENGINEERS/PBS&J

1978
SANYO NORTH AMERICA CORPORATION

1978
SOURCE SERVICES CORPORATION

1979
SAN DIEGO DATA PROCESSING CORPORATION

1980
MCM ARCHITECTS & PLANNERS

1980
OVERLAND DATA

1981
SAN DIEGO NATIONAL BANK

1981
SIERRA OPTICAL

1982
GOLDEN EAGLE INSURANCE CORPORATION

1982
SOUTHWEST AIRLINES

1983
THE ARROWHEAD GROUP OF COMPANIES

1983
DOUGLAS E. BARNHART, INC.

1983
THE EASTLAKE COMPANY

1983
GENETRONICS, INC.

1983
SUNRISE MEDICAL INC.

1984
AGOURON PHARMACEUTICALS, INC.

1984
THE BED & BREAKFAST INN AT LA JOLLA

1984
COMSTREAM

1984
SAN DIEGO CONVENTION CENTER
CORPORATION

I N APRIL 1995, COX CABLE BECAME COX COMMUNICATIONS, A REFLECTION of the company's evolution into a multidimensional national leader with vast resources in the field of telecommunications. Cox has grown as the result of deep roots in the community developed through three decades of customer service, investment in technology, and civic involvement ■ "The future of communications is here," says Bill Geppert, Cox

general manager. "Our customers are the beneficiaries of leading-edge technology and can expect the best, both in service and community commitment."

Cox Communications operates a network that forms the backbone of a sophisticated communications system that will take the San Diego region into the 21st century. In recent years, Cox has invested more than $400 million to install a total of 70,000 miles of fiber-optic

cable, the most recent phase of a multibillion-dollar investment. Today, Cox Communications is the nation's fifth-largest cable system and the largest in California.

Investment in cable technology is matched by the widely recognized Cox commitment to quality customer service. Cox Communications is dedicated to providing the best in customer care. In the 1980s, Cox became the first cable company in the United States

to establish customer service standards that have become the benchmark for the industry. Three times, Cox has won the prestigious Customer Is Key award, national recognition from Cable and Telecommunications: A Marketing Society.

Cox customers have come to expect a crystal-clear television picture, uninterrupted by technical difficulties. Making this a top priority, Cox has built a digital fiber-optic network that is unsurpassed in its capacity to transmit video, voice, and data. The "ring-in-ring architecture," combined with laser transmitters, allows problem-free delivery of the signal.

Cox is finding new ways to use this cutting-edge technology to improve the quality of life for customers. In addition to cable television, Cox offers Cox@Home and Cox@Work—digital Internet access at speeds more than 100 times faster than provided by conventional analog modems—which allow computer users to put the Internet to work in entirely new ways.

Consumers are benefiting from the new choice of Cox for telephone service, including Long Distance by Frontier and, starting in 1998, totally digital local telephone service. And soon Cox will be offering digital television, bringing all the choices of satellite programming without having to buy equipment, and introducing viewers to the new elements of interactive television and continuous commercial-free, digital-quality music.

At the same time that Cox makes new technology useful in the homes of almost 500,000 subscribers, it also provides an intimate connection to the surrounding

IN RECENT YEARS, COX COMMUNICATIONS HAS INVESTED MORE THAN $400 MILLION TO INSTALL A TOTAL OF 70,000 MILES OF FIBER-OPTIC CABLE.

mmunity through award-winning cal programming and charitable vic involvement.

Channel 4 San Diego, telecast more than 741,000 households ver cable channel 4, is a unique indow on the region that was unched by Cox in summer 1996. hannel 4 San Diego provides a orld beyond the three-minute und bite format of typical locally oduced coverage, by exclusive d expanded coverage of San iego area sports, traffic, events, d lifestyles.

The channel's debut as the ox Convention Connexion earned e respect of national news outts through its 14 days of roundne-clock coverage as a full-blown ews channel. The coverage adhered high journalism standards and rned Cox the 1997 Innovator ward for Local Programming om *Cablevision* magazine, the ost prestigious of its annual vards, as well as the Mark Award d a Beacon Award.

In another programming innotion, Channel 4 San Diego is e first station in the country to lecast four hours of continuous orning traffic updates each weeky, enabling viewers to get all the affic news they need before hitng the road.

During baseball season, Chanel 4 San Diego telecasts more an 100 Padres games—a record or games aired in a single season— us original programming that cludes insightful profiles, live ll-in shows, and feature coverge. Basketball fans were thrilled learn that the Los Angeles Lakers ad signed with Channel 4 San iego as the exclusive area televion outlet for 1997-1998 Lakers asketball. Channel 4 San Diego telecasting San Diego State niversity (SDSU) Aztecs football mes, as well as men's and women's asketball games played in Cox rena at SDSU.

The Aztecs sports telecasts d the newly built Cox Arena San Diego State University are

two facets of a many-sided strategic partnership between Cox Communications and SDSU. The unique agreement benefits SDSU students by providing increased fiber-optic connections allowing for more Internet access, a variety of telephony applications, and more opportunities for distance learning.

The Cox commitment to education is extremely important. Besides the special partnership with SDSU, Cox provides free cable service to all schools in the Cox service area, and produces the annual Salute to Teachers awards at San Diego's Civic Theatre (which has netted Cox multiple awards, including four Emmys, in addition to providing a showcase for teacher excellence). Cox distributes a teacher-focused newsletter highlighting worthwhile educational programs coming up on channels carried by Cox. Its Cable in the Classroom program provides commercial-free educational programming for instructional use.

Cable services are no longer restricted to merely television pro-

gramming, and Cox Communications is a prime example of the industry's versatility. By including Internet and telephone services, Cox has poised itself at the forefront of the telecommunications industry. Nationally recognized for leadership in high technology as well as responsiveness to customers, Cox Communications takes pride in exceeding its customers' expectations.

IN ADDITION TO CABLE TELEVISION, COX OFFERS COX@HOME AND COX@WORK—DIGITAL INTERNET ACCESS AT SPEEDS MORE THAN 100 TIMES FASTER THAN PROVIDED BY CONVENTIONAL ANALOG MODEMS—WHICH ALLOW COMPUTER USERS TO PUT THE INTERNET TO WORK IN ENTIRELY NEW WAYS.

THE COX ARENA AT SAN DIEGO STATE UNIVERSITY IS THE RESULT OF A UNIQUE AND IN-DEPTH PARTNERSHIP BETWEEN COX COMMUNICATIONS AND SAN DIEGO STATE UNIVERSITY.

W

ATERFRONT PARKS, OPEN SPACE, SCENIC WALKWAYS, AN bicycle paths are common along San Diego Bay. Thes and other recreational amenities are there for all t enjoy, courtesy of the San Diego Unified Port Distric ■ Established in 1962 to manage the areas on an around San Diego Bay, the Port District works t

develop facilities and services that will offer the greatest public benefit to the regional economy. In its mission to promote commerce, navigation, recreation, and fisheries, it has become an integral part of the area's growth and development.

The Port District is a self-sustaining public agency that has required no tax levy since 1970. Revenues from its three main operational areas—airport, real estate, and maritime commerce—have been sufficient to support Port District operations, service bonded indebtedness, and allow for capital improvements.

The Port District is under the direction of the board of port commissioners, which is composed of representatives from each of its five member cities of Chula Vista, Coronado, Imperial Beach, National City, and San Diego. San Diego has three representatives on the Port Commission because of its larger size and population; the other four cities each have one representative. Commissioners are appointed to four-year terms by the city council of their respective member city. Larry Killeen, executive director, oversees the daily operations of the public agency and a staff of more than 600.

PORT DISTRICT ASSETS

Infrastructure of significant importance, such as San Diego International Airport (Lindbergh Field); major real estate development on the waterfront; marine terminals; numerous parks; and open space are among the many assets of the Port District. It is a major economic engine that fuels the local economy with more than 600 ten ants, including 18 marinas, 6,000 hotel rooms, 12,000 restaurant seats, 25 ship berths, a major ship builder, ship repair facilities, and more.

The Port District leases much of its land and facilities. One example is a waterfront high-rise hotel, which generates anywhere from $5 million to $6 million a year for the Port District. In stark contrast, the San Diego Conventio Center is leased to the City of Sar Diego from the Port District for only $1 a year. The Port District funded the construction of the $208 million center, making it th first debt-free convention center

BOARDWALKS AND WALKING PATHS ARE NUMEROUS ALONG SAN DIEGO BAY AND THROUGHOUT PORT DISTRICT WATERFRONT PARKS (LEFT).

THE PORT DISTRICT FUNDED SAN DIEGO'S WATERFRONT CONVENTION CENTER, A PROMINENT FEATURE ON THE BAY FRONT (RIGHT).

a major U.S. city. This investment by the Port has greatly enhanced the Port's role as a major player in the global trade show and convention arena.

Real estate operations are a major source of the Port District's $31 million annual income. In fact, percent of that amount comes from the agency's 600 tenant leases. Our real estate business segment has been the cornerstone of our success," says David L. Malcolm, chairman of the board of port commissioners. "Our role is to serve as an economic engine for our business partners."

SAN DIEGO INTERNATIONAL AIRPORT

Playing an essential role in the area's transportation needs, some million passengers travel through Lindbergh Field annually. To meet the region's ever increasing air travel demands, Lindbergh Field recently underwent a massive airport construction program for the benefit of the region. Improvements include a new, 300,000-square-foot terminal with eight gates, a completely redesigned airport roadway system, pedestrian overpasses, and new signage.

"As the region grows and becomes more successful in attracting conventions and tourists, and the regional economy continues

to flourish, air travel needs are also being addressed with a recently awarded contract to develop an airport master plan that will outline San Diego International Airport's needs through 2020," says Malcolm.

THE FUTURE

Promoting tourism will continue to be one of the Port District's top priorities, as tourism is San Diego's third-largest industry. In 1996, the city was host to almost 14 million visitors who spent $4 billion in the region.

Also high on the Port District's list of priorities is the restoration of the San Diego & Arizona Eastern rail link to the east and the dredging of San Diego Bay to accommodate larger container vessels.

These needed infrastructure improvements are vital if San Diego is to become a better player in maritime commerce. A convention center expansion and urban redevelopment planning of the South and North Embarcadero areas are already in the works.

The Port of San Diego has been dubbed the San Diego region's gateway. To facilitate redevelopment and ensure prosperity of the area for years to come, the Port Commission is working to ensure that the Port continues its path to enhance and improve the regional economy through prudent use of its resources. Malcolm concludes, "We have joined hands with the region and will work together to take San Diego to the next century."

N

BC 7/39 FOCUSES ITS EFFORTS ON PROVIDING SAN DIEGO WIT
unparalleled news coverage, quality television entertainment, an
extensive information about the area. Neil E. Derrough, presider
and general manager, has been instrumental in making that ha
pen. "Neil is the man responsible for making NBC 7/39 as goo
as it is today," says Douglas Gilmore, vice president of creati

services. "He has had an astound-
ing career and brought all of that
knowledge to this station." Gilmore
says before Derrough arrived in
March 1988, the station was primarily known for airing Padres
games. But when Derrough took
over, the rebuilding process began.

"We did some research at the
time," explains Derrough, "and
found that only 33 percent of the
people in our coverage area even
knew we were an NBC affiliate.
We were not a factor as a major
television station."

But Derrough changed that.
News anchors began identifying
the station more often as NBC,
and program advertisements em-
phasized the affiliation. In addition, news coverage was expanded.
Says Derrough, "We started adding
as much local news as we could.
In 1988, we were doing nine hours
of news per week; now we do 27

hours. News is the most important
part of the way a television station
is perceived locally. In many ways,
it is the personality of the station."

Today's market leader for news
and information in San Diego is
a television station that started
out in 1965 as an independent UHF
station. Owned at that time by

San Diego Telecasters, Inc., KAAR
first decade was a rocky one, begi
ning in 1966 when it was destroye
by a fire and forced to go off the
air for more than a year.

Under new ownership, the sta
tion was revived in 1968 as KCST-T
just in time to begin a long battl
with Channel 6 for its affiliation
with ABC. KCST won out as the
ABC affiliate in 1972, and two yea
later was sold to Storer Broadcasting, Inc., a family-owned broadcasting company with television
stations in the East and Midwes
Finally, in 1977, when ABC switch
its affiliation from Channel 39 t
Channel 10, KCST became NBC
local affiliate.

On October 30, 1987, KCST-T
was obtained by Gillette Commu
nications, and a year later change
its call letters to KNSD. On Nove
ber 20, 1996, after its first year as
San Diego's most-watched televi
sion station, KNSD was purchase
by NBC. And on January 1, 1997,
the station became known as
NBC 7/39. Today, thanks to hard
work, locally focused news, and
a strong bond to the community
NBC 7/39 has become the most-
watched news and entertainmen
station in the San Diego area.

In order to appeal to more Sa
Diegans, KNSD-TV strives for a
local flavor in its news. A prime
example is the station's live, 90-
minute, monthly news program
called *Third Thursday*, hosted by
Marty Levin. The show, which ra
for approximately six years, explore
a variety of important local issue
"When we started adding news,
we took a straight, no-nonsense
approach to it, rather than making local newscasts silly or super
ficial," says Derrough. "We really

NEIL E. DERROUGH SERVES AS
PRESIDENT AND GENERAL MAN-
AGER OF NBC 7/39 (TOP).

NBC 7/39'S 6 P.M. NEWS TEAM
INCLUDES (FROM LEFT) JIM
LASLAVIC, MARTY LEVIN, BREE
WALKER, AND JOE LIZURA
(BOTTOM).

m to bring out the substance of
e local news stories we cover."

N ABUNDANCE OF TALENT

evin is one of the main news an-
ors at NBC 7/39, and his award-
inning work has earned accolades
om the East to the West Coast.
evin, who anchors the 5, 6, and
p.m. newscasts, has been voted
ne of the Best of the Best by
e *Washington Journalism Review*.
Marty has a unique set of talents,"
ys Derrough. "He could be an
chor any place in the country,
ut fortunately, he has chosen us."

But Levin isn't the only strength
f the news team. NBC 7/39 boasts
ome of the area's most recognized
n-air personalities, including
usan Taylor, Joe Lizura, Jim
aslavic, Clark Anthony, and Bree
alker. With this kind of team,
ne station has a depth of talent
good as any television station
the country.

And all this talent has paid off.
1990, KNSD was awarded the
mmy for Outstanding News
tation in San Diego. The station
as kept that title and has been
warded more Emmys during the
90s than all other stations in
an Diego combined. Today, it
the most-watched television

station in San Diego—garnering
more ratings points than any other
station in the marketplace—and
is considered by many to be the
leader in news, entertainment,
and sports programming.

STAYING AT THE TOP

Being on top is particularly satis-
fying for Derrough, who came on
board when the station wasn't a
major player in the area. He feels
part of the reason for its success
is involvement with the local community. In an attempt to become
better involved, the station has

initiated a program known as
NBC 7/39 Listens, in which a news-
person and several station executives go to various communities
and attend local events or civic
group meetings.

"We go to these meetings and
listen to what residents have to
say about their neighborhoods.
The newspeople there listen for
story ideas that can be taken back
to the station, developed, and then
put on the air," says Derrough.
"We want San Diegans to know
we are listening to them. We care
about them."

Hewlett-Packard's presence in San Diego actually began i Pasadena in 1958, when the company made its first acquisitio. At that time, the acquired company—Pasadena-based F.L. Mosele Company—was a producer of high-quality graphic recorders, technology that gave Hewlett-Packard (HP) the ability to creat plotters. These devices were the forerunners of the now-famou inkjet and laser printers that have become synonymous with the Hewlett-Packard name.

In 1968, the company relocated this division to San Diego, where the operation became the first resident of the Rancho Bernardo Industrial Park. The site has changed over the years, and so have the company's products. HP went from making recorders and plotters to developing a complete line of computer peripheral devices for home and business uses. The San Diego site pioneered color printing, beginning with plotters that used fiber-tipped pens and evolving to the world's first color inkjet printer, the HP PaintJet.

Today, HP is a world leader in printers, scanners, and all-in-one devices through its lines of LaserJet, DeskJet, DesignJet, ScanJet, and OfficeJet products. In addition, HP's OfficeJet product line incorporates printer, fax, copier, and scanner functions into a single unit. The company manufactures color copiers and printers in both stand-alone and network versions, and produces pen cartridges for HP's multitude of printing products.

"We offer products that truly have changed the nature of work, making it easier to communicate," says Mitch Mitchell, spokesperson at Hewlett-Packard. "Worldwide, we make some 26,000 products: everything from atomic clocks— which are the world's most accurate—to test and measurement equipment, waveform generators, and laser printers."

THE HP WAY

In 1939, Bill Hewlett and Dave Packard, two engineers educated at Stanford University, founded Hewlett-Packard by combining their product ideas and unique management style. Since its beginning, the company has evolved ir response to changes in the marketplace and in the needs of its customers. HP's mission is to create information products that accelerate the advancement of knowledge and fundamentally improve the effectiveness of people and organizations.

In 1957, Bill and Dave, as the founders are always called, worke with the company's managerial team to develop a set of objectives that would guide HP's future growth. Known as the HP Way, this code incorporates a degree of flexibility into the corporation's overall structure, allowing staff members to work in an open env ronment where they can actively respond to changes in customer needs with improved products.

In describing the premise of the HP Way, Bill says: "I feel that in general terms, it is the policies and actions that flow from the belief that men and women want to do a good job, a creative job, an that if they are provided the prope environment, they will do so." Th company's consumer branding— Expanding Possibilities—incorpo rates and describes HP's abilities to combine future developments in consumer products with the company's superb past reputation for technology leadership and reliable, well-engineered prod ucts. These values provide a solid foundation for HP as it operates in traditional business markets

IN 1998, HEWLETT-PACKARD CELEBRATES 30 YEARS IN RANCHO BERNARDO.

YOLIE ROBLEDO

WITH 11,000 FULL-TIME STUDENTS AND 600 FULL-TIME employees, National University's mission is to create an environment for adult learners that is accessible, challenging, and relevant to a diverse population. ■ The university, which is headquartered in La Jolla, is an accredited, nonprofit institution of higher education,

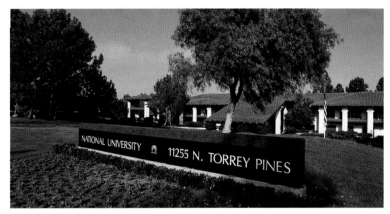

offering 46 degree programs and 16 educational credential programs. National also offers graduate programs in education and business, as well as a unique technology-based Global MBA program. The school's teaching ranks include 112 full-time faculty, 59 associate faculty, and 250 core adjunct faculty.

ACCESSIBLE, CHALLENGING, AND RELEVANT

With 20 campuses throughout the state and nine in San Diego County—including Mission Valley, Chula Vista, Kearny Mesa, Miramar, Vista, and Balboa—National is truly accessible to anyone seeking to better his or her education. "Above all, we create learning opportunities for adult learners," says National University President Dr. Jerry Lee. Learning is a lifelong process and our mission reflects that need in society."

But National's educational reach goes far beyond its multitude of locations. The university has established formal educational agreements with universities throughout the world, including Portugal, Mexico, Colombia, Turkey, Chile, and Ecuador. And National's Global MBA program incorporates the use of digital distance-education technologies, such as videotape, CD-ROM, the Internet, and video teleconferencing.

National also creates learning opportunities by allowing busy professionals and parents to take classes around their schedules. To do this, National offers a unique, one-course-per-month format. "That's one of our strengths as a place for adults to enroll," says Lee. "If you have to miss a month

because of job or family needs, you can do that and come back the next month."

The university has received national attention for its diverse and innovative approach to education. In fact, *U.S. News & World Report*'s "Guide to Colleges and Universities" has ranked National as one of the best universities in the western United States for four consecutive years. The school was also noted as a "best college buy" in *Money* magazine's "1996 Money Guide," and *The Hispanic Outlook in Higher Education* put National on its Hot List of best colleges for Hispanics. *Time* magazine also lists National as one of the best institutions of higher education.

THE COMMUNITY PARTNER

In September 1997, Lee announced that any employee of the university who donates 16 hours of service per year to his or her community will receive two days of paid leave—an initiative that could provide more than 7,200 hours of service. "The most important actions we take in determining the quality of our community revolve around the virtues and values we decide to embrace and live by," says Lee. "My vision for National is that

through mutual respect, encouragement, challenge, and support, we become a vibrant community, giving life to the global village."

With this in mind, National gives $1 million in minority, financial aid, and hardship scholarships each year. In addition, National recently distributed scholarships worth $300,000 for victims of domestic violence. In 1997, some 25 women were able to begin rebuilding their lives though opportunities created by this education program. A sense of community and quality educational programs have given National the ability to contribute to the future of San Diego.

FOR TODAY'S CORPORATE EXECUTIVE, HOME IS WHERE THE LATEST project is. Whether it's across the country or around the world, more companies are relocating executives or placing them on long-term assignments that require extended-stay housing. ■ In the era of downsizing, right-sizing, and outsourcing, many companies have replaced full-time positions with temporary workers and consultants.

These consultants are hired to perform specific tasks or projects. Once the project is completed, the consultant will pack up and move on to the next job in the next city. With these business trends on the rise, there is an increased need for extended-stay options. Oakwood Corporate Housing is meeting these needs.

Oakwood Corporate Housing—a subsidiary of Los Angeles-based R&B Realty Group—provides corporate housing in more than 1,000 cities nationwide. Oakwood operates five apartment complexes in San Diego, as well as numerous other contracted facilities. Founded in 1971, the company manages close to 3,000 corporate apartments in San Diego.

"San Diego is a very vibrant city," says Steven Bergstrom, regional manager for R&B Apartment Management. "In San Diego, we find numerous military contractors need places to stay for extended periods of time. We're also seeing temporary housing needs as a result of the biotech industry. It has been a very busy year."

Oakwood Coronado is San Diego's only extended-stay waterfront community.

THE SAN DIEGO CONNECTION

Bergstrom's list of corporate clients staying with Oakwood in San Diego includes Hewlett Packard, Lockheed Martin, Sony, Matsushita, Callaway Golf, Puget Sound Naval Shipyard, and the U.S. Navy.

Located throughout North County (coastal and inland), as well as in the southern areas of the country near the Mexican border, Oakwood's facilities include everything from studio apartments to deluxe, three-bedroom accommodations. Bergstrom points to the Oakwood Coronado facility as a prime example of Oakwood's premier accommodations.

Oakwood Coronado is located on San Diego Bay, adjacent to the Marriott Hotel. This property has 549 units, composed of a mixture of furnished and unfurnished apartments. The facility also includes covered parking, resort-style pool, conference room, party room, golf driving range, tennis courts, and on-site tennis pro.

"Our business philosophy," explains Bergstrom, "is to provide the best apartments and services we can. Oakwood Coronado is a prime example."

THE SERVICE ADVANTAGE

Oakwood offers a variety of amenities, including apartment complexes with on-site car rental, conference and meeting rooms, beauty and barber shops, business centers, children's play areas, swimming pools, whirlpool spas, fitness

Oakwood Mission Bay is just minutes from beautiful San Diego Bay and Sea World.

nters, tennis courts, and hospi-
lity programs that involve social
nd recreational activities.

Other important amenities
rovided to the corporate traveler
nclude laptop computers, profes-
onal maid services, quality furnish-
gs, and housewares—including
ishes, glasses, electric coffeemakers,
oasters, linens, furniture, plants,
ictures, exercise equipment, mi-
owave ovens, color TVs, cribs,
igh chairs, and roll-away beds.

Oakwood is committed to per-
onalized customer service. This
ommitment is evidenced by the
ompany's 24-hour hot line, which
uts callers in touch with a staff
member at any time, day or night.

As a service-driven company,
akwood strives to shape its busi-
ess to meet the needs of custom-
s. Staff go to great lengths to
ake sure individuals and families
oving to San Diego are satisfied.
he company offers tours for the
milies of business clients, and
akwood's concierges can obtain
erything from airline to theater
ckets. When a client is ready to
ake the move, Oakwood will fax
an Diego maps and directions,
d arrange for move-in, no mat-
r what time of day an arrival is
anned.

On top of its own intensive
uality control program, Oakwood
tains an independent outside
rvice to monitor and rate the

quality of every aspect of its corporate housing services.

A NATIONAL PLAYER

Oakwood dominates the extended-
stay lodging category, the fastest-
growing segment of the hospitality
business. The company provides
residential services—for one month
or longer—virtually anywhere in
the United States.

"Most corporate housing providers see themselves as property
managers," says R&B Realty Group
Chairman Howard Ruby. "We see
Oakwood as a service provider.
Our goal is to provide corporate
housing that meets our customers'
needs."

Inside most large businesses,
there is an employee who is handed
the tough assignment of finding
temporary corporate housing.
These individuals make decisions
that their colleagues have to live
with. Oakwood employees know
that these decision makers have
to cater to a wide range of individual preferences. They are also
under intense time pressure, and
must satisfy people who are feeling
the stress of an impending move—
either temporary or permanent.

Oakwood's clients, therefore,
are expected to accumulate detailed
knowledge of housing options in
diverse locations that conform to
strict budgets. But even under

CLOCKWISE FROM TOP:
MANY FINE AMENITIES, SUCH
AS SWIMMING POOLS, SPAS, FIT-
NESS CENTERS, LIGHTED TENNIS/
BASKETBALL/VOLLEYBALL COURTS,
AND TABLE TENNIS AND POOL
TABLES ALLOW FOR AN ACTIVE
LIFESTYLE AT OAKWOOD.

OAKWOOD'S ON-SITE SERVICES
INCLUDE TENNIS PROS AND HAIR
SALONS, AS WELL AS DRY CLEAN-
ERS AT SELECT LOCATIONS.

OAKWOOD, A TRUSTED NAME IN
CORPORATE HOUSING, PROVIDES
FULLY FURNISHED APARTMENTS
WITH ALL THE COMFORTS OF
HOME.

JOHN MUNNS STUDIO

the influence of all these factors, Oakwood manages to thrive.

SERVING CUSTOMERS WITH TECHNOLOGY

With the largest investment in technology in the industry, Oakwood provides a key building block for maintaining its leadership position.

Clients can make use of the most advanced reservation system in the extended-stay lodging field. A client can make one telephone call and book temporary housing anywhere in San Diego—or the nation.

The company's inventory is available at the click of a button through a sophisticated computer system. The CitySource database has a complete profile on every property, including rate, rent, pet policies, amenities, and recreational facilities. The system also allows Oakwood to maintain the customized housing-need profiles of every individual who has ever used a company facility.

The integrated database enables Oakwood to accept credit cards and personal checks, or offer a client the convenience of a single, detailed master statement each month for all its employees who are staying at Oakwood residences. "All our forms are computer generated," says Bergstrom. "This is a unique service that clients seem to really like."

Oakwood was also one of the first companies in the industry to have its own home page on the World Wide Web, and to provide clients with E-mail access to the entire sales and marketing group.

These days, when Oakwood's sales team goes out on a call, it brings a multimedia presentation to the meeting. Prospective clients can take tours of Oakwood properties while in their own offices, and review inventory in 1,000 cities. The combined use of cellular phones, mobile modems, and laptop computers brings Oakwood's entire database to a client meeting. Consequently, information collection, reservations, and confirmations can be instantaneous.

A WORLDWIDE PRESENCE

With the formation of Oakwood International in 1996, the company has become a global player, with facilities being developed in major cities in Asia and Europe. "Our company is realizing a vision of building a global network of temporary housing services," says company founder Ruby. "We will be the first international company in this field, and we will be the best at providing customer service and quality facilities. We have built our company with a credo that customer service is the only reason for our existence. We stay at the leading edge by thinking about how to make our customers' lives easier, happier, and more productive."

The company's growth into international markets has made Oakwood the only company that can truly provide global short-term residential services.

JOHN MUNNS STUDIO

CLOCKWISE FROM TOP: OAKWOOD MISSION VALLEY, LOCATED JUST OFF INTERSTATES 8 AND 163, ALLOWS EASY ACCESS TO THE DOWNTOWN AREA AND ITS NUMEROUS BUSINESSES AND TOURIST ATTRACTIONS.

NESTLED AGAINST A HILLSIDE IN THE HEART OF MISSION VALLEY, OAKWOOD IS WITHIN WALKING DISTANCE OF MANY FINE RESTAURANTS.

HOME SERVICES PACKAGES COMPLETE EACH GUEST'S HOME AWAY FROM HOME AT OAKWOOD WITH LINENS, DISHES, DECORATOR ITEMS, AND ACCESSORIES.

FROM CELLULAR TELEPHONES TO CD-ROM DRIVES, SONY TECHNOLOGY Center-San Diego (STC-SD) creates a veritable cornucopia of consumer electronic products. The company opened in 1972 with 63 employees as an assembly plant for its Trinitron® color televisions. More than 25 years and 4,000 employees later, STC-SD has become a design, engineering, and manufacturing powerhouse for Sony.

More than 15 million color television sets and 30 million color television picture tubes (CRTs) have been produced at STC-SD, which is also the only manufacturer of computer monitor CRTs in the United States. When an expanded computer display CRT manufacturing facility is finished in 1998, the center will have the capacity to make a total of 6 million CRTs each year for television and computer displays.

But STC-SD does much more than just manufacture CRTs and computer monitors. The site's operations have grown to fully integrate many functions under one roof. "From DVD (Digital Video Disk) players to cellular telephones, digital technology is spreading throughout the consumer electronics industry," says Sony Electronics President Carl Vankowski. "By vertically integrating, STC-SD takes advantage of this technology convergence. Engineers, designers, and manufacturers leverage the experience gained from one product to others."

BEYOND TELEVISIONS

Located in the high-tech neighborhood of Rancho Bernardo, the company's proximity to the Mexican border is ideal for international business and for teaming with Sony's Mexican operations in Tijuana and Mexicali. As a result, STC-SD has become Sony Electronics' North American creative research and design headquarters, seamlessly linking research, development, and manufacturing in one location.

STC-SD's growth in the late 1980s and early 1990s left the facility cramped for space as more

engineers and designers arrived in San Diego. That shortage ended in 1997, however, when Sony opened its Genesis Center for Engineering and Development, a $25 million, 277,000-square-foot building.

The Center is responsible for the design and development of many of the more than 30 different products produced at the 60-plus acre site, and anticipates future expansion of products. The building also possesses a 60,000-square-foot prototype manufacturing line. Says Greg Dvorken, public relations representative for STC-SD, about the state-of-the-art facility: "As the employees figuratively rub shoulders, the cross-fertilization of ideas improves existing products and sparks the beginnings of new ones."

COMMUNITY INVOLVEMENT

Over the years, STC-SD has shared its success with the local community. The center and employees regularly volunteer at area high schools and donate their time and money to the United Way. In addition, the center presents two $10,000 scholarships to students from a local adopted high school each year.

To celebrate STC-SD's 25th anniversary in 1997, Sony presented

a $500,000 endowment to the University of California-San Diego School of Engineering. Also in 1997, Sony sent 800 local students to San Diego's Insights World Conference, where they saw such world leaders as former Prime Minister Margaret Thatcher, management expert Tom Peters, and poet Maya Angelou. "They got a chance to meet these leaders personally and just couldn't stop talking about it," Dvorken says. "That is what creates leaders. You need role models in today's world."

With its strong growth, expanding focus, and commitment to the community, STC-SD has positioned itself for growth into the 21st century and beyond.

THE SONY TECHNOLOGY CENTER-SAN DIEGO'S LATEST ADDITION, THE GENESIS CENTER FOR ENGINEERING AND DEVELOPMENT, IS WHERE ENGINEERS DESIGN SONY'S PRODUCTS OF THE FUTURE.

STC-SD DESIGNS, ENGINEERS, OR MANUFACTURES MORE THAN 30 DIFFERENT PRODUCTS LOCALLY, RANGING FROM COMPUTER DISPLAYS TO WIRELESS PHONES.

WHAT BEGAN IN 1972 AS ONE OF SAN DIEGO'S FIRS environmental consulting companies has become one o the country's most recognized names in the field. Ogde Environmental and Energy Services has grown from humble beginnings in founder Dave Parkinson's garag to become a multimillion-dollar organization boastin

35 offices nationwide and in Europe. Previously known as WESTEC Services, Inc. and ERCE, it is now a wholly owned subsidiary of Ogden Corporation, a multibillion-dollar organization and the world's largest service provider headquartered in New York.

The company's first two contracts were with the U.S. Navy and San Diego Gas & Electric. Today, what was once one of Ogden's first clients is now its largest—the U.S. Navy. Among its most recent contracts is a $210 million hazardous materials management contract in the Pacific Rim, and preparation of an environmental impact statement (EIS) for the homeporting of nuclear carriers in San Diego Bay. Being first in San Diego positioned Ogden at the forefront of the National Environmental Policy Act (NEPA), which was the genesis of environmental protection in the United States.

Ogden employs a staff of 1,000 environmental scientists, engineers, and experts in related fields to meet the varied needs of its clients in both the public and private sectors. The full-service firm provides investigation, characterization, engineering design, remedial action, and construction management through its two divisions, consulting and engineering (C&E) and remediation. The C&E division includes technical disciplines such as geology and hydrogeology; chemical, environmental, mechanical, structural, and civil engineering; toxicology; air quality; chemistry; and regulatory policy analysis. C&E is supported by Ogden Engineering and Construction (OEC), the company's remediation division, which provides project management, contaminated soil excavation, bioremediation, waste treatment, construction, on-/off-site disposal, and post-performance monitoring. This vast array of services allows Ogden to provide any service a client might need to evaluate the potential for contamination, without having to rely on subcontractors.

AN INNOVATOR

Ogden celebrated its 25th anniversary in San Diego in 1997. In a dynamically changing industry in which longevity symbolizes success, company officials attribute their staying power and competitive edge to perseverance. Ogden Vice President and General Manager Donna McClay attributes the company's longevity to an ability to adapt to the ever changing needs of its clients and its ability to control costs.

"Until recently, companies spent a fortune on treatment and removal of contaminated soil and groundwater," says McClay. "Ogden is coming up with new and innovative technologies to assess the true impacts of contamination on human health and the environment—and that reduces remediation costs."

Ogden maintains its competitive edge with strategic hires and state-of-the-art equipment, some of which is found in the company's bioassay lab, where sediment and effluent testing are conducted; in its acoustics and vibration lab; and in its Geographic Information

ystem (GIS), a data management
nd display program used to evalu-
te complex environmental
roblems.

The GIS technology gives Ogden
ne capability to build relational
atabases that can take environ-
nental data and produce maps
o model environmental data, a
echnique that has proved critical
n the land-use decision making
rocess.

Ogden also uses innovative
pproaches to stay ahead of the
ompetition. The Multiple Species
onservation Program (MSCP),
eveloped by Ogden for the City
f San Diego, protects California
ative plants and animals while
llowing compatible land uses to
ontinue. The program's goal is
o conserve natural habitats before
neir native species have declined
o the point that protection under
ne federal and/or state endangered
pecies acts is necessary. Such con-
rvation measures allow land-use
ecisions affecting sensitive spe-
es to stay at the local level. The
rst program of its kind, MSCP
as heralded by U.S. Secretary
f the Interior Bruce Babbitt as
he beginning of a new chapter
n American conservation history."
he program is so innovative, in
ct, it won the 1997 California
hapter of American Planning
ssociation's Focused Issue
lanning Award.

A PROACTIVE STANCE

But Ogden is not solely focused
on the needs of the environment.
Ogden's commitment to the community includes finding a balance
between the needs of each of its
clients and regulatory requirements
that will result in cost-effective
and reasonable solutions to environmental problems.

"There has been a lot of pressure on the regulatory community to be more responsive to the
private sector clients," says Air
and Hazardous Materials Branch
Manager Mehdi Miremadi. "As
a result, Ogden's experts work
with regulators and private individuals in technical work groups
that set future environmental
policies and guidelines."

In order to keep both the
clients and the environment in

mind, Ogden is positioning itself
to help its clients be more proactive—rather than reactive—about
environmental issues. "Not only
can we be called in when there's
a problem that needs to be addressed," says McClay, "but we
are the kind of consulting organization that works with its clients
to be able to anticipate what's
going to happen and to be ready
for it when it does."

Ogden's vision began a quarter
of a century ago when it set up
shop to answer the need for environmental investigation and action.
The company's well-earned reputation for being able to strike the
necessary balance between economic growth and environmental
protection has earned it a spot in
history, as well as a very necessary
place in the future.

SOME OF OGDEN'S BIOLOGISTS
ARE SPECIALISTS IN ORNITHOLOGY
(LEFT).

HORTICULTURAL MANAGEMENT
AND BIOLOGICAL MONITORING
OCCUR ALONG THE SAN DIEGO
RIVER (RIGHT).

AQUATIC SCIENCES IS ONE OF THE
MANY ENVIRONMENTAL CAPABILI-
TIES OGDEN HAS IN SAN DIEGO.

KARLA C. HERTZOG HAS ONLY WORKED FOR ONE COMPANY—TH temporary staffing company her father founded in 1956. Today Hertzog is the owner and president of that company—TOP Staffing Services, Inc.—now San Diego's largest independen staffing services company and one of its largest woman-owne businesses. Originally focused only on temporary clerical busi

ness, today it also offers staffing for light industrial, information technology, and technical services, as well as employee leasing and payroll processing.

Each of its four offices around the county—Carlsbad, Escondido, Mira Mesa, and its headquarters in Mission Valley—has fully computerized training facilities. Rigorous skills evaluation is required of all applicants. Client and applicant histories, as well as the individual's skills, are kept in a database for instant accessibility.

KARLA HERTZOG SERVES AS OWNER AND PRESIDENT OF TOPS STAFFING SERVICES, INC.

THE BEST EMPLOYEES, THE BEST SERVICE

TOPS serves both its clients and its temporary employees. Clients in a variety of businesses expect and get the best temporary employees from TOPS. "San Diego has such a wonderful diversity of businesses," Hertzog says. "Our employees serve manufacturers, banks, call centers, biomedical and high-tech companies, and professional service firms." Technology

companies in particular use TOPS to fill jobs from administration to engineering to computer programming.

"Our clients come to us for quick solutions, quality workers, personalized service, and strong values," Hertzog adds. "They want a staffing company that manages the business like they do."

With nine out of 10 companies using temporary employees—a growing trend—temporary employees are viewed differently. "They

used to be fill-in support," says Hertzog. "Now, they are seen as skilled, valuable employees who hit the ground running." That places a premium on attracting and keeping the best people. TOPS offers excellent benefits and works hard to attract temporary employees, many of whom have been with TOPS for years.

"It's truly a win-win," she says. "We help companies staff for success, while we help hundreds of people every year find meaningfu employment. We also offer training to enhance skills and improv the quality of people we provide to clients."

LOCALLY OWNED AND OPERATED

Being locally owned and operated gives TOPS many advantages, in Hertzog's view. It can respond and solve problems quickly. And all it profits stay in the community.

"We are very proud of our con tributions to the San Diego commu nity," says Hertzog, who donates both money and time to many charitable, educational, and business organizations. She is the firs woman chair of the San Diego County YMCA Board of Directors, a board member for San Diego National Bank, a founding membe of the Greater San Diego Chambe of Commerce Business Roundtabl for Education, an advisory board member of the San Diego City Charter Schools, and a sponsor o several women-in-business events

"I can do all this because TOP has great people," Hertzog adds. "They are the ones who will continue to provide the best service and bring in the best temporary employees for many years to come.

TOPS OFFERS STAFFING FOR LIGHT INDUSTRIAL, INFORMATION TECHNOLOGY, AND TECHNICAL SERVICES, AS WELL AS EMPLOYEE LEASING AND PAYROLL PROCESSING.

SAN DIEGO HOSPICE IS AN INDEPENDENT, NOT-FOR-PROFIT, community-owned health care organization that serves the special needs of terminally ill patients and their families. Its program of care focuses on improving the quality of life for these patients through innovative, effective pain control and symptom management, and by providing emotional and

spiritual support for them and their loved ones.

Since its founding in 1977, San Diego Hospice has been at the forefront of the hospice movement in the United States. It was among the first 100 hospices established in this country, and is the oldest and largest in San Diego County. In 1980, it was selected as one of 4 hospices nationwide to participate in a Medicare demonstration project illustrating the cost-effectiveness and benefits of hospice care.

San Diego Hospice has grown steadily. By the time the organization celebrated its 20th anniversary in 1997, interdisciplinary teams of specially trained physicians, nurses, social workers, chaplains, home health aides, homemakers, and volunteers were caring for an average of 250 patients daily. Most patients are cared for in their homes throughout San Diego County. San Diego Hospice also operates its own inpatient care center, dedicated solely to the care of terminally ill patients. The center is one of only a handful of its kind in the country. Each of the 24 private rooms in the state-of-the-art facility was designed to be homelike, and opens onto lushly landscaped grounds and gardens. The center is used for short-term acute and respite care; once stabilized, patients return home where their care continues.

VISIONARY CARE
Laurel Herbst, M.D., has served continuously as medical director at San Diego Hospice since 1978. Known simply as Dr. Hospice by lawmakers on the Hill in Washington, D.C., Herbst has been a tireless advocate for compassionate care for the terminally ill and the

advancement of the hospice movement since the 1970s. Over the years, she has become a leading authority on pain management and an international influence on hospice care.

Under Herbst's able direction, San Diego Hospice participates in education and research programs through its Center for Palliative Studies (CPS). In addition to serving as a year-round teaching institution for future doctors enrolled in the School of Medicine at the University of California, San Diego, CPS offers education to students in other medical fields, seasoned professionals, and the community at large. Innovative drug studies conducted through CPS have resulted in more effective treatment not only for hospice patients, but for patients suffering from non-terminal illness as well. These efforts are helping to change end-of-life care for all medical professions, as well as meeting the demand from society for more health care options, including compassionate care when a cure is no longer possible.

UNIQUELY QUALIFIED FOR END-OF-LIFE CARE
In 1996, all six staff physicians at San Diego Hospice were among the first to be certified as hospice physicians by the American Board of Hospice and Palliative Medicine. That year, only 127 physicians nationwide passed the certification exam. The majority of other licensed staff at San Diego Hospice are similarly qualified in their fields. Seventy percent of the organization's nearly 400 volunteers also elect to participate in a rigorous training program to be able to work directly with terminally ill patients and their loved ones.

KIM BRUN STUDIOS

Special programs developed by San Diego Hospice have also garnered a national reputation. The Children's Program—including an early intervention program for families with unborn infants who are expected to have a life-threatening or life-limiting prognosis after birth—addresses the special needs of young hospice patients. An extensive bereavement support program, part of San Diego Hospice's continuum of care, offers counsel and support for families and loved ones for at least 18 months after a patient dies.

Throughout its history, San Diego Hospice has been a leader in the development of hospice care and the advancement of compassionate, beneficial care for the terminally ill. Through the efforts of its skilled staff, dedicated volunteers, and generous benefactors—who endeavor to make hospice care available regardless of a patient's ability to pay—San Diego Hospice strives to offer quality of life at the end of life, and continuously seeks to improve end-of-life care for the terminally ill through human caring and medical innovation.

SAN DIEGO HOSPICE IS AN INDEPENDENT, NOT-FOR-PROFIT, COMMUNITY-OWNED HEALTH CARE ORGANIZATION THAT SERVES THE SPECIAL NEEDS OF TERMINALLY ILL PATIENTS AND THEIR FAMILIES.

L IKE MOST OF ITS CLIENTS, DUCKOR SPRADLING & METZGER I fortunate to have a successful business in San Diego. Managin its own business and working with a diverse local and nationa clientele for more than 20 years has given the firm a collectiv experience uncommon to most San Diego law firms. ■ The firn was founded in 1977 by Michael Duckor and Gary J. Spradling

who had worked together for several years at a downtown law firm. Scott Metzger joined the firm as an associate in 1978 and soon became the first new partner.

The San Diego legal community was then quickly coming of age and a number of law firms had implemented an aggressive growth strategy. At the time, the partners saw the need—a need that Duckor Spradling & Metzger continues to serve—for a midsize law firm comprised of experienced lawyers committed to San Diego who are dedicated to meeting the legal services needs of the local business community.

Since then, the growth of the firm has mirrored the ongoing needs of its clients for a full complement of legal services, and it has committed the resources to meet those needs. At the same time, the founders of the firm have remained actively involved on a first-hand basis in the full-time, day-to-day practice of law, as accessible to the firm's clients as ever before.

SCOPE OF PRACTICE

While the work of the firm is as diverse as its client base, the practice remains focused on two major categories: litigation and business

transactions. The firm has also earned a recognized expertise in resolving business disputes, short of protracted litigation, through the dispute resolution procedure of mediation and arbitration.

When a business dispute escalates to a lawsuit, the considerabl out-of-pocket costs often pale in comparison to the burden of the disruption of business, loss of employee morale, and emotional stress. Even the most experienced businessman needs the advice of seasoned legal counsel to enable him to make the difficult decisions necessarily involved in managing the overall litigation effort

DUCKOR SPRADLING & METZGER FOUNDING PARTNERS (FROM LEFT) GARY SPRADLING, MIKE DUCKOR, AND SCOTT METZGER BRING SEASONED LEGAL ADVICE TO BEAR ACROSS A BROAD RANGE OF LITIGATION AND BUSINESS TRANSACTION ISSUES.

ıd resolving disputes. Duckor
ɔradling & Metzger recognizes
ɪat its long-term client relation-
ɪips are its greatest assets. It has
meaningful stake in resolving
:igation matters as effectively
ɪd as efficiently as possible.
ɪperience has also shown the
rm that the cost of resolving
ɪe serious dispute can far exceed
ɪe cost of years of preventive
anning that not only could have
ʻoided the dispute in the first
ace, but also provided peace of
ind in the meantime. Whether
ɪey are looking for insightful
ɪnsultation and advice in their
ɪily affairs, large-scale represen-
tion in complex litigation pro-
ʻedings, or simply a quick answer
ɪ a seemingly simple question,
ɪe firm's clients know that Duckor
ɔradling & Metzger can help and
ill return their calls.

ʻORKING FOR
HE COMMUNITY

ɪembers of the firm dedicate
ɪeir time to lead and support
wide variety of professional,
ɪmmunity, educational, chari-
ble, and religious organizations.
ɪe firm has been especially active
working with the police depart-

ment and community leaders in
implementing gang-related rehabilitation programs. Principals
of the firm were instrumental
in founding the local chapter of
the Association of Business Trial
Lawyers, and firm members are
frequent lecturers in continuing
legal education and industry-
sponsored programs covering
all aspects of business litigation
and legal regulatory developments
in health care, corporate, partnership, and business law, trust and
estates, and employment matters.

Duckor Spradling & Metzger's
sustained growth and recognized
reputation for excellence and client service reflect the value of the

firm's services to its clients and its
contribution to the San Diego
community.

In the end, however, the most
personally rewarding aspect of the
practice is working with people
who, like the members of the firm,
have invested their own time, energy, and effort and have risked
the full extent of their personal
wealth to build their own businesses. Duckor Spradling & Metzger
respects the commitment and per-
sistence of its clients. They deserve,
and the firm is proud to give them,
full personal attention and support. It looks forward to having
the opportunity to continue doing so for many years to come.

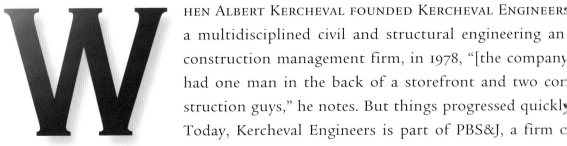

WHEN ALBERT KERCHEVAL FOUNDED KERCHEVAL ENGINEER: a multidisciplined civil and structural engineering an construction management firm, in 1978, "[the company had one man in the back of a storefront and two con struction guys," he notes. But things progressed quickl₁ Today, Kercheval Engineers is part of PBS&J, a firm c

2,200 employees, nationally recognized in engineering, construction management, and program management. The San Diego office is the headquarters for the California operations, which also includes locations in Los Angeles, San Francisco, Irvine, and Riverside. Nearly half of Kercheval's workforce, however, is based in San Diego.

BUILDING BRIDGES

A representative example of the type of projects handled by Kercheval Engineers/PBS&J is the Naval Training Center Bridge in San Diego. The project received an excellent rating from the navy, as well as outstanding evaluations for thoroughness of site investigation, clarity of plans, adherence to schedules, and cooperation and responsiveness.

The navy is typical of the clients served by Kercheval. All over the country, Kercheval Engineers/ PBS&J works with city, county, state, and federal agencies, as well as telephone companies and other public utilities. National clients

have included the U.S. Army, Air Force, and Navy, as well as the Federal Highway Administration. In San Diego, clients have included the Port of San Diego, San Diego Gas & Electric, the Metropolitan Transit Development Board, the San Diego County Water Authority, and QUALCOMM Inc.

COMMUNITY OUTREACH

Kercheval Engineers places great emphasis on community involvement. Al Kercheval, who now serves

as senior vice president of the con pany, has served on the boards of nearly two dozen organizations, including the Greater San Diego Chamber of Commerce and the Urban League of San Diego.

The firm annually participate: in career and job fairs throughou the county—at education levels ranging from elementary schools to colleges and universities. Staff members regularly speak to grouμ of students about career opportu nities in engineering and related fields. Several times a year, student groups are invited to tour the company's offices.

Those tours reiterate the fact that Kercheval Engineers/PBS&J provides a full range of services: project management, constructio: administration and management civil and site engineering, structural engineering, water resource engineering, and telecommunica tions engineering.

"We have a broad range of experience in all these areas," says Kercheval. "We've grown a great deal since 1978, and look forward to more growth in San Diego an all over the country."

KERCHEVAL ENGINEERS/PBS&J PROVIDES PROJECT MANAGEMENT FOR A WIDE VARIETY OF DEVELOPMENT PROJECTS, INCLUDING THE SOUTH BAY BOATYARD AND STORAGE FACILITY IN CHULA VISTA.

MAX BIRNKAMMER

KERCHEVAL ENGINEERS RECEIVED AN EXCELLENT RATING FROM THE NAVY, AS WELL AS OUTSTANDING EVALUATIONS FOR THOROUGHNESS OF SITE INVESTIGATION, CLARITY OF PLANS, ADHERENCE TO SCHEDULES, AND COOPERATION AND RESPONSIVENESS FOR THE FIRM'S NAVAL TRAINING CENTER BRIDGE PROJECT IN SAN DIEGO.

SOURCE SERVICES IS A $300 MILLION NATIONAL COMPANY THAT HAS been providing permanent and temporary staffing solutions to businesses since 1962, and has been in operation in San Diego since 1978. The firm has 32 full-time, degreed recruiters based in San Diego, and technology links to the company's four Los Angeles-area offices provide access to more than 130 trained staffing solutions professionals. "Finding experienced people with the right skills takes time," says Source Services' Managing Director Rick Richards. "Unfortunately, businesses can't always wait. That's why hiring executives turn to us."

EXTENSIVE EXPERIENCE

Source Services' recruiters are truly unique. What sets the company apart from other staffing services is the fact that all employees have in-depth experience in the field in which they work to place permanent, contract, or temporary professionals.

"Our people really know what it means to be in a particular discipline," says Richards. "Our recruiters who place people in finance or accounting have degrees themselves in finance or accounting; most are CPAs. And unlike some companies, most of our recruiting professionals in information technology were developing software prior to placing software engineers in jobs."

PLACEMENT SERVICES

There are five main service offerings in the company's San Diego office: Source EDP (information technology), Source Finance, Source Engineering, Source Consulting, and Accountant Source Temps.

Source EDP focuses on information technology (IT). As computer systems become more critical to business success, companies increasingly need qualified people who understand the latest technological tools and who can utilize them to attain productivity. Source Services' exclusive database includes a diverse group of candidates, ranging from programmers and network engineers to systems analysts.

Source Finance specializes in placing quality accounting and financial professionals across the entire spectrum of experience levels. These candidates are multidisciplined and are skilled at working directly for management, marketing, management information systems (MIS), or operational departments.

Source Engineering helps companies find the most qualified engineering professionals in real-time embedded software engineering, network engineering, ASIC and SC design, hardware design, Telecom and SMT manufacturing, and product design and testing.

Source Consulting specializes in providing information technology consultants for projects including software development, system design, network management, and software implementation. Company consultants are experienced in a wide range of hardware and software environments, and are trained to provide cost-effective solutions to challenging business and IT issues.

Finally, Accountant Source Temps was created to meet the growing demand for temporary accounting and financial professionals. Source Services' database in this arena includes individuals skilled as bookkeepers, tax specialists, CPAs, and controllers.

As a national company, Source Services has tremendous resources in terms of industry knowledge, candidate accessibility, and geographic reach. It is the company's mission to be the first choice in staffing solutions and career development, and this goal is accomplished through customer service, teamwork, and integrity—experience on demand.

SOURCE SERVICES IS A $300 MILLION NATIONAL COMPANY THAT HAS BEEN PROVIDING PERMANENT AND TEMPORARY STAFFING SOLUTIONS TO BUSINESSES SINCE 1962, AND HAS BEEN IN OPERATION IN SAN DIEGO SINCE 1978. THE FIRM HAS 32 FULL-TIME, DEGREED RECRUITERS BASED IN SAN DIEGO, AND TECHNOLOGY LINKS TO THE COMPANY'S FOUR LOS ANGELES-AREA OFFICES PROVIDE ACCESS TO MORE THAN 130 TRAINED STAFFING SOLUTIONS PROFESSIONALS.

A S A REGIONAL CORPORATE HEADQUARTERS, SANYO NORTH AMERIC.
Corporation oversees and supports more than 20 companie
in Canada, the United States, and Mexico. The electronic
and components company has had a presence in San Dieg
since 1978, and on October 1, 1996, Sanyo's North America
headquarters relocated from New York City to San Diego

The headquarters' services to the Sanyo group include property management, information systems, legal and tax assistance, human resources, corporate communications, business development, and finance. Of the Sanyo manufacturing operations in North America, two-thirds are based in the San Diego/Tijuana region.

"This region has a tremendous amount to offer in the areas of high technology and a quality workforce," says Sanyo North America Corporation Chairman and CEO Motoharu Iue. "Strategically, this region has broad appeal. It is convenient to our North American customers, and its proximity to the Pacific Rim and Central and South American markets

is a great advantage. Since the majority of our North American operations are based in San Diego, it made perfect sense to move the headquarters here.

"As the North American headquarters, our San Diego operations are geared toward boosting operational efficiency for the continent," adds Iue. "We're part of a large, worldwide company that is active in many markets. We have our goals and are working toward them, in the spirit of our whole company."

A WORKING SYMBIOSIS
Originally located in Kearny Mesa, today Sanyo North America is located in Otay Mesa, one mile away from the company's manufactur-

ing plants in Tijuana. The Sanyo North America Group is composed of nearly 6,500 employees engaged in manufacturing, sales and marketing, and service and support functions. The North American Group accounts for more than 33 percent of the total overseas sales of Sanyo Electric Co. Ltd., and exports products from San Diego/Tijuana and other North American operations to Europe, Australia, Japan, and Southeast Asia.

Sanyo places a great deal of emphasis on expanding the degree and scope of localized operations throughout North America, beginning with research and development of the product. "Basically the products sold in the Americas should not only be manufactured

ut developed here as well," mentions Iue. The San Diego/Tijuana region is an integral part of that strategy.

Nearly 6,000 employees are based in Tijuana plants, which include the production of TVs, compact refrigerators, video components, rechargeable batteries, laptop computers, and vacuum cleaners. All manufacturing plants in both San Diego and Tijuana are certified under the ISO (International Organization for Standardization) quality system and are recognized by customers as superior manufacturing operations dedicated to producing the highest-quality products.

WORLDWIDE PRESENCE

The parent company of the North American group, Sanyo Electric, is approaching its 50th anniversary and has more than 130 affiliates and subsidiaries, and more than 60,000 employees in more than 39 countries.

Every day, new breakthroughs in technology offer the potential for brand-new ways of manufacturing and, in some cases, the creation of entirely new industries to feed economic growth. Sanyo Electric develops new and exciting technologies to their fullest potential. As a leader in the research and development of clean energy sources, Sanyo is preparing to power tomorrow's new products using highly efficient solar cell and rechargeable battery technology.

As a world leader in environmentally friendly technologies, Sanyo received the Stratospheric Ozone Protection Award from the U. S. Environmental Protection Agency. The award was in recognition of Sanyo's worldwide success in phasing out ozone-depleting substances and developing new, friendlier technologies.

When most people think of Sanyo products, they think of high-value electronic products, ranging from color televisions and CD players to cordless tele-

phones and home theater systems. The company's line of products for the home also includes microwave ovens, refrigerators, vacuum cleaners, air conditioners, and small kitchen electronics. Sanyo also produces cash registers, portable LCD projectors, transcribing equipment, security video, and facsimile equipment.

Some are not aware, however, that Sanyo is the world's largest producer of sealed nickel cadmium batteries—the ones that charge camcorders, telephones, and laptop computers. And Sanyo provides climate-controlling absorption chillers/heaters for places such as New York's Guggenheim Museum.

WORLDWIDE OPERATIONS, LOCAL PRESENCE

Sanyo may be a worldwide company, but it strives to become a source of pride in the communities where it does business. The North American group encourages companies and employees to support local community efforts to improve education, offer cultural activities, protect the environment, and support the economy. These activities include adopt-a-school programs, donations to local children's hos-

SANYO HAS MANUFACTURING PLANTS IN CIUDAD INDUSTRIAL (TOP) AND PACIFICO INDUSTRIAL PARKS (BOTTOM), BOTH IN TIJUANA. NEARLY 6,000 EMPLOYEES ARE BASED IN TIJUANA PLANTS, WHICH INCLUDE THE PRODUCTION OF TVs, COMPACT REFRIGERATORS, VIDEO COMPONENTS, RECHARGEABLE BATTERIES, LAPTOP COMPUTERS, AND VACUUM CLEANERS.

pitals and nonprofit organizations for autistic children, student scholarships, tree planting projects, and teacher recognition programs.

Through both its community service and its status as a major competitor in the electronics and components industries, Sanyo North America Corporation will continue to be a valuable and contributing member of the San Diego community for many years to come.

SAN DIEGO DATA PROCESSING CORPORATION (SDDPC) PLAYS AN important role in San Diego's move into the 21st century. A nonprofit information technology and telecommunications corporation that focuses primarily on customer-driven technologies that enhance the delivery of voice and data services, SDDPC serves the departments within the City of San Diego, as well as certain government and nonprofit entities in the region. Indeed, over the past two decades, SDDPC has helped to bring San Diego into the forefront of technology.

MANAGING THE CITY'S DATA

"SDDPC was founded by the city of San Diego in 1979 in order to help the city keep up with continuously changing data and voice service requirements. SDDPC was created so that it could charge market rates for its services and hire employees without going through the civil service process. The corporation has its own board of directors, who are appointed by the mayor and city council," says Roger Talamantez, president and CEO of San Diego Data Processing.

"We've seen very steady growth," says John Lowry, vice president in charge of finance and administration. "We started with less than a hundred employees and now we've grown to three times that. This year, we have a $52 million budget." The corporation's mission is to excel at providing quality information technology services for the city and the region.

During fiscal year 1997, SDDPC went through a major reorganization, enabling it to provide an integrated approach to service delivery and project management— all to better meet the customer's needs. SDDPC features state-of-the-art client-server technology and is very involved in a year 2000 conversion. The conversion will ensure that applications, totaling more than 6 million lines of legacy programming code in existence for the city and county, will function after January 1, 2000.

The corporation is also heavily invested in geographical information systems. "Several years ago, we developed a system that maps the entire San Diego region. It has more than 100 layers. One layer might consist of all the pipelines, another all the call boxes, another with street information. This was a joint county/city venture, and it is considered world-class," says Chief Operating Officer Ron Wittenberg.

SAN DIEGO AND BEYOND

SDDPC is currently working to service clients outside the city, aiming for a more regional approach to its work. "SDDPC has done that with a project called ARJIS, an automated regional justice information system," says Richard Jennings, vice president in charge of municipal services. Approximately 20 law enforcement agencies within the county have joined together in a common law-enforcement computerized system. This gives local law enforcement agencies access to a larger database and more records. SDDPC has also been instrumental in bringing the city and county libraries together under one common system.

The company is also using its regional approach to connect schools and provide them with cost-cutting measures. Says Howard Taylor, vice president of operations. "We have been involved in a regional telecommunications alliance, which is an attempt by the

ty and county schools to join together and get lower telephone ates."

Like most high-tech companies, DDPC is heavily involved in using ne Internet for getting information around the city and around ne world. "We really look at the internet as a way for the city to ommunicate with citizens—a way o get data out there," says Mary lassis, vice president of INET ervices. This business unit was eveloped in 1997 to further establish SDDPC's presence on the internet. This new unit anticipates nat, by utilizing Internet technology, SDDPC will be able to provide its clients a faster method of ommunicating and conducting ity business. For example, a recent ilot project successfully provided ne public with access to city council meetings over the Internet and ne first implementation of Javaased kiosks for the 1998 Super owl. In addition, the corporation investigating the possibility of roviding residents with other ew services over the Internet, e.g., pplying and paying for various ermits, licenses, or fees such as ark and recreation permits, building permits, business licenses, and arking fines.

NNOVATIVE TECHNOLOGY

om Miller, vice president of itilities/facilities and GIS serices says, "What is most unique bout SDDPC is its involvement n projects that use leading-edge echnologies. This past year, the orporation implemented the ewer/Water Infrastructure Mangement System (SWIM) in addiion to a water, wastewater, and eclaimed water facility maintenance and management system alled SPLASH." This application nd the process put the City of San Diego at the forefront of infrastructure management technology. It is rguably the most advanced product of its kind.

A document and records management system, established for

the Metropolitan Wastewater Department, integrates scanning and imaging systems. More than 20,000 documents have been scanned in putting together the initial database, which supports 200 clients. SDDPC is also working with other city departments to implement this technology.

Another important project for SDDPC was its implementation of a remote-sensing meter-reading system for commercial water customers. This system was a major step in reducing overall operating costs for the Water Department.

The government isn't the only group that benefits from SDDPC's innovations. Plans call for a region-wide, kiosk-based system of government documents that will create a way for visitors and residents to get information about the city and county—from business, health care, tourist attractions, and the performing arts to commercial and cultural activities.

Philip L. Thalheimer, vice president of customer service says, "SDDPC is dedicated to providing the most technologically advanced products and services to its customers." To ensure that the customers' needs come first, a whole division was created dedicated to nothing but customer satisfaction.

Everything SDDPC does—from its ongoing commitment to cus-

tomer responsiveness to its regional presence in public access and telecommunications—is accomplished thanks to a competent, dedicated, and highly motivated staff, which is working harder than ever to propel San Diego into the 21st century.

M

CM ARCHITECTS & PLANNERS IS A MULTIDISCIPLINARY FIRM engaged in the practice of architecture, planning, urban design, and interior architecture. Founded in 1980, MCM has been involved in more than 100 major projects in the United States and Latin America, and has a staff of 2 designers in its San Diego office. ■ "Our practice is guided by strong beliefs and principles," says Founding Partner Joseph Martinez. "Those beliefs are based on the simple concept that the design of forms in space should be generated by the context of their surroundings, while the principles of design should advance our culture."

THE PRINCIPALS OF MCM

Martinez and his partner, Anthony Cutri, the principals of MCM, possess extensive and diverse experience in project design, management, and implementation. They have provided design services for public agencies, municipalities, corporations, and private entities. Both partners received bachelor of arts degrees from the University of California, San Diego (UCSD).

Martinez holds a master's degree in architecture from the Harvard University Graduate School of Design (GSD). While at GSD, he was the recipient of the Alcoa Aluminum Scholarship and the American Institute of Architects

Fellowship. From 1979 to 1993, Martinez was a lecturer in urban design at the University of California, Berkeley; UCSD; and San Diego State University (SDSU). Recognition of his work over the past two decades includes awards from the California/American Institute of Architects and the California Chapter of the American Planning Association.

Cutri holds a master's degree in architecture from UC Berkeley. He has served on the architectural/ urban design faculties of UC Berkeley; the University of Texas, Austin; Columbia University; and the New School of Architecture in San Diego. Additionally, Cutri has served as a principal-in-charge for a wide variety of project types and sizes in both planning and architecture. He has received a Progressive Architecture Citation Award for the energy-efficient Alfred Alquist State Office Building in San Jose, as well as an Orchid Award from the San Diego American Institute of Architects for the Chula Vista Nature Interpretive Center.

"Our intent as a firm is to create good design, that is, to create spaces and structures which exhibit a timeless quality," says Cutri. "We design environments that are inviting regardless of topology and locale. It is our contention that the vitality and beauty of the built environment plays a crucial role in the productive and healthy community. As design professionals, we must assume this responsibility."

MAJOR PROJECTS

The variety of the firm's projects reflects the range and talent of MCM Architects & Planners. For example, the firm is involved in the design for both of downtown San Diego's major convention hotels—the Hyatt Regency and the Marriott Hotel & Marina. Currently, MCM is handling program management for the expansion of the San Diego Convention Center, and, previously, it handled space planning and design for the 1996 Republican National Convention.

Other projects include the Samsung Electronics Office and Manufacturing Facility in Tijuana; the Culbertson Winery & Cafe Champagne, a 26,000-square-foot winery and storage facility in Temecula that includes a full-service restaurant; Bosque de las Araucar-

...s, a new town development in ...tay Mesa, approximately two ...iles northeast of Tijuana; El ...astillo Santa Fe, a $500 million, ...ixed-use development on 24 hect-...es in Mexico City; the Blinder ...enter on Camp Pendleton Marine ...orps Base, a 23,500-square-foot ...cility that includes a chapel and ...assrooms; Fire Station 24 in Del ...ar; and the First Congregational ...enter in Escondido.

Over the years, MCM has mas-...er-planned and designed several ...nner-city projects, the most recent ...f which is the City Heights Urban ...illage. This project is a partner-...g venture between public agencies ...nd private enterprise, including ...he city manager's office, the rede-...elopment agency, the police depart-...ent, the parks and recreation ...epartment, the public library, ...nd San Diego engineering and ...evelopment services, as well as ...he San Diego unified school dis-...rict, the San Diego community ...ollege district, and the metropoli-...an transit district. The develop-...ent occupies nine square blocks ...ith the following proposed uses: ...osa Parks Elementary School; ...ommunity park, public library, ...nd recreation center with joint-use ...ields; midcity police substation, ...ommunity facility, and gymna-...ium; and a community college ...ontinuing education facility.

Also, the firm has designed ...any schools or school-related

projects, including Perkins Elementary School in Barrio Logan; Rancho del Rey Middle School in Chula Vista; a multipurpose facility at Our Lady of Peace Academy, a Catholic high school for girls in San Diego; the National City Adult School; a master plan and seven buildings at the Imperial Valley Campus of SDSU in Calexico; and the career center for UCSD.

Another good illustration of the firm's mission is its work with Cesar Chavez Elementary School. The 7.9-acre site for this K-6 school is located in the Southcrest Park area of San Diego. The design was developed through a three-month

community workshop effort, which included three communitywide workshops, eight task force meetings, and numerous subcommittee meetings with school district personnel. "What we wanted to do was design something that was an educational tool, as well as a community asset. This is very much a joint-use facility. For example, the library can also be used in the evenings or on the weekends," says Martinez.

"In the spirit of aesthetics," adds Martinez, "we geared this project to the users. That's what we do in all our projects, and the end result is very rewarding."

THE FIRM HAS DESIGNED MANY SCHOOLS OR SCHOOL-RELATED PROJECTS, INCLUDING THE NA-TIONAL CITY ADULT SCHOOL (LEFT); A SCIENCE BUILDING AT BELL JUNIOR HIGH (RIGHT); AND A MASTER PLAN AND SEVEN BUILDINGS AT THE IMPERIAL VALLEY CAMPUS OF SAN DIEGO STATE UNIVERSITY IN CALEXICO.

THE VARIETY OF THE FIRM'S PROJECTS REFLECTS THE RANGE AND TALENT OF MCM ARCHITECTS & PLANNERS. FOR EXAMPLE, THE FIRM IS INVOLVED IN THE DESIGN OF ONE OF SAN DIEGO'S MAJOR CONVENTION HOTELS—THE HYATT REGENCY.

SINCE 1980, OVERLAND DATA HAS BEEN A LEADING MANUFACTURER O half-inch tape backup, interchange, and archival solutions fo data storage. The company produces and sells drives, automate tape libraries, and software to meet its customers' informatio storage needs. ■ Overland was cofounded by Martin Gray, who i now the company's chief technical officer. With his expertise i

magnetic tape recording technology, he envisioned connecting nine-track, reel-to-reel tape drives to personal computers for accessing mainframe data. The company's first product was an interconnect card to fill this need.

As the company grew and times changed, Overland added software to its product line in order to make accessing stored data easier—something only a handful of companies could offer at the time. By the late 1980s, Overland offered complete solutions to data storage problems, which included interface cards, software, and tape drives, sold as a value-added reseller.

"We started selling tape drives, accessories, and software—a whole package bundled together," says Robert Scroop, vice president of engineering. "Sometime around 1990, we began designing and manufacturing our own nine-track tape drives, rather than buying them from other people."

The tape drives the company had previously bought were made for high-end computers, and were rugged and expensive. Overland saw an opportunity to deliver a slightly slower machine—better suited to the desktop PC of the time—at significantly reduced cost to consumers. As a result, Overland began manufacturing its own line of nine-track tape drives, known as TapePro.

DRIVING THE INDUSTRY'S FUTURE

By 1992, the company had moved into 18- and 36-track drive technology. And to better serve the needs of its customers, in 1993, Overland purchased Cipher Data's product lines manufactured in Singapore from Conner Peripherals. "That is a great success story," says Vern LoForti, vice president and CFO. "Instead of moving production out of San Diego, we brought it back."

In 1994, the company became involved with today's most advanced data storage technology, called DLT, which is faster and has a greater capacity for storing information than previous systems. "Now we're moving from primarily delivering tape drives

for data interchange to delivering robotic systems for the backup and restoring of data," says Scroop. Overland's engineers are currentl working on a next-generation tape technology and coding technique that it hopes to introduce to the market in the second half of 1998.

All this innovation has not gone unnoticed. Both *PC Digest* and *Byte* magazine have chosen Overland's tape libraries as the best in the industry. In addition, *Business Week* named Overland as one of its hot growth companies of 1997, and added the company's name to its list of the 100 best small corporations in the United States.

To continue its strong growth the company went public in February 1997, increasing its presence and generating additional funds to grow. "Our goal is 25 percent revenue growth each year," Scroop says.

What began as one man's idea has become one of the fastest-growing companies in the data storage industry. And with the ability to quickly respond to market trends and the innovation to stay ahead of the competition, Overland will continue to be a force to be reckoned with for many years to come.

SINCE 1980, OVERLAND DATA HAS BEEN A LEADING MANUFACTURER OF HALF-INCH TAPE BACKUP, IN-TERCHANGE, AND ARCHIVAL SOLUTIONS FOR DATA STORAGE (LEFT).

OVERLAND'S DLT-BASED LIBRARYXPRESS TAPE SYSTEM HAS RECEIVED NUMEROUS INDUSTRY AWARDS FOR ITS UNIQUE SMARTSCALE DESIGN AND OUTSTANDING RELIABILITY (RIGHT).

SOUTHWEST AIRLINES FIRST BEGAN SERVING SAN DIEGO ON JANUARY 1, 1982. Service began with a dozen daily nonstop departures; today, this number has grown to 78. By offering dependable service, along with a sense of fun, Southwest has become San Diego's number one carrier. "We feel like San Diego has embraced us," says Southwest Public Relations Specialist Amy Lyons. "San Diegans have found

at we have good customer service—and we get them to their estinations on time."

The Dallas-based airline has ore than 25,000 employees nationwide, and 252 employees in an Diego. From San Diego's ndbergh Field, Southwest's nonop flights depart from six gates Albuquerque, El Paso, Las Vegas, akland, Phoenix, Sacramento, lt Lake City, San Francisco, San se, and Tucson; connecting serce is offered to 32 other cities. th business and leisure travelers ke advantage of Southwest's w fares.

OOD SERVICE, OOD FUN

any airlines seek to benchmark eir performance against Southest, a company that has come be seen as an icon of employee otivation and customer service. uthwest is proud of its many sts in the industry: It was the st major airline to offer elecnic ticketing, the first to develop Web page, and among the first accept ticketing over the Internet. was also the first to offer emoyees profit sharing.

For the past five years, Southest has earned the Triple Crown r the best on-time performance, st baggage handling, and fewt customer complaints, according to statistics published in the .S. Department of Transportaon *Air Travel Consumer Reports*. addition, Southwest boasts clean safety record—without a ngle crash—and was named the orld's safest airline by *Condé Nast raveler*.

Sporting khaki pants and knit irts, Southwest crew members

PAM FRANCIS

and flight attendants don't dress the way other airlines' staffs do. "We call it Fun Wear," says Lyons. "It started in 1988, when we wore colorful shorts and T-shirts to promote summer Fun Fares. After we started winning the Triple Crown year after year, we got to keep wearing Fun Wear as a reward."

The fun corporate climate at Southwest stems from the personality of the company's cofounder and CEO Herb Kelleher, who has been known to dress up like Elvis, belt out a rap song, and settle disputes by arm wrestling. Flight attendants are famous for their antics, and humor plays a large role in Southwest's unique corporate culture. But each employee's willingness to do his or her best is what lies behind the Southwest Spirit, and this gives the airline its competitive edge.

Southwest Airlines is a rapidly growing company, boasting an unprecedented record of profitability in the industry—24 consecutive years. With its emphasis on service, value, and innovation, the airline will continue to be a vital part of the San Diego community for many years to come.

CLOCKWISE FROM TOP: HERB KELLEHER IS AN UNCONVENTIONAL CEO OF AN UNCONVENTIONAL AIRLINE. HE CHAIN-SMOKES, DRESSES IN COSTUME, DRINKS WILD TURKEY BOURBON, AND CREATED A SENSATION IN DALLAS WHEN HE ARM-WRESTLED THE CHAIRMAN OF AN AVIATION COMPANY OVER A LEGAL ISSUE.

ONE OF SOUTHWEST'S CUSTOMER SERVICE AGENTS DISPLAYS THE AIRLINE'S LEGENDARY POS—POSITIVELY OUTRAGEOUS SERVICE. FOR THE FIFTH CONSECUTIVE YEAR, THE DEPARTMENT OF TRANSPORTATION'S *AIR TRAVEL CONSUMER REPORT* LISTED SOUTHWEST AS HAVING THE BEST ON-TIME PERFORMANCE, BEST BAGGAGE HANDLING, AND FEWEST CUSTOMER COMPLAINTS OF ALL MAJOR AIRLINES.

WHEN SOUTHWEST AIRLINES FIRST STARTED IN 1971, IT WANTED TO BE KNOWN AS A FUN AND ABSOLUTELY OUTRAGEOUS COMPANY. SOUTHWEST OUTFITTED ITS FLIGHT ATTENDANTS IN ORANGE HOT PANTS, LACE-UP GO-GO BOOTS, AND WIDE, HIP-SLUNG BELTS.

Prior to 1981, San Diego's business community did not hav a business bank it could call homegrown. With this in min Robert Horsman, now president of San Diego National Ban (SDNB), and several other local bankers discussed the situatio and decided to form a local banking institution. "We decided w needed a metropolitan business bank in San Diego, so we wen

out and talked with businessmen in the community," explains Horsman. Those conversations led to the formation of SDNB and the installation of its chairman, Charlie Feurzeig, who guided the bank for 16 years and became emeritus chair in 1996. Feurzeig was succeeded by Murray Galinson, the current board chairman.

SDNB shares were traded on Nasdaq until 1997, when the bank was acquired by FBOP Corp. Today, the institution is privately owned.

Although it is no longer locally owned, the bank is—as always— the homegrown bank of San Diego's business community.

BIGGER AND BETTER

"In the summer of 1997," says Horsman, "we merged with Regenc Savings Bank, located in San Dieg thus creating a larger San Diego National Bank. Because of this merger, we can lend up to $30 million to any single customer. Now, we have 11 offices, whereas before the merger we had two, and 35,000 customers instead of 3,500." Today, San Diego Nation. Bank has added individual and retail banking with the same con mitment to personalized service that gave it a reputation as San Diego's premier business bank. Due to the increased size and mag nitude of the bank since merging with Regency Savings, it has the

PART OF THE FAMILIARITY OF SAN DIEGO NATIONAL BANK IS THE TRADEMARK WHALE MURAL PAINTED ON THE OUTSIDE WALL OF ITS DOWNTOWN OFFICE BY WYLAND, A WELL-KNOWN MARINE ARTIST.

THE BANK REMAINS COMMITTED TO PRESERVING THE QUALITY OF LIFE AND UNIQUE LIFESTYLE THAT HAVE COME TO BE SYNONYMOUS WITH SAN DIEGO. DURING THE JULY 1997 MERGER WITH REGENCY, SDNB PRESIDENT ROBERT HORSMAN PRESENTED A $2,000 CHECK ON BEHALF OF THE BANK TO THE BOYS AND GIRLS CLUBS OF EAST COUNTY.

sources to manage San Diego's savings and lending needs to an even greater degree than before. After San Diego Trust left the scene a few years ago, we saw a gap and wanted to fill it," says Horsman.

SAN DIEGO'S LARGEST COMMUNITY BANK

The city's largest independent bank, SDNB serves the needs of San Diegans by offering a complete line of personal and business banking services, and it aims to establish long-term banking relationships built upon trust and mutual respect.

Horsman says his bank's mission is simple: To remain the leading community bank in San Diego County. "We serve our clients in a profitable and ethical manner," he says. "The bank's board members are well-known, successful business owners and professionals who are advocates of the local economy and business community.

"The good news for San Diego County," says Horsman, "is that the real estate and construction industries are on the rebound. A major focus for San Diego National Bank is commercial and construction real estate lending. We are now in a position to facilitate the larger and middle-market loan requests that the bank was unable to do in the past."

In addition to a full line of financial products and services, the bank also offers business customers a unique courier network. SDNB can send one of its couriers to pick up deposits or loan documents, saving busy executives and their employees a trip to the bank. Many clients use courier services on a daily, weekly, or monthly basis.

"We are a billion-dollar bank," says Horsman, "but we are still a familiar face." Part of the familiarity is the bank's trademark life-size whale mural on the outside wall of its downtown office. "Wyland, the well-known marine artist, volunteered to paint the mural during

his West Coast tour if we would agree to light it," says Horsman. "And, of course, we agreed."

ACTIVE IN COMMUNITY SERVICE

In addition to their financial expertise, the bank's management and staff understand and care about the greater community. Through SDNB's associations with local civic and professional organizations, the bank remains committed to preserving the quality of life and unique lifestyle that have come to be synonymous with San Diego.

San Diego National Bank is involved with nearly 80 different civic and professional organizations throughout San Diego County. Included in this long list of organizations are the American Red Cross, Association of Retarded

Citizens (ARC), Catholic Charities, Episcopal Community Services, United Jewish Federation, San Diego Opera, San Diego Blood Bank, San Diego Urban League, Second Chance, Wellness Community, and United Way.

The staff, management, and board of SDNB feel that it is imperative for the bank to be involved in the civic as well as economic well-being of San Diego. "When we merged with Regency, we donated more than $200,000 to different local nonprofit organizations," says Horsman. "Each of our bank branches looked into its neighborhood and told us about groups of people in need of support. We gave them financial support and continue to do so. Even though we continue to grow, we still want to be San Diego's homegrown bank."

VISIONARY IS THE WORD THAT BEST DESCRIBES SIERRA OPTICAL California's largest independent manufacturer of prescription eyewear. The company offers its clients clearer vision through technologically advanced, state-of-the-art processing services and an array of the highest-quality lens products available ■ Sierra Optical was founded in 1981 by Charles Pendrell, now

company president; and Don Dakin, current CFO; with six employees. From a 2,400-square-foot space, Sierra produced 70 pairs of eyeglasses a day. Today, after years of marketing its quality products, the company employs 200 people in a 34,000-square-foot facility, using the most advanced lab technology available in the world. The lab can now manufacture 1,800 to 2,000 pairs of eyeglasses daily.

Sierra's primary market is California; however, with a growing presence in North America, South America, and Europe, plans are being implemented to expand the capacity of this site to handle the expected growth.

"Originally, we acquired the equipment of a test lab that was a part of Signet Optical, now Signet Armorlite, a local lens manufacturer," says Pendrell. "After we purchased the equipment, we started expanding the business." Signet Armorlite manufactures lens blanks, the raw materials that labs like Sierra use to grind prescriptions into, to make a pair of eyeglasses.

LABORATORY OF TODAY
Sierra was the first independent lab in the world licensed to manufacture and distribute Carl Zeiss Optical products. Zeiss is known all over the world for its quality optic lens products and antireflective coatings. "An antireflective or non-reflective coated lens takes all of the reflections off that lens and

neutralizes them so they disappear such as when you are driving at night." says Pendrell. "Antireflective lenses improve a person's night vision significantly. And if you are looking at someone with anti reflective coating on their lenses, you can see their eyes more clearly instead of seeing your own reflection." Carl Zeiss Optical developed antireflective coating more than 50 years ago, and it still remains the leading standard in the industry.

Sierra is a licensed distributor of Varilux products, including Varilux Comfort, the leading choice for progressive addition lenses among patients and eye care practitioners throughout the world. These lenses are especially suited to bifocal wearers, allowing them to read comfortably without the image jump usually found with bifocals. These lenses also allow for a more accurate peripheral vision. In a recent study of bifocal wearers who tried Varilux Comfort, 97 percent of wearers had a successful conversion to the progressive

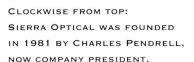

CLOCKWISE FROM TOP:
SIERRA OPTICAL WAS FOUNDED IN 1981 BY CHARLES PENDRELL, NOW COMPANY PRESIDENT.

TODAY, AFTER YEARS OF MARKETING ITS QUALITY PRODUCTS, THE COMPANY EMPLOYS 200 PEOPLE IN A 34,000-SQUARE-FOOT FACILITY, USING THE MOST ADVANCED LAB TECHNOLOGY AVAILABLE IN THE WORLD.

ZEISS' ANTIREFLECTIVE COATING DOME FEATURES ADVANCED BELL-JAR TECHNOLOGY.

ns. Sierra has been so successful ith Varilux Comfort sales that it as recognized as the 1996 Varilux ib of the Year.

Transitions lenses are another onsumer favorite. As the area's ading manufacturer of Transitions, Sierra aggressively markets is lightweight and thin photochromatic lens that changes color variable light and weather onditions.

As the optical industry continues to change, Sierra's emphasis still on the independent practitioner. To aid the practitioner, erra provides new product information, marketing, and certification training. Through seminars, rochures, and Sierra's Web site www.sierraoptical.com, up-tote optical information can be otained for eye care professions as well as consumers.

ECHNOLOGY F TOMORROW

esides its wide array of top-quality roducts, Sierra is a leading testing cility for new optical equipment, aying ahead of the constantly hanging industry. "We work in ose conjunction with our venors," says Pendrell. "If a vendor building a new piece of equipment, the company will ask us to halyze and test it out. We also articipate in the designing of quipment with selected vendors. hey value our ideas and opinions."

Ranked by volume, the company the third-largest optical testing cility in the country, and every ear since 1992, a leading optical ade publication has rated Sierra one of the top 25 laboratories the country.

Sierra's owners have made significant investments in new technology to modernize the company's perations. "Every facet of our peration is computerized," says endrell. "In our assembly proess, 40 percent of the activities e computer assisted." This has hade the company more efficient, elping to standardize the process

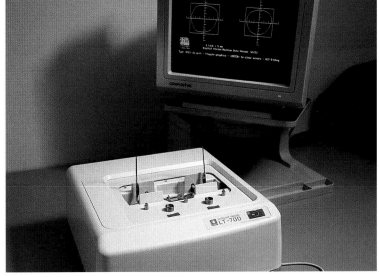

and increase product quality. This is a critical advantage, considering every order is customized for each individual consumer.

But the biggest reason for Sierra's success, says Pendrell, is its emphasis on employee contributions to the finished product. "When you're putting out 1,800 units a day with 200 people, everyone is involved in the process," says Pendrell. "Each person's involvement is very important, as everyone comes into contact with the products and services that we provide."

Sierra will continue to focus on providing high-quality products for consumers, especially those baby boomers who are reaching their 50s and are starting to need special eye care products. And Pendrell believes the market for

antireflective coated lenses will intensify in its growth through consumer awareness and demand.

"It's a matter of education. If you knew the difference between antireflective lenses and traditional lenses, you would never wear traditional lenses again," stated Pendrell. "The U.S. market for antireflective coated lenses is only 8 percent of all lenses sold, compared to 80 percent in Europe and 95 percent in Japan."

As Sierra looks toward its third decade of success, Pendrell and Dakin have focused their company's efforts on producing lighter, thinner specialty lens products. Pendrell concludes, "Our focus is and always will be on quality. We believe our customers' eyes deserve the best."

CLOCKWISE FROM TOP LEFT: LOH SIERRA 1500 IS AN INNOVATIVE WASHUP STATION.

AT THE STATE-OF-THE-ART ANTIREFLECTIVE COATING FACILITY, THE STAFF WORKS TO PRODUCE HIGH-QUALITY ANTIREFLECTIVE LENSES.

NIDEK SATELLITE TRACER IS A COMPUTERIZED SYSTEM THAT ACCURATELY MEASURES EVEN THE SMALLEST FRAMES.

LOH V95, AN AUTOMATIC GENERATOR, PROCESSES GLASS AND PLASTICS.

G OLDEN EAGLE INSURANCE CORPORATION, A SAN DIEGO PRESENC since 1982, is a highly rated provider of commercial insuranc workers' compensation, and home owners insurance to som 100,000 policyholders in California and Arizona. ■ Acquired b Boston-based Liberty Mutual Group in August 1997, Golde Eagle has undergone a vigorous rehabilitation that has bolstere

its financial position. Today's company is rated among the highest in the insurance industry, receiving Excellent marks from the three leading ratings organizations: Best's Rating Service (A), Moody's (Aa3), and Standard & Poor's (AA).

Backed by Liberty Mutual, Golden Eagle Insurance is now busy doing what it does best— providing quality insurance services as a major competitor in the marketplace.

THE LIBERTY DIFFERENCE

By 1996, Golden Eagle Insurance had grown to a company with sales in excess of $700 million. Liberty Mutual's acquisition of Golden Eagle ended a period of growing uncertainty. Its takeover of the old Golden Eagle Insurance Company and the subsequent creation of the new Golden Eagle Insurance Corporation preserved some 1,300 jobs and protected the interest of Golden Eagle policyholders.

A diversified financial services company employing 23,000 people in more than 500 offices worldwide, Liberty Mutual is one of the nation's largest multiline insurers in the property and casualty field,

and has been the leading provide of workers' compensation insurance, programs, and services in the United States for more than 60 years. Liberty Mutual, founde in 1912, ranks 126th among Fortur 500 companies with $8.7 billion i consolidated revenue, more than $40 billion in consolidated asset and $50 billion in assets under management.

With Liberty Mutual's financia strength behind it, Golden Eagle is stronger and more viable than ever. The new company operates under the direction of local man agement, and distribution of the company's products continues through Golden Eagle's network of more than 700 agents and bro kers throughout California and Arizona.

THE PEOPLE DIFFERENCE

What sets the company apart fror its competitors is its people, accorc ing to Fred G. Marziano, Golden Eagle chairman and CEO. "Our employees make the difference," h says. "They are absolutely dedicate and committed. Every minute of their working day is devoted to do ing the best possible job they can.

Golden Eagle is also proud of its record of customer satisfactior "We are known for our ability to be creative, responsive, and competitive," says Marziano. "We routinely work with our agents and insured customers to tailor insurance packages."

The people of San Diego knov that Golden Eagle is committed to them, as well. In October 1997, the company signed a 10-year lease—with a 10-year renewable option—to occupy up to 12 floors in a downtown building on B

GOLDEN EAGLE INSURANCE
CORPORATION IS COMMITTED
TO BEING A VITAL CONTRIBUTOR
TO SAN DIEGO'S THRIVING BUSI-
NESS COMMUNITY, EVIDENT IN
THE RECENT, LARGEST EVER COM-
MERCIAL LEASE TRANSACTION IN
DOWNTOWN HISTORY. BY MID-1998,
GOLDEN EAGLE WILL OCCUPY UP
TO 12 FLOORS AT 525 B STREET.
THIS NEW HOME FOR NEARLY 1,000
GOLDEN EAGLE EMPLOYEES IS
BEING RENAMED GOLDEN EAGLE
PLAZA.

Street, renamed Golden Eagle Plaza. And employees are being relocated from the corporation's nine Greater San Diego locations to this new downtown suite. The new offices accommodate nearly 1,000 employees and encompass more than 160,000 square feet. Some 220 employees remain in Golden Eagle's facility on Camino del Rio in Mission Valley.

"We chose downtown because we like the ambience, the quality of the city, the safety for our employees, and the tremendous facilities surrounding our new offices," Marziano says. "By signing this lease, we have clearly demonstrated our commitment to the San Diego community. And we want to become a major part of that community."

THE EAGLE SOARS

Golden Eagle's plans include expansion of its product lines in California, which should create additional job opportunities in San Diego. The corporation is making further investments in its technical equipment in order to keep the company at the forefront of its industry.

Golden Eagle has also made a major commitment to the San Diego Chamber of Commerce to underwrite its workers' compensation insurance program for members and employees, who receive a 10 percent discount.

Under Liberty Mutual's ownership, the future has never been brighter for the new—and improved—Golden Eagle, where the level of service and a reputation for competitive pricing remain in place. "Liberty Mutual bought Golden Eagle because of its strengths in service to agents and brokers, and its flexibility in underwriting," says Marziano. "Liberty Mutual wants only to preserve those strengths and build on them."

T HE ARROWHEAD GROUP OF COMPANIES IS A DIVERSE ORGANIZATION with one main thing on its mind when it comes to business-insurance. ■ In addition to acting as a managing general agency for other insurance companies, Arrowhead offers its own retail products. "As a managing general agent we were—and are—a wholesale agent. We provide a variety of services for other insurance

companies, essentially becoming their back room," says President J. Richard Hoye. Although 60 percent of the company's business is done in California, Arrowhead also maintains offices in Texas, Louisiana, Washington, Oregon, and Arizona.

The Arrowhead Group of Companies began as Arrowhead General Insurance Agency, origi-

nally established in 1983 by Classified Financial Corporation. At that time, Classified wanted to create a captive general agency that could produce nonstandard personal automobile insurance in Southern California. "In other words," says Hoye, "the company was founded selling high-risk auto insurance." Classified hired Patrick J. Kilkenny, who currently serves as Arrowhead's chairman, to lead the operation in 1984, and a year later sold it to him.

In the 1980s, Arrowhead's business consisted mostly of underwriting, product management, pricing, claims adjustment, and other typical insurance company activities. But in 1988, the company branched out, creating Insurance Express, a retail agency that sells Arrowhead's insurance products, as well as competitor products. In 1995, Arrowhead Specialty Products, Inc. was created to develop, market,

and underwrite other insurance lines.

The Arrowhead Group also successfully entered the California home owners market in 1996. "We had a very good year," says Hoye. "We went from zero applications to 6,000 applications per month. Much of that was due to problems after the Northridge earthquake, when other insurance companies pulled back or got out of the home owners market entirely. We saw this void developing and stepped in."

TECHNOLOGY AND EXPERTISE ARE KEYS TO SUCCESS

Arrowhead has always believed in technology to improve customer relations. With this philosophy in mind, the company installed a new imaging system in 1995, which improved its customer service by providing faster and more accurate information to clients.

DAVE SICCARDI

PATRICK J. KILKENNY CURRENTLY
SERVES AS CHAIRMAN OF THE
ARROWHEAD GROUP OF
COMPANIES.

THE ARROWHEAD GROUP RECENTLY
MOVED INTO ITS NEW HEADQUAR-
TERS, A 95,000-SQUARE-FOOT
OFFICE BUILDING WITH A FULL-
SERVICE GYM AND LARGE CAFE-
TERIA, MAKING A LONG-TERM
COMMITMENT TO STAY IN THE
SAN DIEGO AREA.

ustomer service representatives an now view all active policies within seconds. "We have become very nimble with our information systems and the deployment of technology," explains Kilkenny. During the last half of this decade, windows of opportunity have tended to open and close more quickly than ever before, and much depends on the ability of companies to move data around. We can do that, taking advantage of market opportunities faster than our competitors."

Equally important to the company's competitiveness, says Kilkenny, is its enormous investment in expertise on the part of personnel. "We have four CPAs on board, the head of our claims department is an attorney with extensive experience in transportation law, and we have a lot of professional people here with advanced degrees."

Arrowhead has also found that one of the most important keys to producing a profitable business portfolio is to align with the right retail producers. The company is highly selective in appointing retail producers: In fact, Arrowhead does business with only 600 of the more than 7,000 licensed retail insurance brokerage firms in California.

A WORKFORCE THAT REFLECTS SAN DIEGO

The Arrowhead Group recently moved into a new, 95,000-square-foot office building with a full-service gym and large cafeteria, making a long-term commitment to stay in the San Diego area. Kilkenny says San Diego was originally chosen as Arrowhead's headquarters because of the area's weather and lifestyle. "You can't improve upon the quality of life here," he says, "and that enables us to attract and keep talented individuals from all parts of the country." In addition, area colleges and universities annually turn out highly qualified people for employment, many of whom apply at Arrowhead.

And those employees represent the ethnic and cultural diversity of San Diego. While other companies have had to put special policies in place to ensure they have a diverse workforce, Arrowhead's hiring managers have kept their minds open and hired quality people, reflecting the company's customer base.

SUPPORTING THE FUTURE OF SAN DIEGO

Not wanting only to give jobs to area residents, Arrowhead often gives something back to the com-

▶ DAVE SICCARDI

munity that supports the company. It is a frequent and regular contributor to St. Vincent de Paul charitable activities in San Diego, and donates to local YMCAs as well as hosting several blood drives each year for the American Red Cross. The company also sponsors food drives to benefit other local agencies for the homeless.

As for Arrowhead's future, Kilkenny says it looks bright. "It will involve further product diversification and growth in existing programs," he says. And with an already diverse product line and a desire to remain an innovator in the industry, Arrowhead is well on its way to success in any new project it takes on.

DOUGLAS E. BARNHART, INC.

MUCH OF WHAT MAKES SAN DIEGO A WORLD-CLASS CIT is its world-class buildings and facilities. World-clas structures require the expertise of a quality-minded con struction company to bring to life the design concept. Sinc its inception, douglas e. barnhart, inc. has emerged as on of the leaders in the general building/constructio

management industry in San Diego.

A combination of navy management techniques (adopted by CEO and founder Douglas E. Barnhart), teamwork, and automated management information systems (MIS) provides the cost control, scheduling, coordination, and financial controls that have resulted in the continued success of douglas e. barnhart, inc. These systems, and the philosophy that the client is foremost, have helped douglas e. barnhart, inc. success-

fully complete projects in the San Diego area. These include mixed-use and retail projects, engineering and seismic retrofitting of existing structures, libraries, police stations, schools and universities, television and radio broadcast facilities, stadiums, performing arts centers, churches, casinos, medical facilities, aviation facilities, and government buildings.

Many of these projects have had a major impact on San Diego and have helped the city to be known as world class. The first of these

would be the educational facilities. douglas e. barnhart, inc. has constructed numerous day care centers, as well as elementary, middle, and high schools. The Barnhart Corporation also has built several departmental buildings for institutions of higher learning in San Diego: San Diego Stat University (SDSU), University of San Diego (USD), and University of California San Diego. The Sout Chula Vista Library, the 1995 Gran Orchid winner; the KPBS/Gateway complex at SDSU; and the ◄ Colachis Plaza Fountain at USD represent the many project highlights in Barnhart Corporation's portfolio.

douglas e. barnhart, inc. is par of the San Diego sports scene as well. Acting as the "quarterback," barnhart built a $10 million sport training facility for the San Dieg Chargers. In addition to three football practice fields, a 73,000-square-foot structural steel building houses offices and indoor training facilities for the Chargers The newly-completed Tony Gwyn Stadium was built for the San ◄ Diego State Aztecs baseball team on the SDSU campus. Also, dougla e. barnhart, inc. has constructed numerous high school football stadiums, gymnasiums, swimming pool complexes, and ballparks.

In addition to these projects, douglas e. barnhart, inc. is a leade in the construction of transporta tion facilities. The new Terminal 2 Concourse F project at San Diego Lindbergh Field is the cornerstone of an impressive aviation project résumé. Other landmark projects include the Air Traffic Control Tower at Lindbergh Field; the FAA Terminal Radar Approach

DOUGLAS E. BARNHART, INC. WAS RESPONSIBLE FOR THE RESTORATION OF THE AGING SHILEY THEATRE AT THE UNIVERSITY OF SAN DIEGO FOR THE 1996 PRESIDENTIAL DEBATES. IT WAS IMPERATIVE THAT THE THEATER BE UPGRADED AND ITS 16TH-CENTURY ARCHITECTURAL FEATURES RESTORED SO THAT MILLIONS OF TELEVISION VIEWERS COULD WATCH THE DEBATES.

FOCUSED IMAGES PHOTOGRAPHY

BRADY ARCHITECTURAL PHOTOGRAPHY

THE FAA TERMINAL RADAR APPROACH CONTROL (TRACON) FACILITY AT NAVAL AIR STATION MIRAMAR IS ONE OF THE FIRM'S LANDMARK PROJECTS.

ontrol (TRACON) facility; U.S. Navy aviation facilities at NAS Miramar, NAS North Island, and NAF Imperial Beach; and USMC Camp Pendleton.

In the mass transit arena, Barnhart has constructed major transit centers at Carlsbad, Solana Beach, Santee, and Escondido. The Escondido Transit Center has received national honors, while the Carlsbad Transit Center and Solana Beach Train Station were Orchid winners.

Other significant projects include the restoration of the aging Shiley Theatre at USD for the 1996 Presidential Debates. It was imperative that the theater be upgraded and its 16th-century architectural features restored so that millions of television viewers could watch these debates. Barnhart has also constructed theaters on several campuses. These include the unique School for Creative and Performing Arts in South San Diego, La Costa Canyon High School in Carlsbad, and the $10 million Poway Performing Arts Center in North County.

Law enforcement has also been the recipient of Barnhart construction services. Construction of Southeastern Division Police Station and Eastern Division Police Station was performed by douglas e. barnhart, inc. Recently completed was another police facility in the Poway community.

While douglas e. barnhart, inc. is constantly making its clients' facility plans become reality, the corporation also makes wishes come true for people in need. Barnhart has a long-standing history of donating its services to San Diego communities such as Linda Vista, City Heights, Poway, and Oceanside, and is currently making improvements at the San Diego Center for Children. A student health clinic at Hoover High School bears the douglas e. barnhart, inc. name on its walls as a tribute to its existence. Scholarship funds, donations to Toys for Tots, sponsorships of youth sports organizations, and support to health and education institutions are just some of the examples of ways that Barnhart gives back to the San Diego area. The 1996 Republican National Convention was another recipient of douglas e. barnhart, inc.'s voluntary effort. Also, Douglas Barnhart serves on the boards of the Greater San Diego Chamber of Commerce, and the San Diego International Sports Council, and is a director of the San Diego National Bank.

douglas e. barnhart, inc. is also very involved in the San Diego construction industry. Barnhart managers serve on the board of directors of both the Associated General Contractors (AGC) of America and the Associated Builders and Contractors. Barnhart is

vice chairman of the Contractors State License Board, chairman of the AGC Apprenticeship Training Trust, secretary of the AGC Pension Trust, national chairman of the AGC/U.S. Navy Committee, national board member of the Associated General Contractors of America, and chairman of the AGC Political Action Committee.

The success of douglas e. barnhart, inc. is not limited to San Diego, but includes all of Southern California, Dallas, and Las Vegas.

By constructing the buildings that people live, work, play, and learn in, douglas e. barnhart, inc. has contributed to making San Diego what it is today, a world-class city.

CLOCKWISE FROM TOP LEFT: THE FIRM'S PORTFOLIO INCLUDES THE SOUTH CHULA VISTA LIBRARY, THE 1995 GRAND ORCHID WINNER.

A LEADER IN THE CONSTRUCTION OF TRANSPORTATION FACILITIES, BARNHART HAS COMPLETED SUCH PROJECTS AS THE AIR TRAFFIC CONTROL TOWER AT LINDBERGH FIELD.

THE NEWLY COMPLETED TONY GWYNN STADIUM WAS BUILT FOR THE SAN DIEGO STATE AZTECS BASEBALL TEAM ON THE SDSU CAMPUS BY DOUGLAS E. BARNHART, INC.

Located south of Bonita and west of the picturesque Ota Lakes in eastern Chula Vista is EastLake, one of the larges master-planned communities in San Diego County. Whe completed—likely by the year 2010—EastLake will compris approximately 9,000 dwelling units and a population of nearl 30,000. Created by the EastLake Company—which was founde

in 1983—the project broke ground in 1985, and features three distinct residential neighborhoods, commercial and industrial zoning, schools, parks, lakes, and nature trails.

"Our homes are very attractive to families of professionals," says Paul Nieto, president and CEO of the EastLake Company. "We also have retirees and empty nesters, but about 60 percent of our home owners have school-age kids."

The EastLake Company oversees all development within the community, and is responsible for backbone infrastructure and facility planning. The company markets land to individual builders and commercial, industrial, and retail users. The EastLake Company— which is a wholly owned subsidiary of Los Angeles-based J.G. Boswell Company—has established desig controls that will be implemente throughout the formation of the community.

COMMUNITY OVERVIEW

EastLake is a 3,230-acre, comprehensively planned and balanced development that offers an enviror ment of total quality living. Whe the entire project is complete, it will provide a mix of residential, commercial, light-to-medium industrial, office, recreational, and open-space areas.

The planning and approval pro cess for the community's master plan began in 1983, and three years later, the first two neighborhood: opened: EastLake Hills and EastLak Shores. During the grand openin in April 1986, the company's expectations were surpassed, as 533 homes were sold that year to the first EastLake residents. In the following year, 602 homes were sold, followed by 450 in 1988.

In May 1990, the community's first elementary school was built, and today, EastLake Hills and EastLake Shores boast a 15-acre, man-made lake; a Swim & Tennis Club; private neighborhood parks and a variety of attached and detached homes built by leading area builders. EastLake Business Center was the next phase of devel opment in the community's maste plan, and the center's tenants include UPS, Nellcor, North Island Federal Credit Union, and Kaiser Permanente.

In February 1991, EastLake's third residential neighborhood, EastLake Greens, opened with six new-home products and 21 mode homes designed around EastLake Country Club, an 18-hole champi

EASTLAKE IS A 3,230-ACRE, COMPREHENSIVELY PLANNED AND BALANCED DEVELOPMENT THAT OFFERS AN ENVIRONMENT OF SECURE, QUALITY LIVING.

nship golf course. This 823-acre neighborhood was planned for approximately 2,800 homes with five parks designed for the active Southern California lifestyle.

Two new schools have also been built in EastLake Greens. EastLake High, one of California's most technically advanced learning centers, opened in 1992. The collegelike campus features college preparatory and technical classes, a performing arts center, an evening adult education center, and a shared-use library that is open to the public. For younger children, the year-round Olympic View Elementary School is also conveniently located in EastLake Greens. In all, the master plan calls for two more elementary schools and one middle school.

EastLake Village Center—the first of four retail areas in the community—is being designed as a hub of activity, and features Vons and Rite Aid as anchor tenants. The center provides a place for residents to shop, dine, and share community spirit. The future will bring an entertainment complex with restaurants, boutiques, a hotel, and a theater. To the north of EastLake Village Center, Kaiser Permanente has purchased 32 acres of land for a 3 million-square-foot medical center, which will have medical

office buildings and a major hospital facility.

EastLake is also proud to be the home of the ARCO Training Center, the nation's first warm-weather Olympic training center. Constructed on 150 acres of land provided by the EastLake Company, the center is open year-round and serves local residents by bringing athletes into the community through outreach programs.

A transit center, churches, and day care are additional components proposed in the master plan. Future phases will include the final residential neighborhoods of EastLake Trails, EastLake Vistas, and EastLake Woods, as well as the 86-acre second phase of EastLake Business Center.

DEVELOPMENT PHILOSOPHY

Key aspects of the EastLake planned community program are its diversity and flexibility. The company has the ability to anticipate and respond to market changes over a 25-year development period. Housing prices range from about $130,000 to more than $600,000, with the average dwelling priced at approximately $225,000.

In the lower price ranges, EastLake positions itself to capture a majority of the South County market due to the value-added aspects of the total community. Given a broad range of housing types and prices with emphasis on housing priced below $250,000,

IN FEBRUARY 1991, EASTLAKE GREENS OPENED WITH SIX NEW-HOME PRODUCTS AND 21 MODEL HOMES DESIGNED AROUND EASTLAKE COUNTRY CLUB, AN 18-HOLE CHAMPIONSHIP GOLF COURSE.

EASTLAKE BUSINESS CENTER WAS AN EARLY PHASE OF DEVELOPMENT IN THE COMMUNITY'S MASTER PLAN AND INCLUDES NORTH ISLAND FEDERAL CREDIT UNION (BOTTOM LEFT).

DOLPHIN BEACH, THE THIRD PRIVATE RESIDENTIAL PARK IN EASTLAKE GREENS, OPENED IN THE SUMMER OF 1997 (BOTTOM RIGHT).

a market capture of more than 400 dwelling units per year has been achieved and is foreseeable for future phases.

The development and marketing strategy for EastLake is focused on increasing its South County market share, as well as achieving increased awareness outside its target market area. Growth will occur in an obvious and controlled pattern through a strategy of slow, but steady, growth.

Local street improvements, streetscapes, and neighborhood amenities—as well as the 18-hole golf course—were constructed in the first two phases of development. Residential neighborhoods are centered on activity nodes/parks, which are interconnected by a system of pedestrian/bike pathways and trails.

In addition, a centralized "home-finding" center has been developed as a destination for potential home buyers and as the staging area for matching home buyers with product offerings. The primary purpose for EastLake's HomeFinding Center is to sell the community and lifestyle, with each guest builder participating in EastLake's master marketing and merchandising program.

In assembling its team of construction partners, EastLake welcomes those companies that bring with them expertise and market experience. EastLake's goal is to assemble a team of highly qualified residential builders who are committed to the underlying goals and objectives of the EastLake community on both a short- and a long-term basis.

FOCUS ON SOUTH COUNTY

Into the next millennium, San Diego County will experience major growth in three general geographic areas: the north coastal area, the Interstate 15 corridor near Escondido, and the South County area. Based on recent growth trends, South County has established itself as the fastest-growing of these three areas.

A major benefit of South County is its close proximity to the metropolitan core of the region. South County represents one of the few

major growth areas in San Diego County where a significant number of homes can be purchased in a moderate price range, and where the broadest spectrum of potential housing demand exists.

Chula Vista is the urban center for the South County area and the second-largest city in San Diego County. Regional forecasts conclude that Chula Vista will continue to retain its position in the county as second only to the city of San Diego in terms of size and population. The EastLake/Bonita area boasts three of the top zip code areas for highest household income in San Diego County.

Historically, Chula Vista has captured approximately 5.5 percent of the county's population growth. However, during the next decade, it is anticipated that Chula Vista will capture a higher percentage, largely due to North County's increasingly scarce residential development opportunities, as well as its higher home prices.

According to the California Department of Finances, in 1997 Chula Vista ranked 10th among the fastest-growing cities in the state. Chula Vista will continue to be a major factor in the San Diego housing market because of its ultimate control over large amounts of available and buildable land.

Employment availability is another important factor in determining future housing demand

istribution. Chula Vista's strate-
ic location between the city of
an Diego and the Mexican border
ffers businesses unique manu-
acturing and distribution oppor-
inities, as well as the benefits
om the increased importance
f international trade. Chula Vista
likely to assume increasing sta-
is as an economic and political
irce within the region.

Just 20 minutes from downtown
an Diego and on the urban edge
f existing development, EastLake
in a prime South County loca-
on. The gently rolling property
immediately adjacent to all
rban services and in close prox-
nity to Bonita, one of the most
esirable residential areas of the
ounty. The eastern boundary
onsists of three miles of view
ontage along the upper and
wer Otay lakes. A federally
wned wilderness preserve to
ie east of the lakes provides a
:enic, open-space backdrop.

HISTORY OF THE LAND
he EastLake community is
.tuated on what was once the

romantic Rancho Janal, a sprawling, 4,500-acre ranch of roaming
cattle. Janal is a Native American
term for "spongy ground," which
probably refers to the underground
streams that crisscross the land.

After the Mexican-American
War of 1846, California became
a U.S. territory, which created
difficulties for ranch owners in
proving their rights to the land
grants given to them by Mexican
governors. It wasn't until 1872 that
Don Jose Guadalupe Estudillo
received a property title to the
Janal grant.

In 1869, a San Diego County
surveyor created a stage route from
San Diego to Yuma, which passed
through the Janal ranch. By 1900,
Rancho Janal became the site for
both the upper and lower Otay
dams and reservoir. The dams
were built by E.S. Babcock, who
also built the famed Hotel del
Coronado in 1888.

The history and the environment are important to the EastLake
Company. "We want to be a leader
in protecting the environment,"
says Nieto. "We were the first to

use reclaimed water for landscap-
ing—we were three years ahead of
the state in this aspect of water
conservation. And we were the
first to initiate composting among
our landscapers. That's going to
be a constant in our master plan.
We will continue to emphasize
water and environmental preservation." And along with its master plan and its goal of slow and
steady growth, EastLake is poised
to become one of the most prestigious addresses in all of San
Diego County.

CLOCKWISE FROM TOP LEFT:
FAMILIES ENJOY THE SWIM
LAGOON AT EASTLAKE SHORES.

EASTLAKE CHILDREN HAVE THE
OPPORTUNITY TO LEARN FROM
OLYMPIC COACHES AND ATHLETES
THROUGH AN INNOVATIVE EDUCA-
TIONAL PROGRAM IN COOPERATION
WITH THE ARCO TRAINING CENTER.

THE EASTERN BOUNDARY CON-
SISTS OF THREE MILES OF VIEW
FRONTAGE ALONG THE UPPER
AND LOWER OTAY LAKES.

G

ENETRONICS, INC. IS RECOGNIZED AS THE WORLD TECHNOLOG leader in the field of electroporation. Since 1991, the compan has been developing new ways of using electroporation t improve the treatment of catastrophic illnesses, especiall cancer. Founded in 1983 by Dr. Günter A. Hofmann—who no serves as chairman and chief scientific officer—Genetronic

is headquartered in Sorrento Valley.

Genetronics has developed electroporation into a unique drug delivery system that utilizes brief, carefully controlled pulsed electric fields from the Medpulser™— invented by Genetronics—to open pores in a tumor cell and allow an anticancer drug to enter and kill it. Even though clinical studies using electroporation to administer drugs began in 1994, the equipment used was introduced to the laboratory market in 1985. "We were the first to reduce this technology to practice and are now

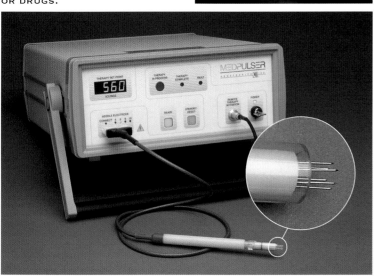

the technological leader in the field," says Lois J. Crandell, company president and CEO.

VANCOUVER HOLDING COMPANY

The company also maintains a holding company in Vancouver, British Columbia, known as Genetronics Biomedical Ltd. Crandell says the Canadian company was established in 1994, a year she calls difficult for finding health care funding in the United States. "Because of this, we were forced to search for funding outside the country," says Crandell. "And as a consequence of that, we found a shell company in Canada and took it over. We began trading on the Vancouver Stock Exchange in January 1995." In September 1997, the company was first listed on the Toronto Stock Exchange, the third-largest exchange in North America.

Canadian loans in 1994 enabled Genetronics to begin its first round of clinical studies for skin cancer treatment at the Moffitt Cancer Center in Tampa. "These areas where skin cancer is found were

immediately accessible to our tecl nology," explains Crandell.

TWO COMPANIES IN ONE

Genetronics Biomedical Ltd. has two divisions: BTX Instruments Division and Drug Delivery. BTX was the company's name initially but it was changed to Genetronic in 1994. BTX now sells laboratory instruments in 40 countries throug a network of 38 distributors worldwide. "The drug delivery component of the company is moving through the development level," says Crandell.

Upon becoming CEO in 1991, Crandell spearheaded the effort to move Genetronics into the therapeutic market. "We are taking the company's products from the laboratory to the clinic," she says "By delivering drugs directly into the tumor at the cellular level, we deliver about one-fiftieth of the systemic dosage of therapeutic chemotherapeutic agents," says Crandell. "This lower dosage eliminates many of the side effects fror chemotherapy. It is a much more humane way to treat a cancer patient."

Genetronics has launched clinical trials to treat head and neck cancer, pancreatic cancer, liver cancer, Kaposi's sarcoma, and malignant melanoma. Crandell says the company hopes to have its first product on the U.S. marke by early 2000 and products in the European market sooner. By continuing to lead the development of this technology, Genetronics will maintain its collaboration with medical researchers to find new and better treatments for cancer and other catastrophic disease in the future.

FOR NEARLY 15 YEARS, TRAVELERS AND LOCALS ALIKE HAVE FOUND a sophisticated, unique place to call their home away from home. Located less than a block from the beach—and across the street from the Museum of Contemporary Art—The Bed & Breakfast Inn at La Jolla offers its guests unparalleled comfort and service in a luxurious setting. ■ Originally built for George Kautz in 1913, the

inn was designed by Irving Gill and is considered one of the renowned architect's finest cubist-style buildings. At the same time, the gardens were designed by Kate Sessions, a well-known horticulturist who also helped create downtown San Diego's Balboa Park.

For several years during the 1920s, the inn was home to composer John Philip Sousa's family. Purchased by the current owners in 1984, the inn now offers 15 deluxe guest rooms, each uniquely decorated in the cottage style. Rooms are elegantly furnished and appointed with fine antiques and fresh flowers, and many have ocean or garden views.

Sales and Marketing Director Marilouise Micuda credits a major renovation and expansion in 1996 for the inn's superior accommodations. "The quality of accessories and artwork in each room is superb," she says. "The aesthetics have been greatly improved and the ambience is very sophisticated, yet relaxed. The inn has an infor-

mal elegance about it. It's very appealing, very peaceful."

The inn is now listed as a historical site in the San Diego Registry and is the only bed-and-breakfast operating in the village of La Jolla, whose excellent restaurants, boutiques, and galleries are within walking distance of the inn.

"We have guests from all over the world," says Micuda, "though the majority come from Southern California. This is a great place for a minivacation or weekend getaway." Micuda also points out that the bed-and-breakfast is a popular setting for small, intimate weddings, and oftentimes, the entire inn is wholly occupied by one wedding party.

AN INTIMATE EXPERIENCE
Although the inn is larger than a traditional bed-and-breakfast, it strives to maintain the same feeling of intimacy. Guests, many of whom are international travelers, are encouraged to dine together and share travel experiences and stories with each other. In addi-

tion, the inn has a library for its guests' reading pleasure.

Adding to this feeling of intimacy are a number of luxuries. Fresh fruit and glasses of sherry are brought to each guest room daily, wine and cheese are offered each day from 5 to 6 p.m., a full gourmet breakfast is served in the dining room or at patio tables in the garden, and pastries and fruit are left out for guests during the day.

In addition to this wide array of thrills for the taste buds, a concierge is available to answer questions and provide information about tours and activities. And the inn maintains a Web page at www.innlajolla.com, which displays photos of each room so guests can make their room selection before calling for reservations.

But even with all these amenities, Micuda says the best thing about The Bed & Breakfast Inn at La Jolla is that its staff pays close attention to the guests' every need, making them feel truly comfortable in their home away from home.

CRAIG TOMKINSON

LOCATED LESS THAN A BLOCK FROM THE BEACH—AND ACROSS THE STREET FROM THE MUSEUM OF CONTEMPORARY ART—THE BED & BREAKFAST INN AT LA JOLLA OFFERS ITS GUESTS UNPARALLELED COMFORT AND SERVICE IN A LUXURIOUS SETTING.

CRAIG TOMKINSON

CRAIG TOMKINSON

THE BED & BREAKFAST INN AT LA JOLLA OFFERS 15 DELUXE GUEST ROOMS, EACH UNIQUELY DECORATED IN THE COTTAGE STYLE. ROOMS ARE ELEGANTLY FURNISHED AND APPOINTED WITH FINE ANTIQUES AND FRESH FLOWERS, AND MANY HAVE OCEAN OR GARDEN VIEWS.

D

RIVING TOWARD THE HOOP IN HIS WEEKLY GAME OF BASKETBALL, TH
teenager's eyes flash with excitement as he maneuvers his Quicki
wheelchair down the lane. He pushes up a shot . . . and scores!
The nursing home resident guides her Guardian rolling walke
along the meandering garden path. Her senses come alive a
she breathes the honeysuckle air and feels the sun warm her face

The fifth-grade teacher taps her desk and calls her class to order, confident that the morning treatment with her DeVilbiss Pulmo-Aide will keep her asthma in check throughout the day.

Sunrise Medical's world is filled with persons, everyday and heroic, whose lives are being touched and improved by the company's assistive technologies. Products manufactured by Sunrise help people in many ways: healing wounds, speeding recovery, providing mobility, facilitating breathing, augmenting voice communication, and assisting in the activities of daily living. The company's products reach end users through its business partners: home health care providers, medical equipment distributors, drugstores, and mass merchants. The products are used in many settings, including hospitals, nursing homes, special education schools, and, of course, the home. Sunrise also markets its products to clinical professionals such as physical therapists, occupational therapists, nurses, and speech language pathologists.

A GLOBAL ENTERPRISE

Founded in 1983 by current Chairman and President Richard H. Chandler, Sunrise has grown to become one of the world's largest manufacturers of home care, extended care, and assistive products. A public company listed on the New York Stock Exchange, Sunrise Medical has sales approaching $700 million. From its corporate headquarters in Carlsbad, North San Diego County, Sunrise management oversees a global enterprise with 4,400 associates (the company's term for employees), 12 factories in North America and Europe, and company-owned distribution organizations in 15 countries. One of the company's important manufacturing centers is its Tijuana plant, just across the border at Otay Mesa, which makes wheelchairs, ambulatory aids, and personal care products. Sunrise products are sold in more than 100 countries around the world, with non-U.S. customers accounting for 44 percent of company sales.

A FAMILY OF MARKET-LEADING BRANDS

Sunrise Medical's brands of medical devices are pacesetters in each of their product markets. In custom manual and power wheelchairs, Quickie in the United State and Sopur in Europe have revolutionized the market by introducing ultralight manual and ultra-agile power chairs that incorporate advanced materials and many end-user-desired features. In seating and positioning products for the disabled, Sunrise's Jay wheelchair cushions and modular backs utilize patented JayFlow technology to maximize pressure relief.

Sunrise's respiratory products including the DeVilbiss oxygen concentrators, PulseDose conserving devices, and Pulmo-Aide compressor nebulizers, assist people with breathing difficulties. In its line of personal care products, the Guardian brand of walkers, crutches, bedside commodes, shower seats, and tub grab bars stands for quality, innovation, and market leadership.

In hospital beds and geriatrically correct nursing home furniture, Sunrise manufactures products such as Joerns beds, Parker bathing systems, and Hoyer patient lifters that consider the comfort and safety of caregivers and residents in need of continuing care. In patient support surfaces, the BioClinic brand of low air-loss mattress systems and Eggcrate foam overlays help treat and protect patients at risk for skin breakdown.

Finally, in augmentative communication, the breakthrough DynaVox and DynaMyte devices and proprietary DSS software as-

SUNRISE MEDICAL'S LINES OF GUARDIAN WALKERS AND DEVILBISS RESPIRATORY PRODUCTS ALLOW USERS TO MAINTAIN THEIR ACTIVE LIFESTYLES (TOP).

SUNRISE MANUFACTURES A WIDE RANGE OF HOME RESPIRATORY EQUIPMENT, INCLUDING AEROSOL, OXYGEN, AND SLEEP THERAPY PRODUCTS (BOTTOM).

...st victims of a variety of condi-
...ons and diseases who have lost
...e ability to speak.

UNIQUE CORPORATE
...ULTURE

...nrise Medical has a unique,
...lues-driven culture centered
...ound its corporate mission: to
...mprove people's lives by creating
...novative, high-quality products.
...he company's drive toward its
...ontinuous improvement is pow-
...ed by its Pursuit of Excellence
...OE) program, composed of five
...anks: Commitment to Shared
...alues, Total Quality Control,
...orld Class Manufacturing,
...perior Customer Service, and
...ssociate Recognition. Also dis-
...nctive is the Sunrise Olympics,
...ith its Sharing Rallies and year-
...d lottery prizes (including auto-
...obiles) for associates who have
...ade exceptional contributions
...uring the year, as well as Sunrise's

Do the Right Thing corporate
ethics program.

Innovation, quality, and education are among the company's hall-
marks. Sunrise introduces more
than 100 new products each year,
many incorporating patented features or technology. Each of the
company's major factories in the
United States and Europe has
earned ISO 9000 certification, the
international standard for excellence in manufacturing. Sunrise
sponsors more than 1,000 educational seminars annually to help
health care professionals understand how today's equipment best
meets the needs of each individual
patient.

A COMPANY WITH
A CONSCIENCE

Sunrise Medical's distinctive corporate culture and dedication to
improving people's lives have received much public recognition
over the years. Sunrise was one
of 12 companies cited for exceptional public spiritedness in the
book *Companies with a Conscience*.
The company has also been recognized in the *Fortune Guide to the 100
Fastest Growing Companies* and in
Empires of the Mind, and has been
featured on network television
shows, including *Good Morning
America* and *60 Minutes*.

In 1992, Sunrise Medical established Winners on Wheels (WOW),
an independent, nonprofit foun-

dation that addresses the social
and educational needs of children
in wheelchairs. WOW has grown to
have 75 "circles" across the United
States that meet biweekly to share
growth and recreational experiences. Sunrise Medical was also the
only home medical equipment company to become an official sponsor of the 1996 Atlanta Paralympic
Games for disabled athletes.

Commenting on what makes
Sunrise Medical special, Chandler
says, "The strength of our company is embedded deep in our
human fabric and corporate culture. Sunrise is composed of a
diverse group of associates all
united by one concern: we really
care about the products we make
and the people who use them. Our
corporate fortunes are interconnected with the disabled, the elderly,
the asthmatic child, the respiratory
sufferer, and others afflicted with
debilitating diseases. Our products
give these people independence
and hope, helping them to ease
their burdens and improve their
quality of life. Both our people and
our products make a difference."

CLOCKWISE FROM TOP LEFT:
IN A SPECIAL WHITE HOUSE
CEREMONY, PRESIDENT BILL
CLINTON PASSED THE TORCH TO
TEAM SUNRISE ATHLETE RANDY
SNOW, WHO OFFICIALLY BEGAN
THE TORCH RELAY OF THE 1996
PARALYMPIC GAMES.

QUICKIE, THE COMPANY'S GLOBAL
WHEELCHAIR BRAND, IS RECOG-
NIZED AS A MARK OF PRODUCT
EXCELLENCE BY WHEELCHAIR
USERS AROUND THE WORLD.

DISABLED ATHLETES, INCLUDING
PARALYMPIC GOLD MEDALIST SCOT
HOLLENBECK, CHOSE QUICKIE
RACING WHEELCHAIRS FOR UNSUR-
PASSED SPEED AND AGILITY.

A

GOURON PHARMACEUTICALS, INC. WAS FOUNDED WITH THE GOAL T·
design, develop, and commercialize innovative drugs for cance·
viral disease, and other life-threatening diseases. ■ San Dieg·
is the home of some of the world's leading research institution·
such as the Salk Institute, the Scripps Research Institute, an·
the University of California. These organizations have provide·

the catalyst for many of the companies that make up the region's biotechnology industry and have furnished the academic environment that inspired the small group of individuals who formed the nucleus of Agouron Pharmaceuticals.

In the late 1970s, pioneering scientists discovered molecular tools that would forever change the way the world approaches the treatment of disease. Advances in genetic engineering and molecu-

lar biology eventually gave rise to entirely new drugs and new ways to intervene in life-threatening diseases. Peter Johnson, then a doctoral student at the University of California, San Diego, was captivated by these developments. "The discovery of DNA restriction enzymes that enabled scientists to clone genes was of profound importance, launching the biotechnology industry and opening up vast new opportunities in drug

discovery," says Johnson, Agouron'· CEO and founder.

A NEW KIND OF PHARMACEUTICAL COMPANY

Armed with these and other new molecular tools, Johnson and his colleagues began to pursue a new approach to research. They starte· to develop a multidisciplinary team of professionals that could harness the most current advance·

AGOURON SCIENTISTS ARE WORKING ON A CURE FOR THE COMMON COLD BASED ON BLOCKING RHINOVIRUS PROTEASE, AN ENZYME USED BY THE COLD VIRUS TO REPRODUCE ITSELF (LEFT).

AGOURON CRYSTALLOGRAPHERS DISCUSS A COMPUTERIZED IMAGE OF THE RHINOVIRUS MOLECULE, CAUSE OF THE COMMON COLD. AGOURON HAS COMPOUNDS IN PRECLINICAL DEVELOPMENT FOR TREATMENT OR PREVENTION OF RHINOVIRUS INFECTIONS THAT AFFLICT MILLIONS OF PEOPLE, PARTICULARLY PROLONGING SYMPTOMS IN THOSE WITH ASTHMA AND EMPHYSEMA (RIGHT).

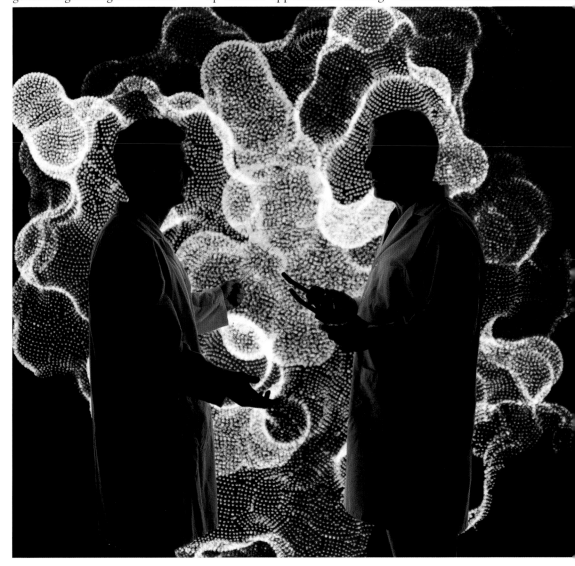

ents in chemistry and biology, and bring them to bear upon practical issues affecting the quality of human life. Most apparent to the group was the need for and feasibility of a more effective and efficient means of discovering and developing new drugs.

The new tools required an environment that fostered creativity and innovation without bounds. These scientists envisioned a company built around the strengths and collegial character of modern science—an eclectic convergence of scientists wielding the latest tools provided by physics, chemistry, computer technology, and genetic engineering. They were inspired by the tradition of the classical Greek agora—the marketplace or town center where the ancient Greeks conducted business, where commerce thrived, and where the learned came to share ideas. This was the intellectual and business inspiration for their new company called Agouron Pharmaceuticals, Inc. Since the company was founded in 1984, its goal has remained the same: to transform drug discovery and deliver the best medicines to those with the most urgent needs in the worldwide health care marketplace.

PROTEIN STRUCTURE-BASED DRUG DESIGN—A PARADIGM SHIFT

In order to understand how Agouron transformed drug discovery, one must understand how drugs work. Virtually every drug molecule works by binding to and altering the activity of some functionally important macromolecule (a large molecule such as a protein). In order for a drug to work, the drug molecule generally inserts itself into a functionally important crevice of its target macromolecular protein called the target, or active site. Using the lock and key model, the drug molecule binds to the active site like a key in a lock, thereby altering the normal biological function of the protein.

This drug-target scheme suggests that if scientists are able to identify the appropriate protein for a given therapeutic agent, and if enough is known about the structure of that protein target (the disease target molecule that plays a key role in a biochemical pathway involved in human disease), it should be possible to design a specific drug to interact with it and thereby block the action of disease progression.

Before the biotech revolution, traditional pharmaceutical companies used conventional screening methods to identify compounds that might confer a therapeutic benefit. But screening involved time-consuming and costly systematic sifting through thousands of compounds before one was found that conferred a therapeutic benefit.

Agouron took a different approach to drug discovery. Scientists at Agouron start from the beginning, using a logical process known as protein structure-based drug design, a method that marshals advancements from disciplines such as molecular biology, protein crystallography, computer simulation, medicinal chemistry, and pharmacology.

First, a disease-related protein is identified as a target and crystallized. Using crystallography and X-ray diffraction analysis, its three-dimensional molecular structure is determined, revealing the unique landscape of the protein. Generally, this 3-D landscape provides deep insight into the structure of the molecule's active site. Agouron scientists knew the tools had become available to approach drug discovery in a more logical manner by studying the exact structure of this target site or protein "lock," then designing and constructing a molecular "key" (drug) to fit it.

X-RAY CRYSTALLOGRAPHY IS AN ANALYTICAL TECHNIQUE THAT DETERMINES THE PRECISE THREE-DIMENSIONAL ATOMIC STRUCTURES OF PROTEINS, PROVIDING AGOURON SCIENTISTS WITH THE CRITICAL STARTING POINT FOR THREE-DIMENSIONAL DRUG DESIGN. THE COMPANY HAS ASSEMBLED ONE OF THE LARGEST AND MOST EXPERIENCED GROUP OF PROTEIN CRYSTALLOGRAPHERS IN THE PHARMACEUTICAL INDUSTRY (TOP).

DR. DAVID A. MATTHEWS, HEAD OF CRYSTALLOGRAPHY AT AGOURON, HELPED TO ESTABLISH X-RAY CRYSTALLOGRAPHY AS AN IMPORTANT TOOL IN DRUG DESIGN IN THE 1970S, IN HIS PIONEERING WORK ON DIHYDROFOLATE REDUCTASE. A CRYSTALLIZED RHINOVIRUS PROTEASE IS SHOWN HERE (BOTTOM).

Once the shape of the active site is determined, thousands of potential compounds are screened before a few lead compounds are identified as active (called hits) against the target. Agouron uses a technique known as combinatorial chemistry, a drug-discovery technology that optimizes lead compounds for drug development by generating screening assays processed by high-speed robotics against disease target molecules (proteins involved in human diseases). Superior hits are selected for drug design.

Design begins on an inhibitor to bind in the active site of the target. Organic chemists synthesize the molecule and biochemists measure its ability to inhibit the activity of the target protein. Simultaneously, crystallographers optimize the design process by recrystallizing the target protein, this time with the newly synthesized drug candidate in place. In a series of repetitive steps, special instrumentation for high-speed data collection and fast computers assist the scientists in determining the structure of this new drug-target complex, and the scientists see in atomic detail how the drug actually binds to the target site's critical clefts and cavities—the lock's "tumblers." This very detailed structural view allows Agouron to correlate performance results and refine the drug design process to produce more favorable properties that bind more effectively to the protein.

ENRICHING THE TECHNOLOGY

This powerful technology has enabled Agouron to build a productive and diverse product pipeline. The application of protein structure-based drug design has produced all of the development programs in the company's portfolio.

Agouron now integrates its protein structure-based drug design technology with combinatorial chemistry, the drug-discovery tech-

nology that optimizes lead compounds for drug design. Agouron accomplished this integration in 1997, when the company expanded its research portfolio and fortified its core drug-discovery technology by merging with Alanex Corporation, a drug-discovery company specializing in high-throughput screening of chemical libraries. The marriage of technologies has produced a complementary drug development platform with wide applicability and staying power to help the company discover many more drug candidates over the next decade and beyond.

HIV PRODUCT DEBUT IS A SAN DIEGO FIRST

Thirteen years after its founding, Agouron gained the distinction of becoming the first biopharmaceutical company in San Diego to market a therapeutic drug from its own research. Agouron's first commercial product, an HIV pro-

tease inhibitor, quickly became one of the most important drugs for the treatment of HIV disease. Launched in March 1997, first-year sales of Agouron's HIV protease inhibitor set a new record in the biopharmaceutical industry.

LEVERAGING THE TECHNOLOGY

Agouron is committed to developing new drugs for the treatment of cancer, the second-leading cause of death in the industrialized world. While much progress has been made in treating certain forms of cancer, most existing anticancer drugs are limited in their application and can be toxic at high dosage levels. Agouron remains dedicated to overcoming the limitations of conventional chemotherapy and developing less toxic and more effective therapies. The company is evaluating several anticancer drugs in human clinical trials and preclinical studies.

CANCER

Broadly defined as uncontrolled cell growth, cancer results from the mutation of certain cells in the body that damage the regulatory system that controls cell growth and division. The underlying objective of most of Agouron's anticancer development programs is to selectively target and interrupt key proteins that are involved in cell growth, proliferation, tissue destruction, and the spread of many cancers.

One important Agouron program focuses on creating drugs that block the destructive qualities of a potent family of enzymes known as matrix metalloproteases (MMPs). The primary function of MMPs is to degrade certain other molecules; in normal tissues this degradative activity is held in check, but when people have certain diseases the MMPs can become destructively hyperactive, degrading healthy tissues with cancer invasion and enabling cancer cells to move to distant parts of the body and invade there, spreading the disease in a process called metastasis.

Agouron's lead anticancer compound in clinical trials is an MMP inhibitor under evaluation for the treatment of prostate, breast, colon, and brain cancers. Research has shown that high levels of abnormal MMP activity have been found in the tissues of patients with cancer and arthritis. Agouron has generated drug molecules that block the activity of certain MMP enzymes and may be effective in inhibiting tumor growth, invasion, and metastasis. Additionally, the company is exploring the utility of MMP inhibitors in the field of ophthalmology, and has launched a collaborative effort evaluating the use of MMP inhibitors in dermatology.

Also being evaluated in clinical trials for the treatment of cancer is a second enzyme inhibitor shown to be selectively active against tumor cells that contain defective p53(-) genes, a common genetic abnormality seen in human malignant tumors. When functional, these genes normally act as a checkpoint repair mechanism during cell division and growth. But when they are altered, they lose a critical mechanism for controlling tumor growth. Roughly 50 percent of all tumors have these defective genes; 70 percent of colon cancers have them.

ANTIVIRALS

In addition to its anticancer programs, Agouron research is concentrated on several important antiviral compounds that block viral proteases, enzymes required for viral replication. As part of the company's continuing commitment to patients living with HIV, a research program is actively under way to discover an anti-HIV drug called an HIV integrase inhibitor. The goal is to design a compound capable of preventing viral DNA from integrating into the host cell chromosomes. If this integration is prevented, the virus cannot successfully complete its life cycle.

Great interest has been generated in Agouron's rhinovirus 3C protease inhibitor for treating respiratory infections and the common cold. While rhinovirus infections are a periodic annoyance to most individuals, they may produce more severe prolonged symptoms in people with chronic pulmonary disease, such as asthma and emphysema.

Finally, the company also has research programs to design selective inhibitors of proteases found in cytomegalovirus (CMV) and hepatitis C virus (HCV). CMV infection is frequently associated with a disease called retinitis, which can lead to blindness and encephalitis in immunocompromised patients, including people with cancer and AIDS. Another viral program targets HCV infection, a significant unmet clinical need particularly in Asian countries, where progressive HCV illnesses can lead to liver disease, cirrhosis, and primary liver cancer.

A FUTURE WITHOUT LIMITS

Over the past 14 years, Agouron has been transformed from a primarily research-oriented organization into the largest pharmaceutical company in San Diego. In 1998, the company employed more than 850 people and continues to grow.

As Agouron moves forward with product commercialization, an exciting new era of prosperity is beginning to dawn along its stretch of San Diego's Biotech Beach. Breaking new ground and contributing to San Diego's economic growth and prosperity, Agouron and the pharmaceutical industry will provide innovative therapeutic products needed around the world. "We're linking science and technology with people in a most fundamental way," says Johnson. "And that's how we will fulfill our mission to develop new, useful products for the most challenging diseases of our time."

AGOURON'S CHEMISTS HAVE PLAYED AN IMPORTANT ROLE IN THE SYNTHESIS AND SCALE-UP OF THE COMPANY'S HIV PROTEASE INHIBITOR, AND HAVE HELPED DRIVE ONE OF THE FASTEST DRUG DEVELOPMENT PROGRAMS IN U.S. PHARMACEUTICAL HISTORY.

ONE OF SEVERAL SAN DIEGO HIGH-TECH SPIN-OFFS FROM TH 1980s, ComStream today is a premier, satellite-based wireles communications company. ComStream's nearly 250 employee represent an extraordinary array of talent and capability. Mos have extensive experience in international, high-growth elec tronics R&D and manufacturing operations. Among th

company's many satellite-transmission pioneers are engineers, sales and marketing specialists, and executives who keep the company at the forefront of industry developments, producing and deploying satellite-based digital communications networks around the world.

"What ComStream is doing for communications technology worldwide is phenomenal," says ComStream president and CEO Robert B. Clasen. "At the same time our satellite networking products are bringing communications to emerging nations in the remot-

est parts of the world, our digital satellite receivers are helping big companies implement leading-edg communications systems to enhance and expand their operations. Indeed, the scope of ComStream products covers a multitude of communications applications— satellite modems, satellite point-to-point earth stations, commercia broadcast systems, world-class satellite telephony interconnect systems, and satellite broadband PC transmission products.

HOMEGROWN BUT NOT HOMEBOUND

Founded in 1984 by managemen and engineers from the satellite communications division of M/A-Com Corporation, ComStream began delivering satellite and data networking products in September 1985. Its first product was a coder/decoder implemented on a single VLSI chip. From that time, ComStream products have been built around the company's proprietary radio frequency, analog, and digital signal processing circuitry. In 1992, Spar Aerospace Limited purchased ComStream, making it a wholly owned subsid iary. Spar is a publicly owned con pany based in Toronto.

Today, ComStream has headquarters and general offices in a new, 100,000-square-foot facility in the Sorrento Mesa area, and maintains business development and customer support offices in Mexico, Colombia, Indonesia, China, Russia, the Philippines, Hong Kong, Singapore, the Unitec Kingdom, and the Netherlands.

Committed to the highest qua ity in every aspect of its business activities and to solidifying its

ONE OF SEVERAL SAN DIEGO HIGH-TECH SPIN-OFFS FROM THE 1980S, COMSTREAM TODAY IS A PREMIER, SATELLITE-BASED WIRELESS COMMUNICATIONS COMPANY. THE SCOPE OF COMSTREAM'S PRODUCTS COVERS A MULTITUDE OF COMMUNICATIONS APPLICATIONS— SATELLITE MODEMS, SATELLITE POINT-TO-POINT EARTH STATIONS, COMMERCIAL BROADCAST SYSTEMS, WORLD-CLASS SATELLITE TELEPHONY INTERCONNECT SYSTEMS, AND SATELLITE BROADBAND PC TRANSMISSION PRODUCTS.

ternational markets, ComStream developed a rigorous strategy to in ISO 9001 certification, the international quality control standard for R&D, engineering, marketing, sales, manufacturing, and distribution processes. In July 1997, the first of ComStream's divisions on certification; the other two expect to receive it in 1998.

SATELLITE COMMUNICATIONS TO CHANGE THE WORLD

Not too many people understand the extent of satellite-based communications or how they are used, according to Clasen. However, thanks to deregulation, improved technology, and decreasing costs, satellites are now so numerous that they form a virtual canopy across the sky, and satellite communications systems are connecting communities and businesses in ways never thought possible before.

ComStream's business divisions address several different areas of this satellite communications technology, and each is dedicated to a specific product line.

The Satellite Products Division (SPD) is the world's leading supplier of satellite modems and earth stations. Its CM701 satellite modem is the industry benchmark for modular, digital satellite modem technology, and is SPD's centerpiece product. The CM701 is the building block component for satellite point-to-point telephony and data networks, and for uplink broadcast applications of audio, data, and video. In two-way communications applications, these modems modulate and demodulate inbound and outbound transmissions over satellite. In broadcast applications, satellite modems modulate the source program material, whether audio, data, or video, to RF for uplinking to the satellite, which then distributes it to the remote receiving sites. ComStream recently introduced the CM601 digital satellite modem for two-way telephony, data, and broadcast applications. The CM601 offers the market a lower-priced alternative with ComStream's proven high-performance and flexible modem technology.

SPD's audio distribution products offer radio networks, service providers, and retailers a satellite distribution system for radio programming, point-of-purchase, instore advertising, and background music. Its data distribution products deliver real-time, high-value data and DVB-standard multimedia services primarily for the financial information industry.

Leveraging ComStream's leadership in broadband digital transmission technology, the Broadband Products Division offers businesses, schools, and government institutions a state-of-the-art MediaCast™ satellite PC/server high-speed receiver card. This high-speed receiver card provides the pipeline for today's bandwidth-hungry computing environments. With the ubiquitous use of the Internet, intranets, and extranets, and with push and streaming media applications, this card offers a communications solution based on a data broadcasting medium that is superior to copper, cable, and MMDS. With this add-on card, information flow takes on a whole new dimension. This integrated broadband solution brings multimedia communications to PCs or servers at speeds hundreds of times faster than telephone lines. It enables content providers to deliver their information quicker and more efficiently. It provides robust back-haul infrastructure—the network infrastructure not seen by users—for Internet Service Providers (ISPs) and content providers. And it enables ISPs to provide high-speed Internet access for business and residential customers, particularly those in emerging markets.

ON THE LIST

"ComStream customers are like a who's who in industry or a roll call at the United Nations," Clasen adds. "We have world-famous corporations like Reuters and Kmart. We have National Public Radio as well as Radio Vatican. Then, we have government ministries from China, Thailand, and Indonesia, among many others. And we have giant corporations like LUKOil in Russia and vast private network systems like MedNet serving Africa and Europe." ComStream has designed and installed digital satellite-based communications networks that deliver data, audio, and video to customers in more than 80 countries. ComStream customers include both private businesses and public organizations. Applications of ComStream's satellite-based telecommunications technologies lend themselves well to the emerging markets of the world, and developed countries deploy the company's wireless technologies to support advanced communications applications.

ComStream's technology reaches a wide customer base. For example, since 1988, Reuters Information Services, the internationally known news agency and financial information service, and ComStream have been working together. ComStream customized a digital broadcast system for Reuters that enables the company to distribute information to thousands of locations all over the world. This is the world's largest financial network, including nearly 20,000 (and the number is growing) satellite receivers. In addition to Reuters, ComStream technology delivers financial information to thousands of banks, brokers, security houses, and governments, including the London Stock Exchange, Hong Kong Stock Exchange, Shanghai Securities Exchange, Shanghai Metals Exchange, Stock Exchange of Thailand, and others.

ComStream helps large merchandisers like Kmart transmit customized point-of-purchase business messages and music directly into retail stores. More than just an entertainment medium, point-of-purchase broadcasting's high-quality audio creates a desirable shopping experience and maximizes advertising effect. Kmart uses the ComStream broadcast

COMSTREAM HAS DEPLOYED SATELLITE COMMUNICATIONS NETWORKS THROUGHOUT THE PACIFIC RIM, AS WELL AS IN INDIA, CHINA, RUSSIA, AND LATIN AMERICA (LEFT AND FAR RIGHT).

twork both regionally and na-
nally with music and advertise-
ents forwarded and stored
thin a specially configured
dio storage/playback system.
is system holds hundreds of
mmercial messages and hours
musical selections. All messages
d selections are stored as audio
ta files and played back in se-
ence according to a play list.
is system permits music and
vertising to be customized by
ographic area, product, or any
arketing segment.

Radio listeners benefit from
mStream's digital audio broad-

cast technology. National Public
Radio (NPR), for example, built a
public radio satellite system that
uses nearly 3,000 ComStream
digital audio receivers and 23
audio uplinks to distribute, via
satellite, radio programming to
its affiliated stations. NPR's radio
satellite system replaced an expensive analog broadcast system and
offers significantly lower transmission costs, an affordable cost
of entry, easy-to-use services, high
audio quality, network security,
and wide area coverage. In addition to NPR, other ComStream
clients include China's Ministry

of Radio, Film & Television; Australia Radio Network; Voice of
Vietnam; Radio Vatican; and many
other radio networks.

Satellite-based communications
systems offer a cost-effective and
easy-to-deploy method to provide
telecommunication services in
rugged or isolated regions of the
world where terrestrial infrastructure is not widely established. To
date, ComStream has supplied
systems for several large rural
telephony network installations.
One of the largest is the Telephone
Organization of Thailand's more
than 1,000-node site. The network
offers thousands of Thai villagers
public telephone service that
reaches throughout the country,
as well as to Laos and Malaysia,
for the first time. The time and
cost to reach these communities
using traditional fixed wire line,
fiber, and microwave-based solutions would have been prohibitive.
But satellite-based technology
made it possible.

THE FUTURE IS NOW

"Even just five years ago, many
people never dreamed satellite
communications would open up
every part of the world, emerging
or developed," says Clasen. "But
we now have full-fledged telecommunications systems being installed
in even the remotest locations,
and the most advanced systems
possible being used to broadcast
commerce, entertainment, and
information to us wherever we
go. And it wasn't because we at
ComStream didn't think it could
happen; we knew it would happen."

Back in 1984, ComStream had
a vision to develop advanced communications technologies, and it
never lost that vision. Committed
to quality and customer satisfaction; committed to seeing every
part of the world connected; and
committed to using the highest
standards in R&D, manufacturing,
and customer service, ComStream
is a San Diego company that sees
the future as now.

I N 1989, DURING THE SAN DIEGO CONVENTION CENTER'S FIRST YEAR O operation, experts predicted it would attract slightly more than a doze conventions and consumer shows. That year, the center actually hoste more than 49 conventions and trade shows and 17 consumer shows. It wa an auspicious beginning for the convention center. ■ The organizatio responsible for overseeing the center, as well as the nearby San Dieg

Concourse, is the San Diego Convention Center Corporation (SDCCC), a nonprofit organization employing more than 800 people. According to the SDCCC, as of fiscal year 1997 approximately 6.2 million guests have attended nearly 2,000 events at the convention

VOLUMINOUS ARCHWAYS WITH
LOOMING SKYLIGHTS; LARGE,
OPEN-AIR DECKS AND TERRACES;
AND PANORAMIC VIEWS OF SAN
DIEGO HARBOR ARE CHARACTER-
ISTICS OF THE SAN DIEGO CON-
VENTION CENTER (TOP).

THE CONVENTION CENTER HAS
BECOME ONE OF SAN DIEGO'S
SIGNATURE ATTRACTIONS—ONE
THAT IS VISITED FREQUENTLY BY
ARCHITECTS AS WELL AS CONVEN-
TIONEERS FROM ALL OVER THE
WORLD (BOTTOM).

center, with an estimated financial impact to the city of $1.6 billion.

"That economic impact is our key contribution to the city," says SDCCC President and Chief Operating Officer Carol C. Wallace. "Our primary purpose is to attract out-of-town trade shows and conventions to generate an economic impact. Our additional mandate is to provide the Concourse and the convention center as venues for local citizens to use and enjoy."

BREAKING GROUND

In 1982, then Mayor Pete Wilson appointed a convention center task force to hold public hearings to assess the city's need for a convention center. The task force included representatives from the City of San Diego, Center City Development Corporation, San Diego Unified Port District,

County of San Diego, and Metropolitan Transit Development Board.

In November 1982, an initiative was placed on the ballot and the residents of San Diego voted to approve both the project and a proposed site along San Diego scenic waterfront. The San Diego Port District paid for the entire project with existing funds at a cost of $160 million. The City of San Diego leases the facility from the Port under a 20-year lease agreement for $1 per year.

The SDCCC, led by a nine-member board of directors consisting of community leaders, was created in 1984 by the San Diego City Council to manage and operate the facility. In August 1993, the city also turned over management of the Concourse, located just a few blocks away from the convention center in the heart of downtown, to the SDCCC.

Construction crews broke ground for the convention center on May 22, 1985. Once completed the project became one of San Diego's signature attractions— one that is visited frequently by architects as well as convention-eers from all over the world. The building is especially renowned for its tented sails covering a special events area; voluminous arch ways with looming skylights; large open-air decks and terraces; a multi purpose amphitheater designed in the ancient Greek forum style; and panoramic views of San Diego Harbor.

SPACE AND SERVICES

In total, the convention center encompasses 760,000 square feet The main exhibit hall consists of

HAWKINS PRODUCTIONS

convenience of location, ambience and maintenance, and trouble-free food and beverage functions.

THE SAN DIEGO CONCOURSE

The San Diego Concourse is a 300,000-square-foot, multipurpose complex that serves smaller trade shows and conventions, and is also home to many of the city's performing arts programs and major social events.

Located within the Concourse is the 3,000-seat Civic Theatre, one of San Diego's prime cultural venues. Elegant and plush, the Civic Theatre is home to the San Diego Opera, the California Ballet, and the La Jolla Chamber Music Society. The theater also attracts major touring shows and Broadway presentations, such as Disney's *Beauty and the Beast*, which attracted 60,000 people for a three-and-a-half-week engagement in 1997.

Other features of the Concourse include the Plaza and Golden exhibit halls, totaling 65,000 square feet; a 10,000-square-foot grand lobby; 18 meeting rooms with capacity for up to 4,300; a 15,000-square-foot Concourse Plaza; and parking for 1,150 vehicles. These features, along with all the convention center has to offer, ensure that San Diego will continue to be a prime convention and performing arts leader for years to come.

254,000 square feet of space. Additionally, the hall includes 32 separate meeting rooms totaling 100,000 square feet; a 40,000-square-foot ballroom; a 100,000-square-foot, column-free pavilion; two 40,000-square-foot lobby and registration areas; a bayside amphitheater that seats 400; and 80,000 square feet of parklike, waterfront terraces. The center can provide food service for up to 6,000 people at a single setting, and has underground parking for 2,000 vehicles. With this list of amenities, it is no surprise that the convention center recently hosted the 1996 Republican National Convention and several activities during the 1998 Super Bowl.

But Wallace is especially proud of the quality of the food service. "We have truly set a new higher standard for convention center

culinary excellence," she says. "Clients who have experienced our exceptional catering and our San Diego spirit—which is an overall philosophy of high service—return frequently." Wallace says San Diego's increased demand as a convention destination necessitates a major expansion of the center in the near future.

Other featured amenities of the center include uniformed doormen to greet guests, concierge service, specially tailored concession menus, audiovisual production and technical enhancements, telecommunications service, a gift/sundries shop, and a business service center. In 1997, the SDCCC received the Prime Site Award from *Facilities* magazine. The award is given to convention facilities that demonstrate a high level of service in the areas of setup and breakdown,

1985-1998

1985
QUALCOMM Incorporated

1985
Sundstrand Power Systems

1986
Cymer Inc.

1986
FPA Medical Management

1986
Jenny Craig, Inc.

1986
Residence Inn by Marriott-La Jolla

1987
Embassy Suites San Diego Bay and La Jolla

1987
Invitrogen Corporation

1987
Safeskin Corporation

)89
LLIANCE PHARMACEUTICAL CORP.

)89
MERICAN SPECIALTY HEALTH PLANS

)89
RAUN THERMOSCAN

)89
YMPHONY TOWERS

)90
)PR CONSTRUCTION, INC.

)90
IIGH TECHNOLOGY SOLUTIONS, INC.

)91
ARONA CASINO/BARONA BAND OF
IISSION INDIANS

)91
IARDX DIAGNOSTICS INC.

)91
IOKIA MOBILE PHONES AMERICA

1992
AMERICAN MANUFACTURING CONCEPTS, INC.

1992
QUINTILES CNS THERAPEUTICS

1993
THE LIGHTSPAN PARTNERSHIP, INC.

1995
AURORA BIOSCIENCES CORPORATION

1995
MORGAN RUN RESORT & CLUB

1995
UNIDEN SAN DIEGO RESEARCH AND
DEVELOPMENT CENTER

1996
ENOVA CORPORATION

1996
JACOR COMMUNICATIONS, INC.

1996
KSWB-TV

QUALCOMM INCORPORATED

THE HISTORY OF QUALCOMM IS IN MANY WAYS THE CHRONICL of San Diego's economic renaissance. The story began in the 1960. when University of California, San Diego professor Dr. Irwi Jacobs and University of California, Los Angeles professor D Andrew Viterbi formed a San Diego-based consulting firm called Linkabit, which grew to become a high-tech dynamo durin

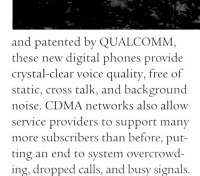

the '70s and '80s. In 1985, the two men went on to establish QUALCOMM, a cutting-edge wireless communications firm that quickly became a magnet for other companies, earning this region the nickname Wireless Valley.

BUILDING A WIRELESS WORLD

What exactly is wireless? "On one level, it's quite complex," explains QUALCOMM President Harvey White. "It's everything from satellite communications to cell sites to semiconductors. But for the average consumer, it's all about freedom and simplicity—with everything you need packed into one little pocket-size phone."

He doesn't mean the old, scratchy-sounding cell phones of the 1980s, however. Those phones, which used analog technology, are being replaced by a new generation of digital wireless phones for cellular and Personal Communications Services (PCS). Using a technology called Code Division Multiple Access (CDMA) that was developed

and patented by QUALCOMM, these new digital phones provide crystal-clear voice quality, free of static, cross talk, and background noise. CDMA networks also allow service providers to support many more subscribers than before, putting an end to system overcrowding, dropped calls, and busy signals.

QUALCOMM'S WIRELESS WONDERLAND

Judging by the looks of QUAL-COMM's corporate headquarters, one would never know this was an office full of die-hard design engineers and patent-penning Ph.D.'s. At first glance, the building looks like something out of Disneyland, with its orange, green, and purple rooftop jutting into the sky. At midday, employees can be found lunching by the koi ponds; mountain-biking in the canyons; swimming in the lap pool; or playing volleyball, basketball, or tennis. This is what the company calls a pleasant business climate.

On closer inspection, however, one also sees the signs of serious work. At the west end of the campus, a huge satellite dish moves slowly from left to right, following an arc across the sky. And up on

the purple roof sits a strange littl rake-shaped antenna. What kind of space-age science project is this

"The antenna connects to a CDMA base station here on the ground," says White, pointing ou a metal cabinet near the back of the building. "This is basically wha you'd find at a cell site out along the highway, only this particular unit is being used to develop and test new features." QUALCOMM manufactures the cell site equipment in a facility here that can produce up to 400 base stations a month—enough to cover severa cities.

Continuing the tour, White turns back to the satellite dish. "This is part of a different system called Globalstar, which we're developing together with Loral Space & Communications and other industry leaders. Through a constellation of 48 satellites, this system will provide wireless voice fax, and data services virtually any where on the planet," says White.

But this isn't the only "satcom" network here. The company also operates the OmniTRACS® system which provides mobile messaging and position location services to commercial trucking fleets in doz-

ns of countries. "This was our first commercial product back in the late '80s," says White, "and it's proven to be quite successful." He leads the way into the OmniTRACS network management center—the hub—which looks like a scaled-down version of NASA Mission Control. "We process over 4 million messages a day through this facility. It's really the information highway of the transportation industry."

The tour concludes with a trip to the Campus Point complex, site of QUALCOMM Personal Electronics (QPE), the company's manufacturing joint venture with Sony Electronics. "This is the world's most advanced wireless phone production facility, with the capacity to build 600,000 units per month," says White. But that's still not enough to meet the rising demand for CDMA phones.

"That's why, in addition to building our own CDMA products, we've licensed our technology to scores of other leading manufacturers around the world. Part of our strategy in establishing CDMA as a global standard was to create a broad base of industry support."

That strategy is working. In the past year, hundreds of CDMA networks have been deployed worldwide, including markets all across the United States, where leading carriers now provide CDMA service to millions of subscribers.

ONLY THE BEST AND BRIGHTEST

With nearly 10,000 employees and more new hires every week, QUALCOMM ranks as San Diego's fastest-growing private employer. "With three world-class universities here and more college graduates and Ph.D.'s per capita than any other major city in the country, we have a great pool to draw from," says Dan Sullivan, senior vice president of Human Resources.

In addition to recruiting locally, the company searches the world over for top-level talent in fields like design engineering. This expertise goes into QUALCOMM's CDMA chip designs, and keeps the company on the leading edge of wireless technology, as evidenced by its portfolio of more than 600 patents (issued or pending).

THE SPIRIT OF SAN DIEGO

Although QUALCOMM now has offices in more than a dozen countries, most of its 10,000 employees live and work in San Diego, where the company's roots run very deep. QUALCOMM has long been a major contributor to programs for education, the environment, the arts, and health and human services. But the company's best-known contribution relates to the facility now known as QUALCOMM Stadium (aka The Q). Through a 1997 naming rights agreement, QUALCOMM provided the final $18 million needed by the city to complete the stadium's expansion.

"This community gives so much to QUALCOMM, in so many ways, that we're happy to give something back," says Dan Pegg, senior vice president of Public Affairs. "There's no better place to live, work, and play than America's Finest City, and we're committed to keeping it that way."

CLOCKWISE FROM TOP RIGHT: WITH 18 MILLION USERS WORLD-WIDE, QUALCOMM'S EUDORA® SOFTWARE IS THE NUMBER ONE NAME IN INTERNET E-MAIL.

BY PROVIDING A MOBILE MESSAGING LINK TO COMMERCIAL TRUCKING FLEETS, QUALCOMM'S OMNITRACS® SYSTEM GIVES DRIVERS, DISPATCHERS, AND SHIPPERS UP-TO-THE-MINUTE INFORMATION ABOUT PICK-UPS, DELIVERIES, ENGINE CONDITIONS, AND OTHER CRITICAL DATA.

QUALCOMM'S NEW CDMA DIGITAL Q™ PHONE COMBINES ALL THE BEST OF A PHONE, PAGER, AND VOICE MAIL INTO ONE VERY COMPACT DEVICE.

THE PAST SEVERAL YEARS HAVE BEEN EXCEPTIONALLY EXCITING and rewarding for San Diego-based Sundstrand Power Systems. Created in 1985 through an acquisition by the Sundstrand Corporation of Solar Turbines' Turbomach division, this successful company is experiencing record growth. The formation of Power Systems combined Turbomach's experience of more than 40 years

in small aerospace gas turbines with Sundstrand's 50 years of experience producing a large variety of aerospace components and subsystems.

Sundstrand Power Systems is a market leader in the design and manufacture of aircraft auxiliary power units (APUs). An APU is a gas turbine engine located in the tail of an aircraft. It is used when the aircraft is at the gate, or in flight in an emergency, to start the main engines, provide electrical power, or provide pressurized air to the air conditioning system. These small engines of up to 550 hp incorporate the most advanced technologies to provide the very high power and small size required for aircraft applications. Sundstrand Power Systems also is a major manufacturer of aircraft fans and blowers, specialty compressors, vapor cycle environment control systems, and small gas turbine engines for ground power and propulsion.

SUPPORTING THE COMPANY
Sundstrand Power Systems' parent company, the Sundstrand Corporation, recorded more than $1.7 billion in sales in 1997. Sundstrand Aerospace—of which Sundstrand Power Systems is a part—accounted for $1 billion of that amount.

But even though Sundstrand Power Systems is a part of a large corporation, it has all the business disciplines in San Diego needed to operate as an autonomous business unit. With more than 600 people in its Kearny Mesa facility, the company is empowered to run as a stand-alone entity, but at the same time benefits from the financial, technical, and support resources of a major corporation.

Power Systems' employees market, design, fabricate, test, and provide worldwide aftermarket support for commercial APUs for small business jets (six to eight passengers), regional turboprop or turbofan aircraft (30 to 80 passengers), and medium-sized aircraft such as the Boeing B737 and Airbus A319-320-321 (up to 200 passengers). With customers all around the world, including the United States, China, India, Africa, South America, Europe, and Canada to name just a few, Sundstrand Power Systems has worldwide recognition and an important responsibility to the airlines of the world. Additionally, high-performance air recirculation fans built by Sundstrand

Power Systems may be found on all Boeing 7 series aircraft and Airbus A319-320-321 aircraft. In 1997, the company had approximately 1,400 APUs in commercial service. Sundstrand Power Systems has recently seen a significant increase in new business. A large majority of the business has recently come to Power Systems from the Asia Pacific region, with the signing of new customers All Nippon Airways, Asiana, Singapore Aircraft Leasing Enterprise, Dragonair, Air Macau, Philippine Airlines, and China Southern, which have all selected Sundstrand APUs for their fleets of A320-series planes. In addition, the largest order ever received for the company's APS 3200 model APU recently came from USAirways for up to 400 APUs.

While products for commercial aircraft applications form the largest part of Sundstrand Power Systems' current business, the company manufactures a significant amount of equipment for the military. APUs for aircraft such as the V-22 tilt-rotor aircraft, the F-16 fighter, the KC-135 tanker, and the UH-60 Blackhawk helicopter

SUNDSTRAND POWER SYSTEMS IS HEADQUARTERED AT THIS 239,000-SQUARE-FOOT KEARNY MESA FACILITY (TOP).

HIGH PERFORMANCE AIR RECIRCULATION FANS FOR THE BOEING 777 AIRCRAFT ARE PRODUCED BY SUNDSTRAND POWER SYSTEMS (BOTTOM).

orm the basis for the current military sales. The company has produced more than 12,000 APUs and engines for military applications.

A TEAM-BASED OPERATION

Much of the recent success of Sundstrand Power Systems can be attributed to the initiation of a team-based operations plan. In 1993, Sundstrand began a strong employee team-based approach to doing business and instituted the enterprise team concept.

To accomplish this, many of the company's employees were organized into one of seven enterprise teams. The teams, which are colocated in the company's facilities, are devoted to the various product lines. The teams are made up of dedicated people who are focused on customer satisfaction and on growing the individual business units. The groups are responsible for all aspects from marketing to aftermarket support and for financial performance. "The results have been outstanding," according to Tim Morris, divisional vice president and general manager. "The level of employee commitment, involvement, and ownership has risen significantly, and shows up in our financial performance and our customer satisfaction metrics. I am very proud of our progress."

TEAMING UP WITH THE COMMUNITY

Another way that Sundstrand Power Systems employees have proved their team spirit is in the community. The company itself has contributed both time and money to a variety of charities in the San Diego area and is at the pacesetter level of participation with the United Way of San Diego. Employees volunteer hundreds of hours to United Way-sponsored Hands-On San Diego, and, throughout the year, go to local schools or community centers to paint and landscape or to work with children and the elderly.

With quality products, a dedicated customer base, a commitment to the community, and a unique, team-based work environment, Sundstrand Power Systems has established itself as an innovator in the aircraft accessories industry. And, as the company approaches the 21st century, it continues to strengthen its position to become a model by which its customers set new expectations.

CLOCKWISE FROM TOP LEFT: THE APS 500 APU IS USED ON THE DEHAVILLAND-DASH 8 AND EMBRAER 145 AIRCRAFT.

THE APS 1000 APU IS USED IN REGIONAL AIRCRAFT SUCH AS FOKKER 50, SAAB 2000, DEHAVILLAND DASH 8-400, AND THE AVRO RJ.

THE APS 3200 APU IS USED ON THE AIRBUS A319/A320/A321 AIRCRAFT.

THE APS 2000 APU IS USED ON THE BOEING 737-300, -400, -500 MODELS, AND A DERIVITIVE IS USED ON THE NEW B-717 AIRCRAFT.

SEMICONDUCTOR MANUFACTURING PROVIDES THE BASIC BUILDING blocks for the equipment that runs a modern, high-tech society. Nearly everything associated with this industry—personal computers, the Internet, consumer electronics, and related software—depends on the continual and rapid evolution of integrated circuits or, as they are more commonly known, computer chips.

Cymer plays an important role in the semiconductor industry by producing illumination sources known as excimer lasers, which provide the special, short-wavelength, deep-ultraviolet (DUV) laser light necessary for high-volume production of computer chips.

LASER PROVIDES THE PERFECT LIGHT

The goal for many integrated circuit manufacturers is to reduce the size of both the chip and the tiny circuits contained within it. Smaller size translates to faster performance and lower cost; performance improves because electrons travel shorter distances, and costs are lowered when more circuits fit on each chip. Next-generation semiconductor chips will have circuits smaller than .30 microns—less than 1/300th the width of a human hair.

In the creation of a chip, it must be patterned through a process called photolithography, which

requires a special light source. Until very recently, that light source had been a mercury-arc lamp, but when the size of chip circuits became too small for this type of light to be adequate, Cymer was able to step forward with its excimer laser. The laser provides the DUV light necessary for patterning chips that are .25 microns and smaller. It took Cymer 10 years to develop and perfect this laser technology, and today, Cymer is a leading producer of high-performance DUV lasers for the semiconductor industry. In 1996, Cymer's shipments of lasers for photolithography applications increased by 438 percent.

Although Cymer's excimer laser may seem akin to science fiction, the reality is that it works well at producing today's computer chips. The laser light is generated by mixing krypton and fluorine gases inside a 2.5-foot chamber. When a brief, 12,000-volt discharge is applied, the atoms of both gases combine into a molecule known as an excited dimer, or "excimer," hence the company name of Cymer.

"Our lasers provide the only usable light effective for patterning chips at .25 microns," says Bill Angus, senior vice president and CFO of Cymer. "The industry made the transition to smaller chips in 1996, and that's when the

emand for our lasers became
aramount. Our lasers are analo-
ous to lightbulbs—a very expen-
ve lightbulb."

ROM STAR WARS
O SEMICONDUCTORS

ymer was founded by Bob Akins,
resident, and Rick Sandstrom,
ce president of advanced research.
oth men received Ph.D.'s from
ne University of California at San
Diego. In the early 1980s, Akins
nd Sandstrom were part of a team
t work on a DUV light source for
ne federal government's Strategic
Defense Initiative, commonly re-
erred to as Star Wars. After this
roject ended, the two men started
ymer to develop this laser-light-
ource technology for the semi-
onductor industry.

"It takes about 10 years for a
ew technology like this to be ac-
epted for production in the semi-
onductor industry," says Angus.
It's a long process of research
nd development." When the in-
ustry moved to develop the next
eneration of computer chips,
ymer's research paid off and
emand for its laser expanded
apidly. Some of the world's top
emiconductor manufacturers—
ncluding Intel, NEC, Toshiba,
litachi, Motorola, Texas Instru-
nents, and Mitsubishi—use
ymer's lasers.

XPANDING WORLDWIDE
ymer's first year as a public com-
any, 1996, saw the company's
evenues and order backlog triple;
ales for that year exceeded sales
f the previous 10 years combined.
n order to meet its additional
roduction needs, Cymer added
37,000 square feet of space to its
xisting offices in Rancho Bernardo,
here the company's corporate
eadquarters, manufacturing,
nd research facilities are located.

Cymer's staff more than doubled
1 1997, and the company is cur-
ently adding worldwide customer
upport facilities to its operations.
ymer now has direct offices in

Europe, Japan, Korea, and Taiwan,
as well as in Boston, Austin, and
San Jose. Cymer is committed to
supporting all its customers glo-
bally as the entire semiconductor
manufacturing industry gradually
adopts DUV lithography.

The factor that truly sets Cymer
apart from its competitors, according to Angus, is the quality of
research it has maintained throughout its history. "Our advanced research put us where we are today,"
Angus says. "Our scientists and

engineers have been more adept
at developing this laser technology than our competitors. We
were the last to the market, but
we had the best solution." With
this level of research, desire for
success, and worldwide name recognition, Cymer has become the
driving force in the computer chip
industry. Having already developed
a 21st-century product, Cymer is
poised to enter the new millennium with a running start on its
competition.

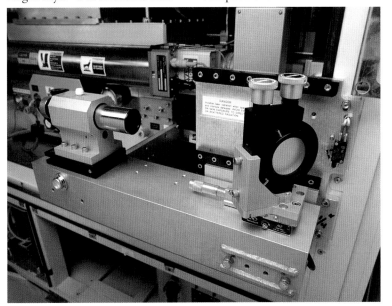

CYMER PLAYS AN IMPORTANT ROLE
IN THE SEMICONDUCTOR INDUS-
TRY BY PRODUCING ILLUMINA-
TION SOURCES SUCH AS EXCIMER
LASERS, WHICH PROVIDE THE
SPECIAL, SHORT-WAVELENGTH,
DEEP-ULTRAVIOLET (DUV) LASER
LIGHT NECESSARY FOR HIGH-
VOLUME PRODUCTION OF COM-
PUTER CHIPS.

FPA MEDICAL MANAGEMENT INC.

FPA MEDICAL MANAGEMENT, INC. IS THE LARGEST NATIONAL PRIMAR[Y] care physician practice management company. Founded in 1986, FP[A] acquires, organizes, and manages primary care physician network[s] that contract with health insurance plans. The publicly traded com[-] pany also provides contract management and support services t[o] hospital emergency rooms. ■ "We're committed to quality and ar[e]

attuned to the needs of physicians," says Dr. Sol Lizerbram, a founder and the chairman of the board of FPA. "We were founded by a group of physicians, so we know what is happening in health care and we can continue to understand the physicians' needs."

FOUNDED BY PHYSICIANS
Before 1986, a group of doctors practicing in San Diego got tired of the time it was taking to handle mounds of paperwork in their practices. "There were five of us," says Lizerbram. "We had nine primary care offices and we were

collectively dealing with 10 HMOs. It was becoming an administrative nightmare. We were having to call every HMO from each of our offices—several times a day."

The group of physicians decided that something had to be done to streamline the process. Thus, Lizerbram, Seth Flam, Kevin Ellis, Howard Hassman, and Michael Feinstein founded FPA in 1986. While two of the company's founders have since left to pursue other opportunities, Lizerbram continues to serve as chairman with Ellis serving as chief medical officer and Feinstein

practicing as an FPA physician. FPA's current management team also includes Dr. Stephen Dresnick[,] the current president and CEO o[f] FPA and founder of its hospital division, Sterling Healthcare Group, Inc.

FPA was ahead of the wave to create more efficiency in the workings of physician and medical groups with managed care organizations. "Eleven years ago, when we were formed, we were not aware of other companies like ours," says Lizerbram. "There were others around, though. And we wound up buying many of them."

STAHL PHOTOGRAPHICS

At first, FPA just serviced the founding physicians. Soon, other physicians got wind of FPA's ability to streamline the process, and began to call. "They heard we had a great service. Physicians wanted to take advantage of our services, and that's how we started to grow."

Enormous Growth

FPA Medical Management went public in October 1994. At that time, the company began to experience enormous growth. In 1994, the company was doing $18 million in business annually, serving 95 primary care physicians and 30,000 HMO members. By 1997, those numbers had ballooned to more than $1 billion in business, 7,700 primary care physicians, and 1 million HMO members.

In 1994, the company had 50 employees; but in 1997, FPA reported close to 5,000 nationwide,

including 700 in the San Diego region. Those employees include doctors; nurses; a corporate management team; and claims, quality, and customer service staff.

Though the corporate management team handles national matters and business of the company, much of the work of the regional San Diego offices is handling the delivery of patient care to local San Diegans. "On the financial side, this is a national business," says Lizerbram. "But health care is practiced locally."

FPA acquires and organizes small primary care practices in specific geographic areas so they can contract with HMOs more effectively. Doctors can participate in two separate ways. They can sell their practices to FPA or they can contract with FPA for administrative services.

FPA assumes the tasks critical to physician practices, including

claims administration, utilization management, health plan contract negotiations, and the operation of management information systems. In 1994, California accounted for 95 percent of the company's revenues. Now, states like Arizona, Texas, Florida, and New York are home to participating physicians. In 1997, California accounted for less than half of FPA's revenues.

Lizerbram says there is still plenty of room for expansion. "There is a lot of potential in the current marketplace," he says. "If you add up the top three companies in our field, the marketshare is only about 5 percent of the 70 million HMO participants in the United States." Though there is room to grow, he adds that the company will never lose focus on its primary concern: "Quality care to patients, and attention to the needs of physicians."

FROM THE ADMINISTRATIVE OFFICE TO THE EXAMINING ROOM, EVERY MEMBER OF THE FPA FAMILY PLAYS A PART IN PROVIDING QUALITY CARE AND SERVICE (LEFT).

FPA'S SIMPLIFIED APPROACH TO MANAGED CARE MAKES LIFE MUCH EASIER FOR PHYSICIANS AND OFFICE STAFF, ENABLING THEM TO DELIVER HIGH-QUALITY CARE IN A TRADITIONAL OFFICE SETTING (RIGHT).

JENNY CRAIG, INC.

T HE PERSONAL WEIGHT MANAGEMENT TECHNIQUES OFFERED BY JENNY Craig, Inc. have withstood the test of time. The company was founded in Australia in 1983, and the corporate headquarters found its way to San Diego in 1986, eventually settling in La Jolla. But the fundamental approach to weight loss offered by Jenny Craig has endured—and the company has prospered

"Our comprehensive weight management program is designed to help our clients develop a balanced approach to eating and build an active lifestyle," says Cofounder Jenny Craig. During any given week, there are an estimated 100,000 people actively participating in the company's program.

IT STARTED WITH JENNY

Like many mothers, Jenny Craig first became interested in weight management after gaining 45 pounds during pregnancy. That was more than 35 years ago, when options for losing unwanted pounds were limited. Perseverance—and a fastidious nature—led to her losing the weight. A willingness to help others led to the creation of the Jenny Craig Weight Loss Program, introduced by Jenny and Sid Craig in Melbourne in 1983. In 1985, the company expanded operations to the United States, with Jenny Craig centers in Los Angeles.

Today, there are approximately 800 centers in 46 states and five

countries worldwide, including the United States, Australia, Canada, Puerto Rico, and New Zealand. All offer one-on-one support to clients. The company employs more than 4,200 people, including 250 in San Diego. About 200 people work in the La Jolla corporate office, and another 50 work in 12 centers spread throughout San Diego County.

Besides personal and peer group support, the company's line of products and services includes four books—*The Jenny Craig Cookbook*, *Jenny Craig's No Diet Required Cookbook*, *Jenny Craig's Little Survival Guide*, and *The Jenny Craig Diabetes Cookbook*—and a line of exercise videos.

A SAN DIEGO STAPLE

When the company first moved to San Diego County, it was located in La Costa and then Del Mar before finding its way to La Jolla in 1996. "If you're looking for a healthy environment in which to work, live, and play, San Diego is the ideal choice," says Craig. "Along with our beautiful weather, geographic diversity, and choice of recreational amenities, San

Diegans enjoy a prosperous economy supported by a wide range of technological resources and business services."

Sid and Jenny Craig believe in giving back to the community. The couple were named Humanitarians of the Year by the San Diego Hospice, and were named to the United Way's Alexis de Tocqueville Society. In 1996, they donated $10 million to the University of San Diego to build the Jenny Craig Pavilion, a multiuse activities facility that will be the home court for the University of San Diego's basketball team.

Perhaps the most rewarding part of widespread participation in the Jenny Craig program is the fact that it has helped millions of people make a difference in their own lives. And with obesity fast becoming one of the most common chronic diseases in the world and one of the leading contributors to premature death in the United States, Jenny Craig is well positioned to help others lose weight, and thereby reduce the risk of such conditions as diabetes, heart disease, hypertension, and some cancers.

A FTER SEVEN YEARS IN THE U.S. NAVY AS A SURFACE LINE OFFICER and Harpoon cruise missile expert, Allan J. Camaisa decided to put his naval experience to use in the corporate world. Thus, in 1990, he initially formed High Technology Solutions, Inc. (HTS) as a consulting firm supporting the Standard missile and Harpoon cruise missile programs. ■ Today, the company has

branched out into information technology solutions and systems integration for the public sector, as well as for the federal government. In fewer than seven years, HTS has not only become a $24 million firm, but it was ranked number 44 of *Inc.* magazine's 500 fastest-growing companies in 1997.

VISUALIZING INNOVATIVE TECHNOLOGY SOLUTIONS

"Systems integration," explains Camaisa, "involves designing customized, Web-based solutions and migrating legacy systems to the client/server, distributed environment." HTS often takes a client's existing software and customizes it to meet specific business needs. That customized information can then be put on a compact disc or a Web site utilizing HTML, JAVA, and VRML, and accessed through secure servers that require a password at several levels. This system has proved ideal for government agencies looking to disseminate and update classified information with a multitude of authorized users.

HTS is also expanding its services in the commercial market. Last year, it purchased TouchMedia in Costa Mesa, thereby expanding its product line to include touch-screen kiosks—essentially "24-hour concierges" that give out information about tourist destination restaurants, hotels, rental cars, and local events. The kiosks can be found in hotels, shopping malls, government agencies, airports, and public places.

Though many of HTS' clients are now private companies, much of its business still comes from contracts with the federal government, including the Department of the

Navy, Veterans Administration, and Department of Transportation. The firm's work for the government ranges from customizing computer programs to helping personnel manage information more efficiently by implementing Web-based solutions, often referred to as E-business.

Camaisa credits much of the company's success to its personnel, who have an enormous amount of subject matter technical expertise in areas such as military weapons systems, logistics support, technical training systems analysis, and software development. HTS is assisting its clients in these vertical markets with ways to disseminate, update, and collaborate on the Internet. These are seasoned professionals with a lot of experience who know what their unique customers need.

"As one of the fastest-growing companies in the United States—with 12 offices nationwide and one in Japan—HTS is ready to expand," says Camaisa, who plans to take the company public in three years. But Camaisa has no plans to move his company from San Diego. "I'm from here, I have seen the

evolution of San Diego, and I feel like a part of the community," he says. It is a community he believes in giving back to by being actively involved in civic activities, ranging from membership on the boards of directors of the Filipino-American Chamber of Commerce, the San Diego Asian Business Association, and the San Diego Chamber of Commerce. The company, with its strong interest, regularly supports charitable causes. This mentality, coupled with the company's drive for success in an ever changing market, will help HTS remain a world-renowned San Diego company for years to come.

HIGH TECHNOLOGY SOLUTIONS' CORPORATE OFFICERS INCLUDE (FROM LEFT TO RIGHT): VICE PRESIDENT JANICE BUXBAUM, CEO/PRESIDENT ALLAN J. CAMAISA, VICE PRESIDENT WILLIAM GREEN, AND CFO SEAN H. JORDAN (TOP).

IN 1997, HIGH TECHNOLOGY SOLUTIONS PURCHASED TOUCHMEDIA, EXPANDING ITS PRODUCT LINE TO INCLUDE TOUCH-SCREEN KIOSKS—ESSENTIALLY "24-HOUR CONCIERGES" THAT GIVE OUT INFORMATION ABOUT TOURIST DESTINATION RESTAURANTS, HOTELS, RENTAL CARS, AND LOCAL EVENTS. THE KIOSKS CAN BE FOUND IN HOTELS, SHOPPING MALLS, GOVERNMENT AGENCIES, AIRPORTS, AND PUBLIC PLACES (BOTTOM).

WHEN BUSINESS OR VACATION TRAVELERS COME TO SAN Diego, they often choose the Residence Inn by Marriott La Jolla as their home away from home. Though there are more than 200 Residence Inn by Marriott properties in the United States, the company's La Jolla location is considered the flagship. ■ Corporately owned and managed by Marriott International, Residence Inn has proved to be an ideal setting for business and leisure travelers alike. At Residence Inn, guests choose from an oversize studio or a two-bedroom suite, allowing them plenty of room to spread out their work—or their souvenirs. All rooms provide separate living and sleeping areas, as well as a fully equipped kitchen.

The property boasts a total of 287 rooms, including 216 studios, 25 two-bedroom suites, and 46 penthouse suites. Room layouts are large enough for working, relaxing, or sharing a home-cooked meal. Penthouse and two-bedroom suites offer privacy for businesspeople traveling together, or families relocating.

"Our rooms are more like condos than traditional hotel rooms," says Ana Escobar, the hotel's director of sales and marketing. "It makes sense that if you're going to be staying someplace for a while,

BESIDES ITS LARGE, COMFORTABLE ROOMS, RESIDENCE INN BY MARRIOTT-LA JOLLA IS ATTRACTIVE TO GUESTS BECAUSE OF ITS CENTRAL LOCATION, PROVIDING EASY ACCESS TO VIRTUALLY ALL OF SAN DIEGO'S ATTRACTIONS (TOP).

"OUR ROOMS ARE MORE LIKE CONDOS THAN TRADITIONAL HOTEL ROOMS," SAYS ANA ESCOBAR, THE HOTEL'S DIRECTOR OF SALES AND MARKETING. "IT MAKES SENSE THAT IF YOU'RE GOING TO BE STAYING SOMEPLACE FOR A WHILE, YOU'D LIKE TO BE AS COMFORTABLE AS POSSIBLE" (BOTTOM).

you'd like to be as comfortable as possible." Escobar adds that about 60 percent of guests at the La Jolla property are corporate employees, 20 percent are government contractors or are conducting navy business, and 20 percent are leisure travelers.

Although Residence Inn is designed to meet the needs of all types of travelers, the hotel is specifically targeted to extended-stay guests. "When corporations send their employees on the road for extended trips—such as training, special projects, or relocation—they find our product, services, and rates very cost efficient compared to those of traditional hotels," says Escobar. "The guests appreciate our efforts to provide a comfortable, homey, and friendly hotel."

GREAT LOCATION
Besides its large, comfortable rooms, there are a multitude of reasons why Residence Inn by Marriott is an outstanding choice for extended-stay travelers. The property is centrally located to virtually all of San Diego's attractions, including the San Diego Zoo, Balboa Park, Wild Animal Park, Sea World, Old Town, and Seaport Village, not to mention downtown La Jolla's shops and restaurants. Within walking distance from the hotel is University Towne Centre Shopping Mall, La Jolla Village Shopping Center, a YMCA health club, and several paths for walking or jogging.

To emphasize its commitment to providing a homey atmosphere, Residence Inn by Marriott-La Jolla welcomes the entire family, including pets. "About 10 percent of our guests bring their pets," says Escobar. "A pet is like a member of the family, and if your family is relocating to San Diego, it's so convenient to stay in a place that accepts pets."

A SENSE OF COMMUNITY
Complimentary breakfasts—every day of the week—are another hallmark of Residence Inns. But breakfast isn't the only complimentary

meal. Guests enjoy a social hour very evening from 5 to 7, which includes a light meal and cocktails served outdoors. This daily event also gives guests the opportunity to mingle with the hotel staff and with each other. Since guests are most often staying at the property for extended periods of time, the social hour fosters a sense of community among "neighbors."

In the summer, the Residence Inn also offers a chance to mingle every Thursday around an outdoor barbecue, where guests enjoy plenty of grilled hamburgers and hot dogs. They can then hit the volleyball courts for some bumping and spiking action.

If a private meal is more to a guest's liking, the kitchens in each room can be put to good use. Each fully equipped kitchen contains a microwave oven, toaster, coffeemaker, china, and pots and pans.

But great opportunities for socialization and community spirit aren't the only memorable features of Residence Inn. If a guest's day is filled with business meetings or other activities, the hotel offers a unique courtesy shopping service. Guests fill out a shopping list and leave it at the front desk, and a Residence Inn employee will venture out to a nearby supermarket to purchase all the requested items, which are placed in the guest's room by the end of the day. After a tough day at work, guests can also take advantage of a number of activities-related amenities offered by the Residence Inn, including two large swimming pools, five heated spas, picnic facilities, and volleyball and basketball courts.

Or if it's time to just relax in the room, there are plenty of ways the hotel makes it easy to unwind. In-room amenities include complimentary newspapers (*USA Today*, the *Wall Street Journal*, and the *San Diego Union-Tribune*), daily housekeeping service, and 24-hour-a-day

message service. In addition, in-room cable TV and "On-Command" movies are available. There is also a coin-operated laundry facility on the premises, and one-day valet dry cleaning is available. All these amenities make the guest's stay even better.

With this long list of services and amenities, it is not surprising that occupancy levels hover above 90 percent at the Residence Inn by Marriott-La Jolla. But even with the property's great record of suc-

cess, the hotel's rates remain very reasonable. "When corporations send an employee on the road, they save money in several areas by choosing Residence Inn," says Escobar, "especially on food expenses—since the employee has access to complimentary breakfasts, evening socials, and an in-suite kitchen. We provide all guests a true home away from home." General Manager Rick Brown adds, "If guests try us just once, they will never go anywhere else."

EMBASSY SUITES STRIVES TO MAKE A RETURN CUSTOMER OUT OF EVERY guest, and the unique hotel chain goes to extra lengths to make that happen. With two locations in the area—in San Diego Bay and La Jolla—Embassy Suites has been expertly serving business guests and vacationers to San Diego for more than a decade. ■ Whereas in most hotels a guest stays in one room containing a bed and

bath, at Embassy Suites all accommodations are two-room suites consisting of a living room and separate bedroom. The hotel also offers such value-added amenities as remote-controlled, color televisions with cable; phones with voice mail; and a galley kitchen, complete with a microwave oven, refrigerator, coffeemaker, and wet bar. A hair dryer, ironing board, iron, and complimentary shuttle to and from the airport are additional conveniences at the San Diego Bay location.

In addition, both locations offer their guests a full, cooked-to-order breakfast each morning and a two-hour manager's reception each evening, complete with cocktails, soft drinks, and snacks. And small touches—such as a complimentary morning newspaper, a gift shop, express checkout, guest laundry, valet service, and room service—all make a stay at Embassy Suites practical and comfortable. The San Diego Bay location also has a delicatessen and a barber and beauty shop.

Talene Lanuza, sales and marketing director at Embassy Suites La Jolla, says the costs of most of these amenities are built right into the price of the suite at both hotels. "We don't want to nickel-and-dime our clientele. Our customers are savvy travelers; we aren't going to insult them by adding extras onto their bill," she says.

DIFFERENT HOTELS, ONE GOAL

Although the San Diego Bay and La Jolla hotels offer the same high level of service, there are many differences that set the two apart.

For example, the San Diego Bay location, which offers full-service exercise facilities, a whirlpool, a sauna, and an indoor heated pool, is perfect for both business travelers and families on vacation. Not only are business clientele just minutes from the San Diego Convention Center and the downtown business district, but also they can take advantage of the hotel's 4,500 square feet of flexible meeting/banquet space, meeting rooms for up to 200, and a well-lighted work space in every suite, which also make excellent small meeting rooms.

The hotel's proximity to the Seaport Village and the Gaslamp District, which has some of the city's finest restaurants, makes it an ideal spot for families. It's also only a few blocks from the San Diego Zoo, Sea World, the Coronado Ferry, harbor cruises, and ships to Mexico and Catalina Island.

But vacationers don't have to leave the hotel to find entertainment. Barnett's Grand Cafe seats 206 people, and serves dinner with selections from a menu featuring California and continental cuisine. If guests are in the mood for a more casual atmosphere, the 125-seat Winning Streak Sports and

James Bar—with its video wall, sports memorabilia, and games—serves lunch and dinner from a contemporary menu.

Only five miles from downtown La Jolla and located in the Golden Triangle of San Diego, the hotbed of the city's biotech industry and financial district, the La Jolla site is a great home away from home to business travelers and vacationers. The hotel can provide 3,200 square feet of space for corporate meetings, and is within close proximity of University Towne Center, home to almost 200 shops and restaurants; the Birch Aquarium at Scripps; the University of California, San Diego; the world-class Torrey Pines Golf Course; SeaWorld; and the beach.

The La Jolla location is also known for its fine dining. The Coast Cafe offers great food served indoors or on the outdoor patio. P.F. Chang's China Bistro, located on the front lawn, offers traditional Chinese dishes served with contemporary flair. The adjoining lounge features a large-screen television and seasonal, weekend entertainment.

Every Guest, Every Time

Embassy Suites' philosophy is a simple one: Satisfy every guest, every time, guaranteed. In fact, the chain has put that guarantee in writing. "We believe in 100 percent satisfaction, so if you aren't happy with your stay, you don't

have to pay. It's that simple," says Michael Krizanic, Embassy Suites San Diego Bay's director of sales and marketing.

To aid in customer satisfaction, all hotel employees are qualified to act as a concierge and can provide guests with directions, activity suggestions, and tickets to San Diego's myriad of attractions. "We want to promote contact with our staff on the part of guests. They should feel comfortable asking questions of any employee they see," says Lanuza.

Embassy Suites' focus is customer service, and as a result, the company regularly conducts surveys to measure guest satisfaction. "It gives us an idea of how we are doing," says Lanuza, "and our scores have always been very high." The La Jolla hotel in particular often scores at the top of the charts. "Two of our employees have received

Chairman Awards, the highest honor an Embassy Suites employee can get from the national chain," she says.

In order to maintain a high level of customer satisfaction, both hotels keep renovating and upgrading their facilities, although never at the expense of the client's comfort. "We do it behind the scenes, on an ongoing basis, so it never gets in the way. People always say we look better than when we first opened," says Lanuza.

With a host of amenities, a hardworking staff, and a corporate dedication to customer satisfaction, it's no wonder that Embassy Suites San Diego Bay and La Jolla have become two of the most popular destinations with business and pleasure travelers alike. As the hotels continue to grow, so will their commitment to making return customers out of every guest.

CLOCKWISE FROM TOP LEFT: WITH TWO LOCATIONS IN THE AREA—IN SAN DIEGO BAY AND LA JOLLA (SHOWN HERE)—EMBASSY SUITES HAS BEEN EXPERTLY SERVING BUSINESS GUESTS AND VACATIONERS TO SAN DIEGO FOR MORE THAN A DECADE.

BOTH EMBASSY SUITES LOCATIONS OFFER THEIR GUESTS A FULL, COOKED-TO-ORDER BREAKFAST EACH MORNING AND A TWO-HOUR MANAGER'S RECEPTION EACH EVENING, COMPLETE WITH COCKTAILS, SOFT DRINKS, AND SNACKS.

THE LA JOLLA SITE IS A GREAT HOME AWAY FROM HOME TO BUSINESS TRAVELERS AND VACATIONERS. THE HOTEL CAN PROVIDE 3,200 SQUARE FEET OF SPACE FOR CORPORATE MEETINGS, AND IS WITHIN CLOSE PROXIMITY OF UNIVERSITY TOWNE CENTER, HOME TO ALMOST 200 SHOPS AND RESTAURANTS; THE BIRCH AQUARIUM AT SCRIPPS; THE UNIVERSITY OF CALIFORNIA, SAN DIEGO; THE WORLD-CLASS TORREY PINES GOLF COURSE; SEAWORLD; AND THE BEACH.

SAN DIEGO IS THE HOME OF INVITROGEN CORPORATION, A LEADING biotechnology company that develops, manufactures, and markets molecular biology research tools and services. The company was founded in 1987 and in the intervening years has experienced rapid growth. "Invitrogen started very small and without any venture capital investment. It's a true entrepreneurial success

story," says Glenn Davies, Invitrogen's director of sales and marketing. The company currently offers more than 500 products, and is the market leader in gene expression and PCR cloning, technologies that are at the center of the biotechnology revolution.

Invitrogen sells its products worldwide. In order to better serve its European customers, the company established a European subsidiary in the Netherlands in 1993. Because of Invitrogen's rapid expansion, the company relocated its San Diego headquarters from

Sorrento Valley to a 60,000-square-foot facility in Carlsbad in early 1997. Invitrogen now employs more than 170 people, and provides an exciting work environment with many opportunities for growth and development. Invitrogen's workforce is highly educated, with nearly 70 percent of the employees holding advanced degrees.

Invitrogen's products are used by scientists in both academic (e.g., National Institutes of Health, universities, and medical schools) and industrial (e.g., pharmaceutical

and biotechnology) institutions. Researchers around the world use Invitrogen's products to study a variety of diseases, including cancer, AIDS, and genetic disorders. Invitrogen's products are used in basic research, but also have applications in developing pharmaceuticals and techniques that will improve human health and advance science.

TECHNOLOGY LEADERSHIP
In the early years, Invitrogen did not have the resources necessary to form a full research and devel-

BY IDENTIFYING THE NEEDS OF SCIENTISTS IN THE LIFE SCIENCE RESEARCH MARKET, INVITROGEN HAS BEEN ABLE TO DEVELOP A PRODUCT LINE THAT ALLOWS RESEARCHERS TO OBTAIN THEIR RESULTS QUICKLY AND COST EFFECTIVELY.

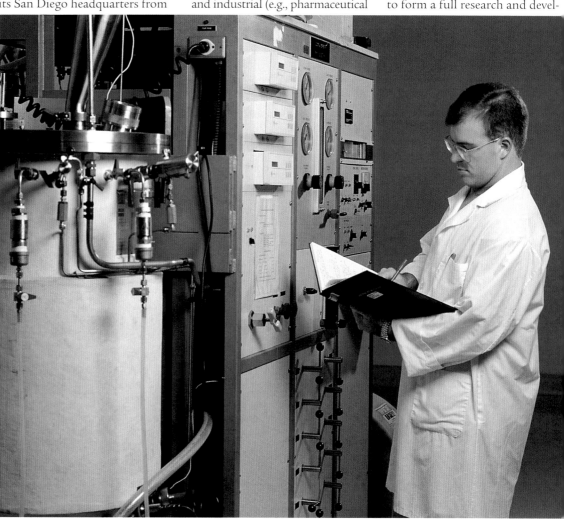

ment department. Therefore, the company focused on becoming a leader by acquiring technology licenses and using the company's resources to turn the technologies into products and services. The company currently holds more than 60 licenses, over half of which are exclusive, and owns the patent for the TA Cloning® technology, which is the most widely used method for PCR (polymerase chain reaction) cloning.

INNOVATIVE PRODUCTS

Invitrogen has always had a strong focus on the introduction of new, innovative products. This has set the company apart from its competitors. The company has been willing to take risks on new technologies and maintain its vision of producing high-quality products that allow researchers to obtain their results more efficiently and cost effectively.

Invitrogen is the leader in recombinant gene expression. Gene expression is the technique of producing a particular protein (usually human) in a foreign host such as insect, yeast, bacterial, or mammalian cells (e.g., mouse, rat, monkey, and human). The protein that is produced is called recombinant protein. Gene expression allows researchers to study characteristics of a particular protein and to produce large quantities of the protein for use in pharmaceutical applications. Invitrogen offers the widest selection of products for gene expression and has introduced at least one new product in this area every year since 1993. Some of the company's expression products include the Ecdysone-Inducible Mammalian Expression System, the *Drosophila* Expression System, the *Pichia* Expression System, and the pBAD Expression System. Each product has unique characteristics that address certain needs for researchers expressing their proteins of interest.

The *Drosophila* Expression System (DES™) was introduced

in 1997. It is a nonviral, insect-based system that represents a revolution in recombinant protein expression. Insect cells grow rapidly in culture and use many of the mechanisms of protein expression, as do mammalian cell lines. This means that recombinant proteins that are mammalian in nature can be produced in their native form more quickly and less expensively than if the researcher were to use mammalian cells.

Invitrogen has been a leader in PCR cloning technology since the introduction of the TA Cloning® Kit in 1990. It is the method by which very small amounts of DNA are amplified to produce large amounts that can be used in a variety of applications in clinical and academic research. The TA Cloning® Kit was the first product that allowed researchers to clone—make a hard copy—of their PCR product for future use. The company has continued to expand its PCR cloning product line and in 1997, introduced the TOPO™ TA

Cloning® Kit. This kit reduces the time required for PCR cloning dramatically and simplifies the entire process. In 1998, the company will continue to expand the TOPO™ Cloning product line.

In 1998, the company is setting its sights on the cell biology market. Invitrogen researchers have been working diligently to clone and express thousands of genes from a variety of species. This will allow researchers to purchase a particular gene of interest without investing the time and effort in cloning it themselves. These products will save researchers weeks of time.

By identifying the needs of scientists in the life science research market, Invitrogen has been able to develop a product line that allows researchers to obtain their results quickly and cost effectively. "In the bigger picture," says Davies, "our products may enable researchers to develop pharmaceuticals or identify the cause of disease and, in the long run, greatly benefit mankind."

INVITROGEN NOW EMPLOYS MORE THAN 170 PEOPLE AND PROVIDES AN EXCITING WORK ENVIRONMENT WITH MANY OPPORTUNITIES FOR GROWTH AND DEVELOPMENT.

I N THE LATE 1980S, THE FOUNDERS OF SAFESKIN CORPORATION IDENTIFIED A emerging market and cornered it. Neil Braverman, Richard Jaffe, and Irvin Jaffe realized that protective gloves made of latex and synthetics were be coming more of a necessity in the medical industry, especially as the AID epidemic began to spread. Today, the company is a leading manufacture and distributor of latex and synthetic gloves for the medical, dental, an

high-technology communities.

When Safeskin was founded in 1987, it established offices in San Diego and Boca Raton. But in 1996, the headquarters for the international company was formally established in Del Mar, California, firmly cementing Safeskin's position in the San Diego business community.

MEETING A NEED

Braverman and the Jaffes noticed the trend that gloves were being worn for extended periods of time in the medical industry. At the time, most gloves used by doctors and other medical personnel were powdered, which were unsuitable for long-term use as powder tends to dry the skin. Safeskin remedied this problem by initiating a line of powder-free gloves.

Along with powder-free gloves, Safeskin also introduced a line of gloves that contain a reduced level of chemicals that adversely affect the skin over long-term use. As the Safeskin company name implies, the product line protects wearers not only from outside sources, but also from irritation and ad-

verse side effects that come from extended wear. When this produ was introduced, Safeskin was the only manufacturer to offer these innovations.

"Our company was born out of the need for protective devices in dealing with the AIDS epidemic," says Jeff Martin, Safeskin vice president of marketing and business development. "When we first hit the market, there was a strong demand for our product. Our founders felt latex gloves at that time were barrier products. But they realized health care workers

AS THE SAFESKIN COMPANY NAME IMPLIES, THE PRODUCT LINE PROTECTS WEARERS NOT ONLY FROM OUTSIDE SOURCES, BUT ALSO FROM IRRITATION AND ADVERSE SIDE EFFECTS THAT COME FROM EXTENDED WEAR.

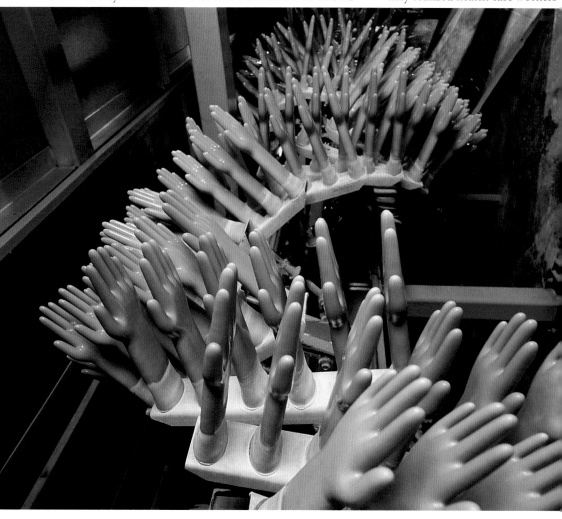

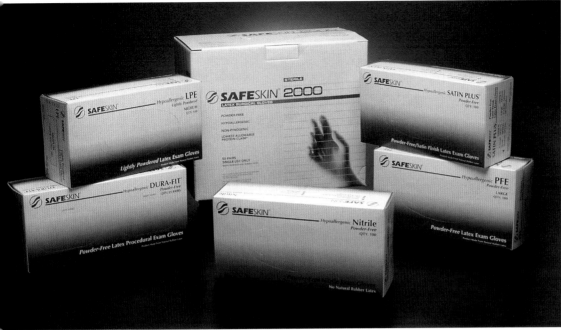

SAFESKIN CORPORATION CURRENTLY MAINTAINS AN EXTENSIVE PORTFOLIO OF NATURAL LATEX RUBBER AND SYNTHETIC POWDER-FREE GLOVES. THEY COME IN THREE BASIC TYPES—MEDICAL EXAMINATION GLOVES, STERILE SURGICAL GLOVES, AND CLEAN-ROOM GLOVES.

ould have to wear gloves all day, ot just for a few minutes. We cognized that workers would eed protection from their own loves, too."

FULL PRODUCT LINE

afeskin currently maintains an xtensive portfolio of natural latex rbber and synthetic powder-free loves. They come in three basic rpes: medical examination gloves, erile surgical gloves, and clean- oom gloves. Examination gloves re a non-sterile type commonly ound in most doctors' offices. erile surgical gloves, as the name nplies, are used by surgeons in ne operating room. Clean-room loves are used by high-tech com- any employees in the construc- on of microprocessors and other ninute and particle-sensitive omponents.

Safeskin produces gloves for a ride variety of clients in the medi- al field, alternate care market, nd science-related companies. In ne medical and acute care fields, afeskin provides gloves mostly o hospitals, including 5,000 fa- lities based in the United States. Alternate care markets include rimary care physicians, extended are providers, nursing homes, and ental offices. Scientific field cus-

tomers include microelectronics companies, pharmaceuticals manufacturers, and biotechnical research firms. With this wide variety of clients, the company is number one in the U.S. marketplace for powder-free medical gloves.

QUALITY AND GROWTH

To help manufacture the highest-quality gloves possible, Safeskin employs more than 4,500 people worldwide. Most of these employees work in the company's manufacturing plants in Malaysia and Thailand, while about 100 people are employed at the company's San Diego headquarters. Another 100 salespeople are deployed throughout the United States.

And Safeskin is continuing to grow through strategic acquisitions. The company in 1997 acquired Tactyl Technologies, which is based in Vista in North San Diego County. Tactyl has developed a synthetic product that is a premium alternative to natural latex rubber. The purchase of Tactyl immediately gave Safeskin a 50 percent share of the synthetic surgeon's glove market.

Despite its rapid growth, Safeskin plans to maintain its headquarters in San Diego. "We're pleased to be located in San Diego

for a number of reasons," says Martin. "Of course, there are a number of high-tech and biotech industries in this area that we serve. But San Diego is also close to our Pacific Rim customers. Safeskin's goal is to become the number one service leader within its markets."

But Safeskin's number one goal is to provide its customers with a consistently high level of service. To do this, the company follows four core values when dealing with customers: always exceed customer expectations; deliver promptly on all commitments; do the right thing; and be the best.

As part of its drive to do the right thing, Safeskin is very involved with the San Diego community, especially at the university level. In connection with University of California, San Marcos, the company invites seniors to work with Safeskin staff members on actual business situations. Other community involvement includes a major sponsorship of INSIGHTS, San Diego Chamber of Commerce, Junior Seau Foundation, and AIDS Walk. And this involvement in the community, along with its drive to satisfy its customers, will assure that Safeskin remains an industry leader for years to come.

ALLIANCE PHARMACEUTICAL CORP.

THE DEVELOPMENT OF NEW PHARMACEUTICAL PRODUCTS IS long and laborious process, requiring extensive laboratory testing. Pharmacology and toxicology studies must be done, and fo good reason," notes Duane Roth, chairman, president, and CE of San Diego-based Alliance Pharmaceutical Corp. "It's th nature of the business because our products have to be saf for use with human beings."

Alliance currently has three products in clinical development: LiquiVent®, Oxygent™, and Imagent® US. These products are based on the company's perfluorochemical (PFC) and emulsion technologies. PFCs are biochemically inert compounds that may be used by doctors for therapeutic and diagnostic applications. The primary drug substance in both Oxygent and LiquiVent is perflubron, a unique PFC that can transport respiratory gases throughout the body. According to Roth, an exciting future is ahead for these technologies.

THE BIOTECHNOLOGY COMMUNITY

Currently, San Diego is a hotbed for biotechnology companies. Established in 1989, Alliance is one of the largest players in this field, employing approximately 250 people, 80 percent of whom are in scientific or technical positions. The company's local operations include its laboratories and manufacturing facilities on Science Park Road and corporate headquarters on Genesee Avenue.

Connection to the community is important to Alliance. "We're very close to the local university system," says Roth. "We're very good at taking the knowledge that's available in the universities and developing it into useful products intended to aid acute care patients."

In terms of dedication to the community, Roth leads by example. He was the 1996 volunteer president and 1997 cochair of BIOCOM/Sa Diego, a local organization that promotes issues related to the biomedical industry, and is also a member of the boards of directors for the California Healthcare Institute, the San Diego Economi Development Corporation, and the Greater San Diego Chamber of Commerce.

In 1996, Roth served as chairman of the annual American Hea Association (AHA) Healthy Choic Heart Walk. In doing so, he kept San Diego in first place as a fund raiser for AHA in California. Rot also has been recognized for his community service efforts by AT&T, which gave him its 1996 International Business Leadership Award for contributions to the city of San Diego, and by San Diego Citizens Against Lawsuit Abuse, which gave him the 1997 Making a Difference Award.

USEFUL PRODUCTS

In 1997, all three of Alliance's pharmaceutical products were in Phase II clinical trials. Phase I typically involves administering an investigative drug to healthy volunteers for an initial safety assessment. Although safety is monitored throughout clinical development, Phase II studies focu on determining proper dosage an further evaluation of the drug. Phase III trials involve testing the product on a larger number of patients to confirm previous findings.

The FDA, which regulates the progression of the trials and the drug approval procedure, has granted fast-track status to LiquiVent. The liquid drug has the potential to help treat patients

CURRENTLY, SAN DIEGO IS A HOTBED FOR BIOTECHNOLOGY COMPANIES. ESTABLISHED IN 1989, ALLIANCE PHARMACEUTICAL CORP. IS ONE OF THE LARGEST PLAYERS IN THIS FIELD, EMPLOYING APPROXIMATELY 250 PEOPLE, 80 PERCENT OF WHOM ARE IN SCIENTIFIC OR TECHNICAL POSITIONS.

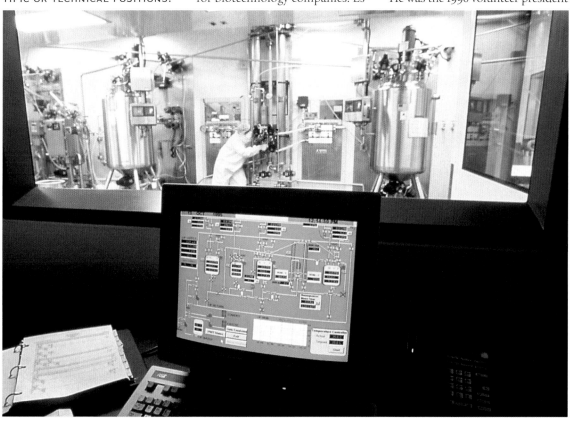

ith acute respiratory failure, a condition resulting from serious infection, traumatic shock, severe burns, or inhalation of toxic substances. Patients suffering from these conditions frequently develop inflammation in their lungs, which leads to blockage of airways and inadequate gas exchange.

Patients with lung dysfunction are routinely placed on mechanical ventilators to improve blood oxygenation. Unfortunately, however, the high pressure needed to force air into the lungs can cause further damage. Initial clinical trials show LiquiVent improves lung oxygenation without limiting side effects or damage. This unique oxygen-carrying liquid also removes debris and, in essence, helps clean out the lungs.

Oxygent, an intravascular oxygen carrier that can be injected into the bloodstream, acts as a temporary blood substitute to provide oxygen and remove carbon dioxide. Developed in conjunction with Johnson & Johnson affiliates Ortho Biotech Inc. and the R.W. Johnson Pharmaceutical Research Institute, Oxygent is administered to patients according to Alliance's patented procedure for augmented hemodilution—a method for conserving the blood of a surgical patient. Oxygent also reduces the need for blood transfusions during surgery.

With the use of Oxygent, patients enjoy a significantly reduced risk of the infectious disease transmissions associated with traditional blood transfusions. It is estimated that more than 3 million people in the United States annually receive one or more units of blood during elective surgery. Oxygent use would help avoid the risk of bacterial infections resulting from these transfusions, as well as the spread of hepatitis and HIV.

Imagent US, an ultrasound contrast agent, employs technology similar to that of underwater SONAR. It is being developed to be used for diagnosis and patient

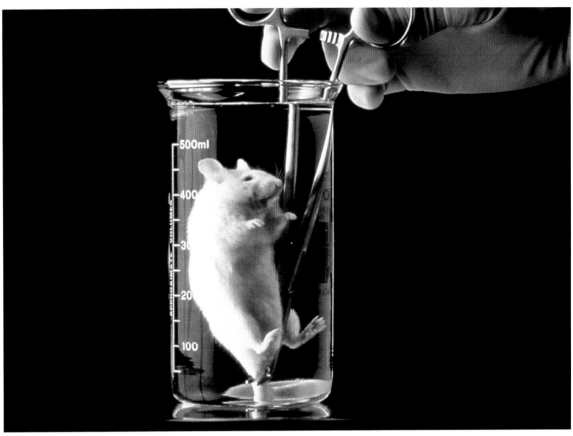

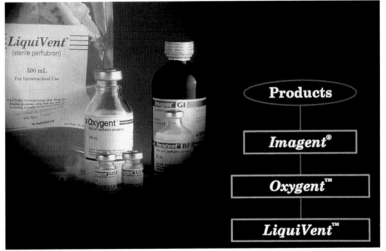

evaluation by doctors, and should be especially helpful in assessing the condition of heart disorders.

Ultrasound imaging is a versatile, low-cost, low-risk, noninvasive technique. Though it lacks sensitivity compared to technology such as magnetic resonance imaging, ultrasonography is in widespread use by both office- and hospital-based physicians. The process of using Imagent US is best understood by picturing a series of microbubbles traveling

though the bloodstream. The bubbles circulate freely for several minutes until they shrink and collapse, but the echoes they create may help doctors determine the condition of certain tissue areas.

"We're very enthused about the future of these products," says Roth, "and about Alliance's ability to create other products. Our only restriction is that our work be innovative. We don't do things that are easy—that's for sure."

INITIAL CLINICAL TRIALS SHOW LiquiVent IMPROVES LUNG OXYGENATION WITHOUT LIMITING SIDE EFFECTS OR DAMAGE. THIS UNIQUE OXYGEN-CARRYING LIQUID ALSO REMOVES DEBRIS AND, IN ESSENCE, HELPS CLEAN OUT THE LUNGS (TOP).

ALLIANCE CURRENTLY HAS THREE PRODUCTS IN CLINICAL DEVELOPMENT: LiquiVent®, Oxygent™, AND Imagent® US. THESE PRODUCTS ARE BASED ON THE COMPANY'S PERFLUOROCHEMICAL (PFC) AND EMULSION TECHNOLOGIES (BOTTOM).

Alterative medicine is a booming business in California. And a San Diego-based specialty HMO, American Specialty Health Plans (ASHP), has become the leading specialty HMO in California for complementary health services, such as chiropractic, acupuncture, and traditional Chinese herbal supplements. Formerly known as American Chiropractic Network Health Plan, this specialty HMO covers more than 3 million Californians and is the third-largest specialty HMO in the state, out of approximately 60 plans.

CALIFORNIA'S FIRST CHIROPRACTIC HMO

ASHP President and CEO George DeVries says that when he and his two partners started the company in 1987, it provided chiropractic networks and administrative services. DeVries worked out of a spare bedroom in his Huntington Beach condominium. "We set up a chiropractic network and provided customer service, claims administration, and utilization review of chiropractic services," he says. In early 1989, DeVries moved the firm to San Diego.

In 1992, DeVries began the arduous application process to become a licensed HMO in California. It took two and a half years and 15,000 pages of documentation until finally, in September 1994, his company became the first licensed chiropractic HMO in the state.

After that, business took off. "We made $26,000 our first year in business, and it wasn't until our fifth year that revenues exceeded $1 million. In our 10th year, revenues were $48 million, and in 1998, we are projecting $75 million," says DeVries.

This first specialty chiropractic and acupuncture HMO allowed managed care systems to be applied to chiropractic and acupuncture care, stabilizing costs and enhancing the quality of service. Today, a statewide credentialed network of more than 1,500 chiropractors, 600 acupuncturists, and 1,000 radiology and clinical laboratory providers participate in ASHP's network. ASHP averages one participating chiropractor within a three-mile radius of a member's residence in urban areas of California. The network operates a credentialing process for each of its providers, reviewing the provider's education, professional licensure, malpractice insurance history, office facilities, and other related areas.

AN HMO SERVING OTHER HMOS

ASHP is a specialty HMO used in addition to traditional medical HMOs. It contracts with most of the major HMOs in California to provide their chiropractic benefits. ASHP's clients include Aetna/US Health Care, Blue Shield HMO, Blue Cross/California Care, CIGNA Healthcare, Community Health Group, Health Net, HealthMax/Health Plan of the Redwoods, HMO California, Kaiser Foundation Health Plan, One Health Plan, PacifiCare, Prudential HealthCare Plan, Sharp Health Plan, United HealthCare, and Universal Care. Growth plans for the specialty HMO include the development of clients for the new acupuncture and traditional Chinese herbal supplement benefit. American Specialty Networks (ASN), an affiliate of ASHP, is currently developing networks for provider groups, such as certified massage therapists and other providers throughout California.

DeVries, who was named San Diego's Entrepreneur of the Year in Health Services in 1997 by Ernst & Young, Nasdaq, and *USA Today* chose San Diego as the company's headquarters because of his long affection for the area. Originally from Iowa, DeVries says that after high school, he had planned to

AMERICAN SPECIALTY HEALTH PLANS (ASHP) EMPLOYS MORE THAN 300 WORKERS IN ITS SAN DIEGO HEADQUARTERS.

LINDA O'NEILL

LINDA O'NEILL

tend the University of North arolina in Chapel Hill, but first ook a 52-hour bus trip to Los ngeles to visit a friend. He stayed ree weeks with that friend and ent one day visiting San Diego. fter visiting San Diego, I had to e here. So, when I got back home anceled my acceptance to Uni-rsity of North Carolina, and orked two jobs for a year," he ys. "I applied to the University California San Diego, came out ere for college, and stayed."

N Evolving HMO

May 1997, the HMO formally anged its name from the Ameri-n Chiropractic Network Health an to American Specialty Health ans. DeVries says the reason for e change was that the company ad expanded from a single, spe-alized area of chiropractic into upuncture. In November 1997,

ASHP received approval from the California Department of Corporations (DOC) to add acu-puncture services, as well as tradi-tional Chinese herbal supplements that are recommended by an acupuncturist.

The name change reflects the company's evolution into other areas of complementary and alter-native health care. DeVries believes there is a growing demand for acupuncture and chiropractic ser-vices among its subscribers. ASHP has already contracted with more than 600 licensed acupuncturists throughout California. "As with our chiropractic providers, we apply high credentialing standards with our acupuncture providers," says DeVries. ASHP has also drawn on the expertise of the acupunc-ture community in developing its clinical guidelines and quality standards.

DeVries says the State of Cali-fornia allows acupuncturists to recommend traditional Chinese herbal supplements. "ASHP's sister company and distributor, American Specialty Health Products, has a mutually exclusive contract with Sun Ten Laboratories in Irvine and Taiwan. Our distributor will pro-vide about 150 traditional Chinese herbal supplements to ASHP mem-bers via mail order. Sun Ten is the leading manufacturer of traditional Chinese herbal supplements world-wide, selling its products on six continents and in 22 countries," he says. "We anticipate a strong, positive response to this new prod-uct. It's another mark of innova-tion for us."

DeVries says his company is unique among HMOs. "We have chosen areas that are difficult for most health plans to understand, and it has given us a particular niche. We are special because of our ability to innovate and create managed care products that don't exist," he says. "Consumers are demanding more choice and flex-ibility in their health care options. I believe that acupuncture will become a standard benefit rider within managed care over the next few years as chiropractic has be-come in the past decade. ASHP has positioned itself to take a leader-ship role in that development."

ASHP HAS BECOME THE LEADING SPECIALTY HMO IN CALIFORNIA FOR COMPLEMENTARY HEALTH SERVICES, SUCH AS CHIROPRACTIC, ACUPUNCTURE, AND TRADITIONAL CHINESE HERBAL SUPPLEMENTS (LEFT).

IN 1997, ASHP BECAME THE FIRST HMO IN THE NATION TO OFFER AN ACUPUNCTURE AND TRADITIONAL CHINESE HERBAL SUPPLEMENT BENEFIT (RIGHT).

I N 1987, A QUIET REVOLUTION TOOK PLACE IN THE WORLD OF THERMOMETR A product known as a noncontact infrared ear thermometer was created allowing a person's body temperature to be measured cleanly, convenientl and in less than three seconds. But it was expensive, making it unobtainabl for many people. When the ThermoScan Instant Thermometer was unveile in 1990, the face of thermometry began rapidly changing, putting cutting

edge technology in the hands of the consumer.

Today, the ThermoScan Instant Thermometer is the instrument of choice for health professionals who take millions of temperatures in doctors' offices and hospitals each year with infrared thermometers. With that in mind, it's not surprising its manufacturer—Braun ThermoScan—is the world's leader in infrared thermometry.

BRAUN THERMOSCAN'S 80,000-SQUARE-FOOT FACILITY IS LOCATED IN THE SORRENTO VALLEY AREA OF SAN DIEGO.

A HISTORY OF INNOVATION

ThermoScan, as it was originally known, was founded by entrepreneur Jon Lindseth. Lindseth hailed from Cleveland, Ohio, but when he needed engineering expertise for his new enterprise, he found it in San Diego. In the early 1980s, Lindseth began a partnership with Jacob Fraden, Ph.D., who was working to develop an affordable, noncontact, instant thermometer for home use.

"Originally, ThermoScan wanted to make thermometers for everyone to use," says Randall Steward, former president of Braun ThermoScan. "We owned the rights to a patent for a less-expensive infrared ear thermometer than the one on the market at the time, and we wanted to make a thermometer that could be used by consumers

at home, as well as by physicians in their offices or in hospitals."

Back then, Steward explains, infrared ear thermometers could only be used by physicians. They were bulky and expensive, costing approximately $1,000. "Our mission was to change the way the world takes its temperature," says Steward.

MAKING TECHNOLOGY AFFORDABLE

Infrared thermometers operate by measuring the naturally occurring electromagnetic radiation emissions from the auditory can and tympanic membrane. Emission are measured by placing a sensor in the path of the thermometer's field of view.

"The best way to describe our thermometers," says Steward, "is that they work a lot like cameras The hard window in an ear thermometer basically acts like the lens of a camera, beginning the optical path that infrared light will take from ear to thermometer

Since the introduction of the ThermoScan Instant Thermomete Braun has made more than 150

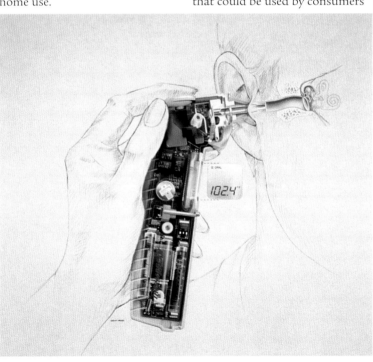

THE EAR THERMOMETER TAKES A TEMPERATURE IN ONE SECOND BY MEASURING THE INFRARED HEAT GENERATED BY THE EARDRUM AND SURROUNDING TISSUE.

improvements to its product, as well as developing a variety of thermometers for physicians and the average consumer alike. Although infrared thermometry is not new to medical professionals, Braun ThermoScan's PRO-Series and HM-Series thermometers incorporate an advanced, patented technology that makes them more durable and affordable.

Designed for physicians' constant use, Braun ThermoScan's professional thermometers are created with durable hard windows and a shutter mechanism that are protected in a metal housing and coated with low-friction material. Braun's Home Use model is slightly less sophisticated, but it's also less expensive, giving consumers an affordable, accurate, and easy way to take temperatures. "The beauty of this kind of thermometer is that it takes the body's temperature in the ear, without discomfort, and in just a second. Infrared technology works that fast," says Steward.

AN INTERNATIONAL PRESENCE

In November 1995, ThermoScan was acquired by the Gillette Company and now operates as a division of Braun, which is headquartered in Kronberg, Germany. That acquisition allowed the company to expand its international capabilities. "Before the acquisition, less than 5 percent of our sales were international," says Steward. "Now, it's closer to 50 percent."

Braun ThermoScan's San Diego office focuses on the technical and operations side of the business, leaving most of the marketing and sales to Braun and Gillette. "We are the only Class II medical device produced in all of Braun and Gillette, so we have the regulatory expertise and are responsible for worldwide manufacturing of professional products," says Steward. Consumer products, which comprise 90 percent of the company's business, are manufactured in Asia.

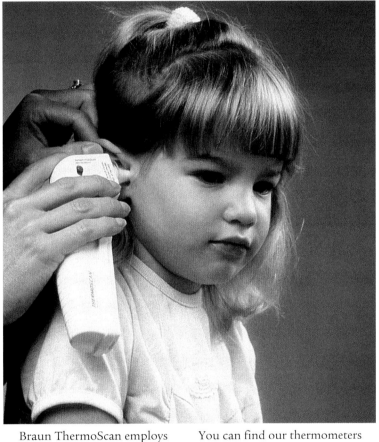

THE HM-SERIES THERMOMETER GIVES CONSUMERS A FAST, EASY WAY TO ACCURATELY TAKE THE TEMPERATURES OF ALL FAMILY MEMBERS.

Braun ThermoScan employs 150 people in its 80,000-square-foot San Diego facility, which includes a 25,000-square-foot warehouse for distribution of its professional products. The company hopes to venture into the personal health care market and develop new diagnostic products in the next several years.

"In six years, we've gone from zero to a $170 million company, with just one product," says Steward. "We've maximized the capability of one product, selling it globally.

You can find our thermometers in 35,000 stores throughout the United States, everywhere from big chains to independent pharmacies, warehouse clubs, and department stores."

What began as two men working to develop a less expensive, more durable product has become an industry leader with an international presence. And with this history of innovation and a goal of constant improvement, Braun ThermoScan will continue to revolutionize health care on an international basis.

A LMOST IMMEDIATELY AFTER ITS GRAND OPENING IN 1989, SYMPHON Towers became a leading landmark in downtown San Diego Today, it serves as the city's benchmark for innovative design quality construction, and tenant service. ■ Five years passed from inception to completion of Symphony Towers, San Diego' largest private, mixed-use project. It includes a Class A, 34-stor

office tower; the 27-story Marriott Suites Hotel; a five-level parking structure; and the elegantly restored, 2,255-seat Copley Symphony Hall. The 1.2 million-square-foot project occupies a full city block in the heart of downtown San Diego.

BUSINESS AND ART PERFORMING IN HARMONY

In 1984, the block bordered by Seventh and Eighth avenues and A and B streets in downtown San Diego was home to a 75,000-square-foot office building and parking structure. Additionally, the once-beautiful Fox Theater—which opened in 1929 and closed in the early 1980s—was located here. While Symphony Towers' developers were planning the project, the San Diego Symphony Orchestra was also eyeing the property—hoping to acquire and restore the theater for its own use. A deal was reached between the two parties that allowed the orchestra to move forward with its plans.

But keeping the theater presented another hurdle—providing parking for the office tower and hotel. Much of the theater was

below ground level, making underground parking structurally impossible. The solution was a huge, elaborate truss system suspended above Symphony Hall, and supported by the hotel and office towers at each side. The resulting "structural bridge" contains five levels of parking, which accommodates more than 600 vehicles, and preserves the beauty and structural integrity of the theater.

The truss system also helped solve a difficult logistical problem—the site's steep slope and the hotel's problematic foundation, which is approximately 20 feet higher than the office building's foundation. Project engineers designed the

truss system in an inverted V in order to counteract the gravitational pull on the buildings. The six-story truss system is so strong that it's topped by a 12th-floor sky bridge between the two towers that includes retail space, a restaurant

CLOCKWISE FROM TOP RIGHT: SYMPHONY TOWERS, SAN DIEGO'S LARGEST PRIVATE, MIXED-USE PROJECT, INCLUDES A CLASS A, 34-STORY OFFICE TOWER; THE 27-STORY MARRIOTT SUITES HOTEL; A FIVE-LEVEL PARKING STRUCTURE; AND THE ELEGANTLY RESTORED, 2,255-SEAT COPLEY SYMPHONY HALL.

THE BUILDING OWNERS AND MANAGERS ASSOCIATION NAMED SYMPHONY TOWERS ITS 1994 INTERNATIONAL BUILDING OF THE YEAR, MAKING IT THE TOP STRUCTURE IN ITS CLASS THROUGH-OUT NORTH AMERICA.

AN 80-FOOT SYMPHONIC MURAL AND RICH GRANITE AND BURLED MAHOGANY FINISHES GRACE THE MAIN LOBBY OF SYMPHONY TOWERS.

lounge areas, meeting rooms, and hotel and office lobbies.

TIMELESS DESIGN

With its exterior mix of glass and inset red granite, the office structure embraces a timeless design. Burled mahogany paneling adds a touch of richness to the elevator cars and lobby areas. The bay windows that protrude from the top floors offer unmatched panoramic views of the city. The top floor is also home to the private University Club, one of San Diego's most prestigious social organizations.

The building offers unusual tenant amenities like valet parking and shuttle service between Symphony Towers and the local courts. Tenant parties are common, as are free community concerts by top local musicians each summer and during the December holiday season.

In many respects, the hotel perfectly complements the office tower. Marriott Suites offers vital public spaces, such as meeting rooms and restaurants, that are used by office tenants.

Attention to detail from Symphony Towers' office staff, engineers, security guards, parking garage workers, and janitors keeps the building looking and operating at its peak. Such dedication has not gone unnoticed by building management professionals. For three consecutive years from 1991 to 1993, Symphony Towers was named San Diego's Office Building of the Year by the local chapter of the Building Owners and Managers Association (BOMA). Then, in 1994, BOMA named Symphony Towers its International Building of the Year, making it the top structure in its class throughout North America. The building has won many other awards, including honors for energy conservation and lobby decorations during the holiday season.

In addition to servicing the business community, Symphony Towers has opened its doors for many charitable events and has

served as a rehearsal hall for the Old Globe Theatre. Building management, along with many tenants, has made Symphony Towers a part of San Diego City Schools' Partnership in Education program. Dozens of students from Crawford High School—the district's business magnet school—have participated in job-shadowing days at Symphony Towers. And each year, building management gives a college scholarship to a graduating Crawford business student.

The operation of the building fits well with the overall philosophy of its owner, SPP Investment Management, a leading Swedish pension fund. SPP has interests in cities around the world, as well as in nearly a dozen communities in the United States. SPP's U.S. portfolio is currently valued at approximately $500 million, an amount that may very well double by the turn of the 21st century, according to David Sherwood, chief executive officer for SPP Investment Management's real estate portfolio.

"We are always looking to acquire high-quality assets in the best locations—much like Symphony Towers," Sherwood says. "We like to develop strong relationships

with tenants, the project management team, and brokers. It's our belief that the investment of goodwill pays off over a long holding period."

It is a philosophy that has worked well. In fact, within three years of its opening—while the downtown office vacancy rate topped 20 percent—Symphony Towers was 97 percent leased. Such success, along with its countless amenities and its award-winning design, makes Symphony Towers San Diego's most prestigious corporate address.

SYMPHONY TOWERS OFFERS SOME OF THE BEST VIEWS IN DOWNTOWN SAN DIEGO.

THE TOP FLOOR OF SYMPHONY TOWERS IS HOME TO THE PRIVATE UNIVERSITY CLUB, ONE OF SAN DIEGO'S MOST PRESTIGIOUS SOCIAL ORGANIZATIONS.

FOR SAN DIEGO COUNTY AND THE BARONA BAND OF MISSION INDIANS Barona Casino is more than just a source of income—it's a source of magic. ■ The Barona Band of Mission Indians, established by the Executive Order of 1891, is recognized by the U.S. government as a sovereign entity. The tribe—which has made its home in this area for more than 5,000 years—is governed by a general council composed of approximately 240 voting members.

Since opening in 1991, the casino, which is located on the Barona Indian Reservation just 30 minutes northeast of downtown San Diego, has poured not only income, but new hope into the Native American community. Barona, the first Native American-owned casino to integrate a central theme into its casino and marketing, is also the largest facility of its kind in California, with 115,000 square feet of gaming and hospitality space.

AS CLOSE AS IT GETS TO LAS VEGAS

"Anyone who enjoys the sights and sounds of a visit to Las Vegas will get just as much enjoyment at Barona Casino," says Karol Schoen, Barona Casino general manager. "We are in the entertainment business, and we pride ourselves on being as close to Las Vegas as it gets without actually going there. We have all the fun and excitement of Vegas, and our staff is extremely friendly."

Barona offers nearly 1,000 video and video poker gaming machines, 29 card tables for Joker's Wild 21 and poker, a 1,500-seat bingo hall, a satellite wagering facility for off-track betting, a gift shop, a food court (offering four different styles of food), and a 240-seat, Las Vegas-style buffet. And for large groups heading out to enjoy the casino's excitement and food, Barona offers free busing Monday through Friday for groups of eight or more from as far north as Oceanside and as far south as the Mexican border.

A trip to Barona Casino has been very worthwhile to many patrons. In 1996, the prize payouts totaled $245 million. Poker jackpots have paid out as much as $20,000, individual bingo players have won as much as $82,000, and progressive jackpots on video machines have paid off as high as $165,000.

OVERALL ECONOMIC IMPACT

The growth and success of Barona Casino over the years has enabled the Barona Band of Mission Indians to achieve an unprecedented level of economic self-sufficiency.

BARONA, THE FIRST NATIVE AMERICAN-OWNED CASINO TO INTEGRATE A CENTRAL THEME INTO ITS CASINO AND MARKETING, IS ALSO THE LARGEST FACILITY OF ITS KIND IN CALIFORNIA, WITH 115,000 SQUARE FEET OF GAMING AND HOSPITALITY SPACE (TOP).

TRIBAL CHAIRMAN CLIFFORD LACHAPPA VISITS A PATIENT AT CHILDREN'S HOSPITAL, JUST ONE OF THE MANY LOCAL AND NATIONAL ORGANIZATIONS BARONA HAS SUPPORTED (BOTTOM).

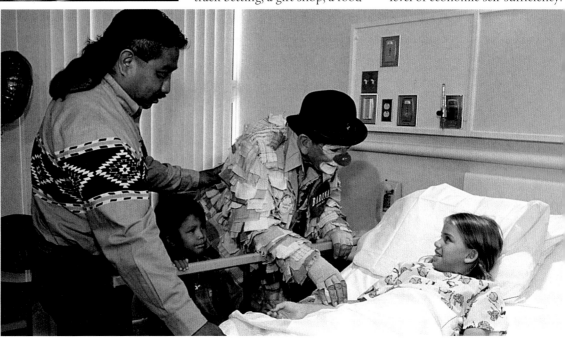

past of poverty has been replaced
a future of unlimited potential.
dian gaming revenues have en-
led tribal leaders not only to
e back to the community, but
so to begin building the physical,
ucational, and cultural infra-
ructure necessary to ensure the
ture of the tribe.

Since the casino opened, the
rona Band has been able to es-
blish educational programs for
e young—such as Head Start—
d a college scholarship program.
e tribe has also built a gas station,
new homes for tribal families,
d a $2 million sewage treatment
ant, and has also invested nearly
.5 million in improving and main-
ining roadways. The tribe has
cently completed a $2 million
pansion of its community cen-
r to include a museum, tennis
d basketball courts, a new school,
library, and a new building for
e Head Start program.

Through Indian gaming revues, unemployment on the
servation has been eliminated—
ing from 70 percent to zero.
dian gaming is the cornerstone
which tribes such as Barona
ve begun to build a commu-
ty, renew its culture, and share
good fortune with others,"
ys Tribal Chairman Clifford
Chappa. "The impact of such
reversal from poverty and despair
likely to impact many future
enerations."

This good fortune has allowed
e tribal leaders to help and give
ack to the community outside the
servation as well. Barona Casino
ploys approximately 1,100 people,
ly 3 percent of whom are Native
ericans. And just as the casino
eates jobs for non-Native Ameri-
ans, it is also a source of tax dol-
rs for non-Indian governments
d communities. The millions
dollars the tribe has spent on
nstruction projects go to bol-
er the overall local economy.

Since 1994, Barona Casino has
invested more than $1.5 million
charitable contributions and

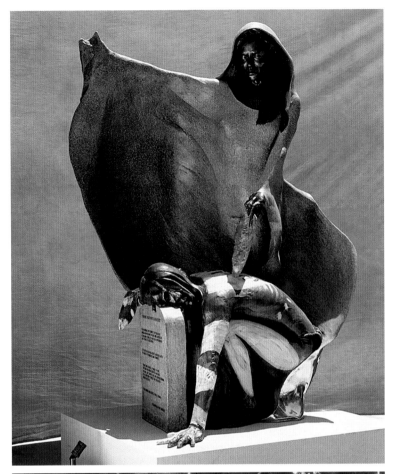

sponsorships throughout San
Diego County. There are close to 60
local and national organizations
Barona has supported, including
Children's Hospital, Greater San
Diego Inner-City Games, Sharp
HealthCare Research and Education
Program, Boys and Girls Club of
Ramona, California Highway Patrol,
La Jolla Playhouse, San Diego Blood
Bank, SDSU/Aztec Athletic Foun-
dation, MADD, and many others.

With the great success the
casino has experienced since its
opening, it's obvious why the tribe
is so proud of its accomplishments.
Schoen says the casino truly reflects the spirit of the tribe. "From
the experience and entertainment
we offer, to the great things the
casino has done for the tribe and
the community," she says, "it sums
things up to say we believe in
magic."

BARONA OFFERS NEARLY 1,000
VIDEO AND VIDEO POKER GAMING
MACHINES, 29 CARD TABLES FOR
JOKER'S WILD 21 AND POKER, A
1,500-SEAT BINGO HALL, A SAT-
ELLITE WAGERING FACILITY FOR
OFFTRACK BETTING, A GIFT SHOP,
A FOOD COURT (OFFERING FOUR
DIFFERENT STYLES OF FOOD),
AND A 240-SEAT, LAS VEGAS-STYLE
BUFFET.

AMONG THE FEW PRIVATELY OWNED BIOTECH COMPANIES IN SAN Diego, MarDx Diagnostics has positioned itself to become world leader within the biotech arena. Located in Carlsbad MarDx Diagnostics was recently ranked among the top 25 local biotech companies by the *San Diego Business Journal*. Working diligently to provide its extensive diagnostic product line to

leading laboratories, both in the United States and abroad, MarDx Diagnostics has achieved its success through perseverance, innovation, quality, and exceptional commitment to customers.

MarDx Diagnostics made its mark in the medical industry with test kits that detect and assist in the diagnosis of Lyme disease. Lyme disease is the most commonly reported tick-borne illness and, left untreated, can lead to severe health problems. Faced with this emerging disease, MarDx rose to the challenge and applied its R&D resources to the development of assays that assist physicians in the diagnosis of this disease. MarDx developed the first Lyme western blot assay to receive FDA clear-

ance. Trademarked as MarBlot® kits, MarDx Diagnostics has developed additional western blot kits to aid in the diagnosis of autoimmune disorders and infectious diseases. MarBlot® kits are used by commercial laboratories, hospitals, and research centers around the world.

Led by a core team with more than 100 years' combined experience, MarDx is poised to continue as an industry leader. Arthur Markovits, president and founder, received his M.S. in public health from UCLA and began his career in 1969 with a privately held diagnostic company in New Jersey. Markovits holds patents in immunofluorescence and is a world-renowned authority on autoimmune disor-

ders. Joan Markovits, vice president of finance and cofounder, holds an M.B.A. in international business management, and has created and maintained all of the company's business plans. Barry Menefee, vice president of scientific affairs, began his career at MarDx Diagnostics soon after the company's inception. Menefee holds a Ph.D. in molecular biology from the University of Arizona. Rounding out the management team are Arnie Aquilino and Jon Knowles. Aquilino serves as vice president of sales, marketing, and operations, and holds an M.S. degree in molecular biology and an M.B.A. in business management. Knowles serves as vice president of regulatory affairs and holds a

LED BY A CORE TEAM WITH MORE THAN 100 YEARS' COMBINED EXPERIENCE, MARDX DIAGNOSTICS IS POISED TO CONTINUE AS AN INDUSTRY LEADER. PICTURED FROM LEFT TO RIGHT ARE: JOAN MARKOVITS, CO-FOUNDER AND VICE PRESIDENT OF FINANCE; ARNIE AQUILLINO, VICE PRESIDENT OF SALES, MARKETING, AND OPERATIONS; JON KNOWLES, VICE PRESIDENT OF REGULATORY AFFAIRS; BARRY MENEFEE, VICE PRESIDENT OF SCIENTIFIC AFFAIRS; AND AUTHUR MARKOVITS, PRESIDENT AND FOUNDER.

doctorate in public health from the University of North Carolina.

Among the many reasons for MarDx's phenomenal growth is the friendly business atmosphere of the San Diego area, which offers a well-rounded and solid environment for both business and personal growth. MarDx Diagnostics has grown fourfold since moving to Carlsbad in 1991. As Joan Markovits says, "San Diego is a good place to do business; it ranks up there with the biggest centers of the world. With the ground links to L.A. airports, distribution of our products domestically and internationally runs smoothly." There are also personal reasons why MarDx made the move to the Carlsbad. "We chose the San Diego area for the quality of life," she adds.

Menefee says that San Diego has proved to be a treasure trove of knowledgeable workers. "The workforce is outstanding," he says. "We get many of our employees from local colleges, including the University of California, San Diego."

Much of MarDx Diagnostics' success can be attributed to its entrance into foreign markets. As with many American companies, MarDx Diagnostics shifted its new product focus from the domestic marketplace to the world market. The opportunities afforded in the emerging health care systems in the international community, coupled with a less expensive registration process, have fueled MarDx Diagnostics' tremendous growth. According to Knowles, "Experience gained in the European market, along with the modernization of U.S. regulatory policy, will facilitate the introduction of more new products into the domestic market in the coming years."

MarDx stands out from its competitors due to its unwavering commitment to customer ser-

GLYN JONES PRODUCTIONS

GLYN JONES PRODUCTIONS

LOCATED IN CARLSBAD, MARDX DIAGNOSTICS WAS RECENTLY RANKED AMONG THE TOP 25 LOCAL BIOTECH COMPANIES BY THE *SAN DIEGO BUSINESS JOURNAL.* WORKING DILIGENTLY TO PROVIDE ITS EXTENSIVE DIAGNOSTIC PRODUCT LINE TO LEADING LABORATORIES, BOTH IN THE UNITED STATES AND ABROAD, MARDX DIAGNOSTICS HAS ACHIEVED ITS SUCCESS THROUGH PERSEVERANCE, INNOVATION, QUALITY, AND EXCEPTIONAL COMMITMENT TO CUSTOMERS.

WITH A RECORD OF EXCELLENT PRODUCTS AND SERVICE, MARDX DIAGNOSTICS IS POSITIONED FOR THE YEARS AHEAD WITH A VISION TO INCREASE ITS ABILITY TO PROVIDE THE HEALTH CARE INDUSTRY WITH QUALITY DIAGNOSTIC PRODUCTS.

vice. "Everything starts with a good product," says Aquilino, "but our service and support team is really unique. We aren't just a vendor; we are a partner with our customers."

With a record of excellent products and service, MarDx Diagnostics is positioned for the years ahead.

"We look forward to the millennium," states Joan. "The future holds great promise for increasing our ability to provide the health care industry with quality diagnostic products. MarDx Diagnostics will continue to be an industry leader for years to come."

HELSINKI-BASED NOKIA MOBILE PHONES IS ONE OF THE WORLD'S leading telecommunications companies, employing more than 36,000 people in 45 countries and having net sales in 1996 exceeding $8.5 billion. ■ The company's focus is wire-line/wireless communications, which are commonly known as mobile phones. In fact, NOKIA was a pioneer in mobile telephony and is currently the world's second-largest manufacturer of mobile phones, as well as a leading supplier of digital cellular networks. The company is also a significant supplier of advanced transmission systems and access networks, multimedia equipment, satellite and cable receivers, and other telecommunications-related products.

FOCUS ON RESEARCH

NOKIA Mobile Phones' research and development facility in San Diego is a high-tech paradise that includes state-of-the-art tools, technologies, and methodologies. The work at this location is driving innovations in the design, manufacture, and sale of mobile phones.

At NOKIA, employees work within small, collaborative teams, where open communication is the rule and risk taking is encouraged. In San Diego, employees are developing code division multiple access (CDMA) digital telephones, which offer some enhancements over existing technologies. "We have already introduced our first CDMA phone," says John Gelm, the center manager for San Diego research and development.

"Our first product was introduced in 1997: a handheld digital phone. This is a cellular phone that operates in both digital and analog modes," says Gelm. Although NOKIA still manufactures analog-only phones, Gelm's branch does not. The San Diego center is involved in technology development and works closely with NOKIA's manufacturing facility in Texas. Production takes place worldwide at seven such facilities.

WORLDWIDE CELLULAR MARKET

In 1996, there were more than 100 million mobile phone subscribers worldwide. NOKIA supplies cellular phones and accessories internationally for all major digital

NOKIA MOBILE PHONES' RESEARCH AND DEVELOPMENT FACILITY IN SAN DIEGO IS A HIGH-TECH PARADISE THAT INCLUDES STATE-OF-THE-ART TOOLS, TECHNOLOGIES, AND METHODOLOGIES. THE WORK AT THIS LOCATION IS DRIVING INNOVATIONS IN THE DESIGN, MANUFACTURE, AND SALE OF MOBILE PHONES.

and analog standards, and sells these products in 120 countries. "Anyone buying cellular phones could be buying a NOKIA phone. We are one of the biggest manu- facturers for both consumers and businesses," says Gelm.

NOKIA began manufacturing mobile phones in 1981, and since then, the company has had more than 2,100 patent applications granted and pending worldwide.

Cellular and wireless phones are becoming almost as widespread as wired ones, and NOKIA believes that its phones must become as easy to use as the average home or office phone, while providing all the new services made possible by technology. Although the com- pany manufactures a wide range of cellular phones for all major digital and analog networks, all of its phones bear a family resem- blance. The large display and clear keypad layout tell customers at a glance: "It's a NOKIA."

The San Diego facility concen- trates its efforts on leading the latest developments in digital technology. "There are a lot of exciting things happening there and many opportunities for engi- neers," says Gelm, who adds that the employees at his facility are mostly engineers, many with ad- vanced degrees. "It's a mix of soft- ware and radio frequency engineers," he says, citing their specialties.

"We have a wide range of talent and a culturally diverse workforce."

SUCCESS NOW AND INTO THE FUTURE

Digitalization—a specialty of San Diego NOKIA—has ushered in a completely new telecommunica- tions age. People's ideas about the nature of telecommunications will fundamentally change in the next decade, and NOKIA is becom- ing a vital part of that evolution.

The company has worked hard at becoming a focused telecom- munications business. NOKIA divested its interests in cables, color televisions, and chemical businesses in order to concentrate on what it does best, and this strat- egy helped to make NOKIA a glo- bal market leader in digital cellular phones by the end of 1996.

The future need for telecommu- nications has no limits. Networks are poised to handle increasing numbers of users and increasing amounts of transmitted informa- tion. For NOKIA, this means data

quality must be vastly enhanced, resulting in clearer images and sounds.

NOKIA believes the only way to shape the future is by listening— to customers, to the market, and to others in the industry. The com- pany employs more than 10,000 people dedicated to research and development at more than 28 re- search centers in eight countries. Its research and development units are placed in the world's leading technology centers.

San Diego NOKIA's future will involve substantial growth, says Gelm. "We had just a handful of employees in 1991 when we began here, and now we have consider- ably more than 250," he says. "Our goal is to reach at least 350-plus employees in order to keep up with the demands for wireless and cel- lular phones, expand our product portfolio, and keep researching and developing new technologies."

DPR Construction, Inc.

WHEN FOUNDED IN 1990, DPR CONSTRUCTION, INC. SET out to challenge "customary practices" and to reexamine the relationships between building contractors and owners, developers, architects, and engineers. With an emphasis on a collaborative approach and early involvement, DPR streamlines the communication processes

anticipates and solves problems before they crop up, and identifies long-term and short-term customer objectives for each project. DPR then establishes aggressive schedules to meet those objectives and commits the resources in manpower and expertise to deliver promises—with no excuses.

DPR's rapid rise to one of the nation's largest, safest, and most

respected contractors has always drawn attention to the firm's annual revenue increases. Although revenues are approaching the $2 billion level, DPR's leaders point to many things besides gross earnings when talking about their success. The company is fueled by a number of synergistic forces that include enlightened founders, a bright and innovative workforce, a commitment to excellence, and a team mentality committed to a shared vision.

While gross earnings are the bottom-line goal for any company, there is one overall goal that drives the company: DPR exists to build great things. This desire to build great things is evidenced by the projects DPR builds, the relationships DPR's employees enjoy with its customers, and the company itself.

DPR has also gained success by aiming its creative strength

at very specific markets. Its areas of construction have centered primarily on the biotechnology, pharmaceutical, microelectronics, health care, and corporate office markets. By keeping the company focused on technically complex work, DPR has been able to develop in-house expertise aimed at serving its customers' needs. Providing expertise not normally expected from a builder has allowed DPR to differentiate itself from other firms serving the same markets.

A DIFFERENT TYPE OF LEADERSHIP
While several elements set DPR apart from its competitors, one profound difference is its leadership philosophy. The firm's 1,500 employees and 11 nationwide offices operate with an entrepreneurial and autonomous spirit on a local basis while still maintaining a seam-

DPR CONSTRUCTION, INC. IS RECOGNIZED AS ONE OF SAN DIEGO'S LARGEST AND MOST SUCCESSFUL BUILDERS OF PRIVATELY OWNED FACILITIES. ALMOST 10 PERCENT OF THE COMPANY'S TOTAL BUSINESS ON AN ANNUAL BASIS IS DONE IN SAN DIEGO COUNTY ALONE.

THERE IS ONE OVERALL GOAL THAT DRIVES THE COMPANY: DPR EXISTS TO BUILD GREAT THINGS. THIS MOTTO IS EVIDENCED BY THE PROJECTS DPR BUILDS, SUCH AS THE NATIONAL ASSOCIATION OF MUSIC MERCHANTS (NAMM) CORPORATE OFFICE IN CARLSBAD, CA; THE RELATIONSHIPS DPR'S EMPLOYEES ENJOY WITH ITS CUSTOMERS; AND THE COMPANY ITSELF.

ss company feel to employees and customers alike.

One visible indicator of the team approach that permeates the company is that DPR's principals and founders work in an open-air environment alongside the engineers, estimators, and administrative staff. They are not sequestered at the top of a pyramid organization or guarded by executive secretaries. This isn't an attempt to be trendy, say DPR's founders. It purposefully reflects the corporation's desire to eliminate barriers between senior managers and employees. It also makes senior executives immediately accessible to anyone who needs their input. As a result, DPR's corporate footwork in the competitive arena is swift and decisive.

In another attempt to remove barriers common in a corporate environment, DPR eschews titles. Employees' business cards carry only their name, the company name, the area office address, and phone numbers. DPR leaders believe authority springs from experience and accountability, not from a title. In discussing a project, for example, those who demonstrate real knowledge will have an opportunity to be heard, regardless of their position within the company. DPR's entrepreneurial spirit recognizes the talents in all its people and enables them to exercise their talents free from interference and micromanagement.

CUSTOMER SERVICE COMES FIRST

While working to create an ideal business from the inside, DPR never loses sight of who really needs to be kept happy: its customers.

DPR's construction teams truly listen and help clients define what they need in terms relevant to the client. They present options that can be understood, and they explain the impact and ramifications of every option. Whether a project involves a multimillion-dollar manufacturing facility or

a small building renovation, helping each customer understand the full consequences of project decisions is part of DPR's emphasis on teamwork and full communication among team members.

DPR's in-house experts in mechanical, electrical, and ultra-high-purity piping systems exemplify this spirit of teamwork and customer advocacy on technically complex projects. DPR understands that technical competency and speed of project delivery are key elements in the successful construction of its customers' projects. To support these requirements, the company has developed a keen understanding of current and proposed regulations, and its employees recognize the changing nature of these regulations and help DPR's customers anticipate future requirements.

SUCCESS STORIES

Guiding DPR's communication process and its desire to build great things are four core values: Integrity, Enjoyment, Uniqueness, and Ever Forward. The last two of these core values are what embody the company's refusal to rest on its laurels or be perceived as stagnant.

Using these values as benchmarks, DPR's San Diego success stories include facilities created for customers such as NAMM, Carlsbad by the Sea, Ligand Pharmaceuticals, Advanced Tissue Sciences, Alliance Pharmaceuticals, SGS-Thomson, Hewlett-Packard, ScrippsHealth, Kaiser Permanente, and the UCSD Burn Center.

DPR Construction, Inc. is recognized as one of San Diego's largest and most successful builders of privately owned facilities. Almost 10 percent of the company's total business on an annual basis is done in San Diego County alone. What is even more significant is that in an industry that generally purchases construction on a "low bid" basis, more than 95 percent of DPR's work companywide is done on a negotiated basis—a pro-

cess where the project team and their qualifications are the primary selection criteria.

Always guided by its core values and its vision to build great things, DPR has also been able to create an impressive list of nationwide success stories. Beyond its success in the field, the company has also been recognized by *Forbes, Inc.,* and others for its impressive development as a company. Additionally, *Inc.,* Merrill Lynch, and Ernst & Young recognized DPR as 1994 Entrepreneur of the Year in Construction.

DPR's outlook for the future remains constant: to continue to build great things. To DPR greatness is not an end point, it's a path—a long, arduous, sometimes tortuous trail of continual development and improvement.

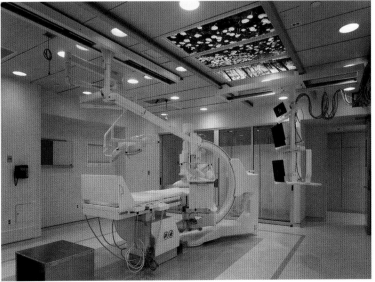

A S A LEADING MANUFACTURER OF BASEBALL-STYLE CAPS, AMERICAN Manufacturing Concepts, Inc. (AMC) has created innovative head wear for some of the largest active sportswear, surf, golf, resort, and entertainment companies in the world. ■ The company's client list includes Mossimo, Liz Claiborne, No Fear, The Gap, Disney, and Universal Studios, among others. "We have

a flair for taking consumer trends and putting them into a hat," says AMC President and Cofounder Tom Smith, who shares with his business partner Steve Cunliffe a fashion/apparel background that spans 36 years. The pair have also developed fashion accessories for clients such as Ocean Pacific, LA Gear, Jimmy Z, and Newport Blue.

Since the company's founding in 1992, sales have increased more than 20 percent per year, and today, AMC produces more than 3 million hats annually at its 40,000-square-foot facility in Chula Vista. Smith attributes AMC's success to quality products, on-time deliveries, and a talent for keeping its finger on the pulse of the fashion industry.

A COMMITMENT TO QUALITY

Knowing that consumers are particular about the hats they wear,

AMC is committed to customer satisfaction. To ensure high-quality products and on-time deliveries, the company maintains in-house control of all aspects of the business, from fabric buying, cutting, digitizing, embroidering, and assembling, to final hat blocking and shipment.

Specific manufacturing techniques are used to provide comfort as well as fashion, and in AMC's step-by-step hat construction process, special attention is paid to turning out a wrinkle-free product. In order to avoid wrinkles from the very beginning, caps are constructed by individually sewing each panel together on single-operator machines.

AMC has been a leader in developing improvements to current industry standards in one-size-fits-all cap design. The company was the first to introduce the new

Flip-n-Grip™—a soft-buckle-closure system. This plastic closure is far superior to those made of metal, which can rust and become uncomfortably hot when worn in the sun.

Another notable feature of AMC caps is the superior quality of their brims, which are made of polyethylene rather than cardboard. "When you wrinkle cardboard, it stays wrinkled," says Smith, "So once you lose a cardboard brim, you lose it forever. Polyethylene is a plastic with a memory. It bounces back and doesn't wrinkle."

AMC's embroidery department operates around the clock, using the industry's most advanced embroidery techniques. AMC was the first to offer 3-D embroidery domestically, and AMC's digitizing department inputs client logos into computers stitch by stitch. For most logos, this requires inputting 5,000 stitches, but some—

SINCE THE COMPANY'S FOUNDING IN 1992, SALES HAVE INCREASED MORE THAN 20 PERCENT PER YEAR, AND TODAY, AMERICAN MANUFACTURING CONCEPTS, INC. (AMC) PRODUCES MORE THAN 3 MILLION HATS ANNUALLY AT ITS 40,000-SQUARE-FOOT FACILITY IN CHULA VISTA.

uch as those AMC has produced
or Disney World—may need as
many as 20,000 stitches. For better
quality, embroidery work is done
on flat panels prior to hat assembly.

To ensure excellent form, AMC
uses crown blocking, which is the
last step in the manufacturing
process. This consists of steaming
and pressing the crown to remove
any wrinkles. "If we did not put
the shape to it, the brim would
be straight across," says Smith.
"We shape our own hats, like most
baseball players and kids do."

A Legendary
Head Wear Division

AMC was the first to introduce
the six-panel, low-profile cap to
the golf market. In 1993, AMC
launched Legendary Headwear,
today's fashion and design head
wear leader in the golf industry.
The business of translating fashion ideas into hats of style and comfort has led Legendary Headwear
to introduce gambler- and safari-
style straw hats made from high-
quality raffia and Panama straws.

In keeping with the legendary
theme of its designs, this line also
features a vintage driver's cap that
is reminiscent of the golden years
of golf. Legendary Headwear's products have also been updated with

today's fabrics and fits, such as the
Terry Fleece line, water-resistant
golf caps, and ladies' larger-brimmed
visors for improved sun protection.

Keeping up with changing
trends and consumer needs has
meant developing a quality team
of experts. At the end of its first
year, AMC had 30 employees, 90
percent of whom are still with
the company today. "We pay our
sewers at a higher rate than our
competitors, so we attract a better-
quality sewer," Smith says. Today,
AMC employs 300 sewers, 12 cutters,
eight fabric handlers, 50 embroider-
ers, and seven digitizers, in addition to staffing its administrative
offices and shipping department.

Although AMC has been solic-
ited by a number of cities to relocate its thriving business, Smith
says the company's commitment
to quality includes staying in San
Diego to take advantage of the
high-quality sewers who reside in
the city's South Bay community.

In preparation for the future,
American Manufacturing Concepts
will continue to maintain the high
standards that have always been
its hallmark. In meeting the fashion, design, and manufacturing
needs of a new generation of consumers, AMC will work closely with
its client companies to provide
superior head wear for a variety
of uses in the new millennium.

SAN DIEGO IS HOME TO ONE OF THE LARGEST OFFICES OF QUINTILES Transnational Corp., the world's leading provider of contract research, and sales and marketing services to the pharmaceutical biotech, and medical device industries. More than 500 employees work at the Sorrento Valley offices of Quintiles CNS Therapeutics which focuses on therapies for central nervous system disorders

SAN DIEGO IS HOME TO ONE OF THE LARGEST OFFICES OF QUINTILES TRANSNATIONAL CORP., THE WORLD'S LEADING PROVIDER OF CONTRACT RESEARCH, AND SALES AND MARKETING SERVICES TO THE PHARMACEUTICAL, BIOTECH, AND MEDICAL DEVICE INDUSTRIES (TOP).

(FROM LEFT) DAN BUSH, PH.D. AND WAYNE DAVIS, PH.D. JOIN KEVIN L. KEIM, M.S.,PH.D., PRESIDENT OF QUINTILES CNS THERAPEUTICS, IN SETTING THE STANDARD FOR CNS DRUG DEVELOPMENT (BOTTOM).

San Diego offers global companies such as Quintiles a rare nexus of resources, expertise, and geography: The city is home to leading medical and scientific research and is a world-class gateway to the emerging markets of the Pacific Rim and Latin America. This combination makes San Diego an extremely attractive location for Quintiles.

From the opening of Quintiles' first office in San Diego in 1992 (formed when Quintiles joined with what was then International Clinical Research), the growth has been nothing short of remarkable. The office started with 10 employees, and now typically hires that many in a month. Quintiles Transnational went public in 1994

(Nasdaq: QTRN) and now has a market capitalization of more than $3 billion.

CENTRAL NERVOUS SYSTEM WORK

Kevin L. Keim, M.S., Ph.D., president of the company, says the International Clinical Research (ICR) group that preceded Quintiles CNS focused on mostly psychiatric work, but now its research is much broader.

"When I joined the group in 1991, I was able to take advantage of the need to expand clinical studies into the neurology area," says Keim. "As we currently stand, San Diego primarily does psychiatric and neurology subspecialty work for Quintiles Transnational. We are the center of their global CNS therapeutic group."

Keim says the company manages drug development and clinical trial studies for most major drug companies. Businesses in the pharmaceutical and biotechnology industry, he explains, increasingly out-source management of their clinical studies, and Quintiles is able to assist them through its

contract work. "We contract medical services, business consultations clinical trial management, biostatistical and data processing, and medical/scientific report writing, and we help with regulatory issues," says Keim. "We advise our clients how to write a protocol, strategically design their drug development plan, and help them overcome any regulatory hurdles they may have encountered. They don't always have the right experts on their team to do that, and we are able to complement the total effort."

The San Diego office has a medical staff that includes physicians, board-certified neurologists and psychiatrists, and nurses. These specialists work as a team to integrate their central nervous system expertise across all stages of the drug development process. Worldwide, Quintiles CNS Therapeutics has between 5,000 and 8,000 patients receiving experimental medications at any one time. Other personnel in the San Diego office engage in clinical trial and project management, regulatory services, and medical writing.

CLINICAL TRIALS AROUND THE WORLD

Quintiles Transnational has offices and research centers around the world and has partnered with today's biomedical pioneers to speed development of new medicines to the market. Quintiles has helped study the safety, efficacy, and cost-effectiveness of drug therapies in every major therapeutic category. This process has involved hundreds of clinical trials around the world with tens of thousands of patients.

YEARS OF INDUSTRY EXPERIENCE

Quintiles CNS Therapeutics' expertise comes from years of experience bringing key central nervous system compounds through the development and drug registration process. Quintiles' Phase I units—the first phase of a clinical drug trial—have extensive experience in the first human studies with a variety of antidepressant, antipsychotic, anticonvulsant, and anxiolytic drug candidates.

In central nervous system studies, it is rare to find quantifiable points that demonstrate a drug's safety or efficacy, and as a result, a study's design is not necessarily straightforward. This means that instead of taking the patient's temperature, the researcher must measure his or her mood; instead of noting the presence/absence of bacteria, the investigator must quantify cognitive function. The process requires specialized expertise to determine how to measure psychiatric and neurological functions consistently and accurately. This is why the services of Quintiles' specialized CNS team in San Diego are so important. The group is a specialty research organization with its own integrated global drug development capabilities. "I think we are unique among the contract research organizations in that we are the only company in the business that has a dedicated group for this thera-

peutic area," says Keim. "We have set the standard for CNS drug development."

The global experience of the CNS group is particularly important because of geographic differences in psychiatric and neurological medical practice—and even in ways of defining central nervous system diseases. There are major offices in Europe and the Pacific Rim area, including Japan, China, Singapore, Australia, and South Africa.

THE MARKET LEADER

Quintiles Transnational is the market leader in providing contract pharmaceutical services worldwide, and its 1997 net revenue of $814 million established another industry record.

Maintaining customer loyalty requires the company's staff to be astute professionals who know the broad business environment, understand the customer's concerns, and are committed to service excellence. And this commitment to excellence has allowed the company to expand rapidly. Today, Quintiles Transnational has 11,000 employees in more than 75 offices in 27 countries. In addition to its

contract work, Quintiles Transnational also provides health care policy consulting and health information management services to the health care industry.

Keim says the San Diego group plans to maintain its presence as an important employer in the San Diego area. "When I first came here, we had only 20 employees," he says, "and now we have more than 500." With such rapid growth in such a short time span, Quintiles CNS Therapeutics is positioned to maintain an influential role both in the city it calls home and in the worldwide medical community.

AMONG THE MORE THAN 500 EMPLOYEES WHO WORK AT THE SORRENTO VALLEY OFFICES OF QUINTILES CNS THERAPEUTICS IS JUDEE SEDLER, DIRECTOR OF HUMAN RESOURCES (TOP).

THE SPECIALISTS AT QUINTILES CNS THERAPEUTICS WORK AS A TEAM TO INTEGRATE THEIR CENTRAL NERVOUS SYSTEM EXPERTISE ACROSS ALL STAGES OF THE DRUG DEVELOPMENT PROCESS (BOTTOM).

THE LIGHTSPAN PARTNERSHIP, INC.

THESE DAYS, EDUCATORS ARE WORKING HARDER THAN EVER TO ME[...] the challenging task of educating children. Research shows th[...] for the greatest achievement, teachers need to supplement t[...] classroom experience with additional opportunities for lear[...] ing. Providing these educational opportunities is the goal [...] The Lightspan Partnership, founded in San Diego in 19[...]

The Lightspan Partnership offers curricula for kindergarten through sixth grade in reading, language arts, and mathematics. This learning program consists of a product line of CD-ROM-based programs supplemented by Internet programming for students to use in the classroom and at home. In these programs, the company combines standards-based curricula, the interactive power of computer technology, and the reach of modern telecommunications.

"We were founded on the premise that we could make a difference for kids and increase their achievement," says Susan Richardson, vice president of product marketing. "And we're doing it in an innovative way. We add time for learning to each day by using the qualities that draw kids to television and video games to address reading/language arts and mathematics curriculum content."

SOLVING PROBLEMS

"Prisoners of Time," a report recently commissioned by Congress, identified a key problem hindering education: the lack of time in the typical school day for learning. In addition, research has shown that student achievement is further hurt by the lack of parental involvement, the lack of teacher access to professional development, and inequitable access to educational technology. By creating a connection between schools and homes, The Lightspan Partnership helps solve all these problems.

Using new, affordable technol[...] ogy that allows schools to purchase equipment for every child[...] Lightspan is forging a new scho[...] home connection with its produc[...] This connection makes it possi[...] for families to work with their children to help them succeed. When students and family men[...] bers work together on interacti[...] educational content in their hom[...] this significantly enhances the learning that takes place in scho[...] and extends learning beyond th[...] time limits of the school day an[...] the physical boundaries of the school building.

Lightspan's learning progra[...] is so much fun that participatin[...] students are spending 30 to 60 minutes each day using it. This[...] is time they would have spent wit[...] entertainment TV or video gam[...] "We have a wonderful, diverse gr[...] of in-house developers who creat[...] our product," says Richardson. "We use a triangle to visualize our product development goal. At the center of this triangle is[...]

LIGHTSPAN FLAGSHIP CHARACTER MARS MOOSE™ IS A LOVABLE BLUE MOOSE FROM ANOTHER GALAXY WHOM STUDENTS JOIN ON A SERIES OF EXCITING, INTERACTIVE ADVENTURES IN WHICH THEY TEACH HIM TO READ (TOP).

AN ANIMATOR AT LIGHTSPAN CREATES THE PROGRAMS THAT MAKE LEARNING COME ALIVE THROUGH THE USE OF WONDERFUL CHARACTERS WHO SERVE AS POSITIVE ROLE MODELS (BOTTOM).

rriculum content, which is tied national and state standards. omprising the three sides are aracters, stories, and interactive mes, which connect to make e content engaging, memorable, d fun."

Part of making the learning perience fun is the use of wonderl characters who serve as positive le models. For example, the flagip character Mars Moose™ is a vable blue moose who has come Earth from another galaxy where ey no longer use reading to communicate. Kindergarten to second ade students join Mars Moose 1 a series of exciting, interactive ventures in which Mars Moose's w friends teach him to read. ajor areas covered are print and xt recognition, phonics and deding, vocabulary and comprension, and critical-thinking and udy skills.

Another character who inhabs Lightspan games is Cali, a iendly creature from the land Googol. Along with characters ana and Ben, Cali takes students a number of exciting mathemati-l adventures, helping out with ometry and spatial sense, numr sense, operations, facts, and plications.

The Lightspan adventures can played on personal computers,

as well as on Sony's PlayStation™ game console.

The company also has two Internet products. At the Lightspan Web site, http://www.lightspan.com, customers can learn more about this new way of learning and participate in a free demonstration. Schools that subscribe to The Lightspan Network can enter the site's rich worlds of learning. Another Internet product is Lightspan Local Connect, which helps schools create their own Web site and provides two-way communication between students, teachers, and families.

MORE THAN JUST SOFTWARE

Mars Moose, Cali, and the other Lightspan characters go on learning adventures in classrooms and on kids' television screens all over the country. Headquartered in San Diego, The Lightspan Partnership employs some 200 San Diegans, and has a national sales and service force of approximately 100. The company headquarters houses research and development, administration, marketing, sales management, and a professional services group.

So far, Lightspan's software seems to be making a difference. "One of the first things educators ask us is, 'How do I know this will

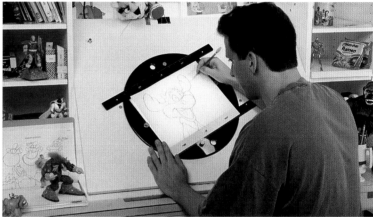

work?' We've done research on our customer base, and we know this is working because we're getting very powerful results," says Richardson. "Students are spending more time learning, their families are getting involved in the learning process, and this is adding up to significant increases in student achievement and higher test scores."

With a firm grasp on technology and a commitment to contribute to the education of America's children, The Lightspan Partnership is taking a leading role in creating new and effective learning programs. Always striving to improve its product, the company will continue to harness the power of technology to offer the education community the best programs possible to help all children achieve their highest potential.

AURORA BIOSCIENCES CORPORATION IS IN THE BUSINESS C industrializing and accelerating the drug discovery process. Sinc the company was formed, Aurora has been on the cutting edge c helping biotechnology and pharmaceutical companies do fast and more efficient research, save money, and, ultimately, save an improve lives. ■ San Diego-based Aurora has its roots with D

Roger Tsien and Dr. Charles Zuker, two noted professors at the University of California, San Diego. In 1995, the pair teamed up with a venture capital company to form Aurora, and within two years the company had expanded to 90 employees—including experts in the fields of engineering, informatics (software), genomics, and biochemistry.

The company's primary mission is to advance drug discovery. Other companies outsource to Aurora, which is developing automated systems for ultra-high throughput screening. "Our goal is to make the drug discovery process more efficient for companies," says Paul Grayson, senior vice president of corporate development for Aurora. The company has also formed a syndicate of pharmaceutical companies that will receive an ultra-high throughput screening system and screen development assistance from Aurora in return for research

funding, licensing fees, milestones, and royalties.

Aurora's portfolio of fluorescent assay technologies is designed to enable screening of compounds against nearly all major classes of human drug targets—including receptors, ion channels, and enzymes—in most therapeutic areas. Typically, biotechnology companies spend many years incurring significant costs as they test and identify drugs and the causes of disease.

Many companies have used combinatorial chemistry to quickly create libraries of thousands, even millions, of small molecules for screening against established and novel targets. The number of those potential targets has increased due to advances in genomics. However, this increasing number of targets and compounds has created severe bottlenecks in the drug discovery process. Efficiency in this arena is linked to speed. Since time is money in this industry, faster discovery may allow biotech and pharmaceutical companies that use Aurora's proprietary technology to get to market earlier.

Aurora is also setting new industry standards with its trademarked

product called NanoPlates, a proprietary device used to hold compounds during testing. Compared to standard plates for use during screening assays, which contain 96 "wells," NanoPlates have 3,456 wells, allowing for significantly less compound to be used per assay, reducing consum able costs. This increased density is also optimally suited to allow faster testing. "What we're doing is a unique integration of technolc gies," says Grayson. "We're combining engineering, informatics and biochemistry together to solve problems."

With demand for Aurora's revolutionary products at an all-time high, Aurora has moved into an 81,000-square-foot facility in the Torrey Pines area of San Diego. Basing its operations in the San Diego area is a natural and practical idea, says Grayson. "San Diego has world-renowned research institutes, such as the University of California, Scripps, and the Salk Institute," he says. "And there are many biotech and technology companies in the area that would make ideal collaborators."

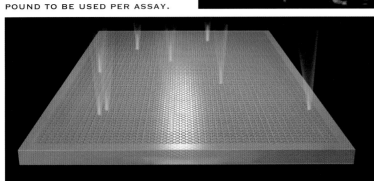

HETHER THEY'RE ON A LONG-AWAITED VACATION OR AT-tending a crucial business meeting, travelers of all kinds list Morgan Run Resort & Club as one of the desirable, prestigious destinations in San Diego. The flagship property of Del Mar-based Cobblestone Golf Group, Morgan Run is a relaxing and uncomplicated retreat located in

rene Rancho Santa Fe—a location nowned as an intimate hideway for the rich and famous.

From its inception, Morgan un has been designed to complement this prestigious community. he resort is so beautiful a setting at it is often the location for television shows, movies, and commercial photo shoots.

Located 20 minutes from downwn San Diego and Lindbergh irport, and only minutes away om coastal Del Mar, the resort isted from 1958 until 1995 as the 'hispering Palms Country Club. obblestone purchased the property in 1994 and promptly invested o million to renovate every aspect f the facility. "We've created an mosphere that is both upscale nd very comfortable," says Linda pichell, director of sales at Morgan un.

OR BUSINESS OR LEASURE

oday's Morgan Run Resort & lub has 89 rooms, including seven ites with wet bars and fireplaces nd seven executive king rooms. ll rooms have patios or private alconies, and many boast spectacular golf course views.

Recreational activities are endss. In addition to access to other obblestone golf clubs in the area, Morgan Run guests are invited enjoy an on-site, 27-hole championship golf course, as well as a riving range and a short-game ractice facility. The resort also as 11 tennis courts, four of which re lighted; a fitness center; an utdoor swimming pool; and a hirlpool.

While these amenities make ne resort an excellent spot for a

vacation, Morgan Run has also become a destination for business travelers. The property can accommodate groups ranging in size from 10 to 250 people in 4,100 square feet of meeting space (six beautifully appointed rooms) and 4,500 square feet of outdoor patios that overlook the golf course.

Businesspeople also come for the resort's high level of service. "When people bring groups to our property, they usually remark about our personalized, high level of service," says Apichell. "We're a private resort, but we're also accessible and very affordable to many people."

Groups also like the self-contained aspect of Morgan Run. "When a group is here, attenders can hold productive meetings, and then relax without having to go somewhere else," says Apichell. "They can play golf, watch sports in the lounge, or just spend time in front of one of our fireplaces."

With its picturesque location, wide array of amenities, and high level of service, Morgan Run has become a favorite of business and leisure guests alike. Dedicated to making return customers out of every guest, the resort is bound to be an industry leader for years to come.

WHETHER THEY'RE ON A LONG-AWAITED VACATION OR ATTENDING A CRUCIAL BUSINESS MEETING, TRAVELERS OF ALL KINDS LIST MORGAN RUN RESORT & CLUB AS ONE OF THE DESIRABLE, PRESTIGIOUS DESTINATIONS IN SAN DIEGO.

U NIDEN CORPORATION HAS TRULY MADE ITS MARK ON THE WIRELES communications industry. It is not only the world's largest manu facturer of cordless telephones—producing more than 10 millio units per year—but also a leading innovator of new technologie that will push wireless communications into the 21st century. Uniden is committed to developing new products that combin

the latest advances in wireless telephone and computer communications. As the company prepares to bring new products to market, the Uniden San Diego Research and Development Center plays a vital role in laying the necessary groundwork.

"Our charter is to develop and deliver leading-edge wireless and multimedia communications products to consumers demanding high value at the lowest possible cost," says Uniden San Diego President Hiep Pham. "Our tag line is Communications with Vision," he says. "We want to develop products that look to the future."

UNIDEN IS COMMITTED TO DEVELOPING NEW PRODUCTS THAT COMBINE THE LATEST ADVANCES IN WIRELESS TELEPHONE AND COMPUTER COMMUNICATIONS.

BUSINESS OPPORTUNITY

Uniden Corporation—which was founded in 1966—reported 1997 sales approaching $1 billion and currently employs more than 17,000 people worldwide. For most of its 32-year history, the Japanese company has been a traditional consumer electronics manufacturer. The burgeoning popularity of wireless voice and data products presented a major business opportunity for Uniden.

In 1995, the company chose San Diego's Sorrento Valley as the site of its research and development center, largely due to the city's reputation as the Wireless Capital of the World. San Diego offered many advantages, including access to skilled graduates and faculty from the University of California San Diego and, of course, the ideal climate and lifestyle.

PRODUCTS FOR A WIRELESS WORLD

Less than two years after its inception, the Uniden San Diego Research and Development Center unleashed a stream of wireless products. These included cellular telephones, data terminals, and modems.

Uniden San Diego's first offering was a cost-effective analog cellular phone, the PCD-1000, priced to compete by providing functionality without costly frills. Moving to the forefront of wireless technology, Uniden has designed a new type of wireless modem, the Uniden Data 1000. This modem operates over a cellular system configured to deliver information in cellular digital packet data (CDPD) format. CDPD takes advantage of existing cellular infrastructure

by sending small packets of data during idle periods, with no dialup required.

Uniden foresees many uses for the Uniden Data 1000. Mobil workers can use the modem with a laptop computer to stay in touc with their offices. Credit card ver fication, alarm system managemen and even remote monitoring of vending machine inventory can all be completed through the system. In addition, the Data 1000 can be purchased at a fraction of the cost of competing products.

Uniden San Diego also produces the Uniden Data 2000, a portable, wireless CDPD PC card that makes it easy and convenien to stay connected to information and resources while on the road. The card allows its user to retriev E-mail, connect to the Internet, and respond quickly to business needs while out of the office.

In 1998, Uniden will launch more sophisticated cellular phone: The first, the Uniden 8360LX, wil use time division multiple access (TDMA)/IS-136 technology, whic is popular in North and South America. In addition, phones usir global systems for mobile commu nication (GSM), which is popula in Europe, and code division mul tiple access (CDMA) are currentl in development.

COMPUTER BUSINESS

In computing, Uniden offers its own network computer, a simple and cheaper alternative to standard personal computers. Namec the Network Computer, each uni allows users to transmit and receive E-mail, and to gain access to the World Wide Web and offic networks using the Internet Pro-

col (IP) standard. Its cousin,
e Wireless Network Computer,
fers wireless access from up to
o feet indoors and 1,500 feet
itdoors from a source line.

Because they have no hard
ive, floppy drive, or CD-ROM,
twork computers typically cost
out one-half to one-third the
ice of an equivalent PC. Appli-
tions do not reside on the com-
iter, and are delivered through
corporate network or via the
ternet on an as-needed basis.
he Wireless Network Computer
lows companies to quickly set
o a network without the tedious
sk of laying wiring from termi-
al to terminal. In addition, com-
iters may be relocated at will
ithout disrupting the network.

Uniden has developed a stand-
one telephone/computer hybrid
lled the Internet E-mail phone,
hich features a keyboard and
as the ability to send and receive
-mail. This new device provides a
w-cost solution for those who
eed an on-line connection, but
o not wish to purchase a PC, or
ho require a separate terminal
or E-mail and Internet access.
nally, the Uniden San Diego

center spawned PerfecTV for the
Japanese market, a digital set-top
box that receives programs and
special events via satellite.

IMPACT ON SAN DIEGO
To feed the pipeline, Uniden San
Diego has rapidly increased its
research and development staff.
The center currently employs
about 250 people, including 200
engineers, and is hiring additional
staff. Uniden's San Diego employees take part in a variety of charitable activities, such as the annual
Toys for Tots campaign and the

San Diego Science Alliance Technical Forum for high school students.
Uniden San Diego also donated
1,000 network computers to 100
of California's economically challenged schools.

In fall 1998, Uniden San Diego
will relocate to a larger headquarters
in San Diego: a 10-story, 270,000-
square-foot building in Sorrento
Mesa featuring amenities such as
a cafeteria, tennis courts, and a gym.
By 2001, the company intends
to have more than 1,000 people
working on development projects
for wireless and multimedia products. With constant efforts such
as these, Uniden is assured of maintaining its leadership position in
improving wireless communication
technology in the 21st century.

UNIDEN CORPORATION IS NOT
ONLY THE WORLD'S LARGEST
MANUFACTURER OF CORDLESS
TELEPHONES—PRODUCING MORE
THAN 10 MILLION UNITS PER
YEAR—BUT ALSO A LEADING IN-
NOVATOR OF NEW TECHNOLOGIES
THAT WILL PUSH WIRELESS COM-
MUNICATIONS INTO THE 21ST
CENTURY.

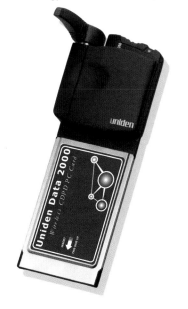

UNIDEN SAN DIEGO PRODUCES
THE UNIDEN DATA 2000, A POR-
TABLE, WIRELESS CDPD PC CARD
THAT MAKES IT EASY AND CONVE-
NIENT TO STAY CONNECTED TO
INFORMATION AND RESOURCES
WHILE ON THE ROAD. THE CARD
ALLOWS ITS USER TO RETRIEVE
E-MAIL, CONNECT TO THE INTERNET,
AND RESPOND QUICKLY TO BUSI-
NESS NEEDS WHILE OUT OF THE
OFFICE.

I N 1998, THE PROPOSED MERGER OF ENOVA CORPORATION, THE PARENT COMPAN of San Diego Gas & Electric (SDG&E), and Pacific Enterprises, the paren company of Southern California Gas Company, will bring a new name expanded utility services for residents and businesses in San Diego an beyond. The new name is Sempra Energy. Sempra is derived from the Lat word "semper," meaning "always"—and the new company plans to make th

name as familiar to customers as SDG&E has been since 1881. The name was carefully chosen through extensive market research with energy customers in key markets across the country. It suggests to customers that they can always depend upon Sempra Energy to provide them with innovative and competitively priced energy solutions, reliability, and trustworthiness—all traits necessary for success in the newly deregulated marketplace.

A FORTUNE 500 COMPANY FOR SAN DIEGO

Sempra Energy will be the only Fortune 500 company in San Diego and will have 6 million customers— the largest customer base in the United States. The merger is a direct response to the dramatic transformation of the energy marketplace in California and the nation—and the intense competition that deregulation will bring to provide energy and energy-related services to customers. For the first time, in 1998 utility customers in California were able to buy electricity from an energy provider other than their local utility. Regardless of the provider chosen by SDG&E customers, all electricity is delivered over SDG&E's power lines.

EXPANDING SEMPRA ENERGY'S BUSINESS

"Domestically, we're going to do our retail marketing through Sempra Energy Solutions, our retail energy-services marketer set up in March 1997 to introduce new energy-related services and products to customers," says Stephen L.

ENOVA CORPORATION IS PARTNERING WITH HOUSTON INDUSTRIES TO BUILD AND OPERATE A $280 MILLION POWER PLANT IN BOULDER CITY, NEVADA, JUST 40 MILES OUTSIDE OF LAS VEGAS (TOP).

CHAIRMAN AND CHIEF EXECUTIVE OFFICER OF ENOVA CORPORATION STEPHEN L. BAUM STATES, "WE PLAN TO CONTINUE TO MOVE AGGRESSIVELY IN THE NEW MARKETPLACE TO EXPAND OUR BUSINESS, BUT, ALONG THE WAY, WE WILL ALSO MAINTAIN OUR STRONG COMMITMENT TO—AND INVOLVEMENT IN—THE COMMUNITIES WE SERVE, ESPECIALLY SAN DIEGO, ORANGE COUNTY, AND LOS ANGELES" (BOTTOM).

Baum, chairman and chief executive officer of Enova Corporation.

"We have already signed up major customers from Bangor, Maine, to the back lots of Hollywood, and from Las Vegas to Los Angeles, along the way acquiring CES/WAY, the largest independent energy-services company in the United States, based in Houston," says Baum. "These efforts complement our acquisition of Sempra Energy Trading (formerly AIG Trading Corp.), a wholesale energy trading firm based in Greenwich, Connecticut."

The company also is partnerin with Houston Industries to buil and operate a $280 million powe plant in Boulder City, Nevada, just 40 miles outside of Las Vega This will be one of the first powe plants that will cater to the competitive marketplace by supplyin utilities throughout the Southwest with electricity. The plant will provide enough power for 480,000 homes.

"In addition, we will reach ne customers through our international subsidiary," Baum adds. "We and our project partners were the first private companies licensed to build natural gas facil ities and deliver that commodity to customers in Mexico. We have projects under way in Mexicali and Chihuahua.

"We plan to continue to move aggressively in the new marketplace to expand our business," Baum concludes. "But, along the way, we will also maintain our strong commitment to—and involvement in—the communitie we serve, especially San Diego, Orange County, and Los Angeles

JACOR COMMUNICATIONS' SLOGAN IS "THE NOISE YOU CAN'T IGNORE." ITS chairman is the legendary real estate tycoon Sam Zell, and its CEO is Randy Michaels, one of the best-known, most creative programming directors in the radio industry. In less than two years, Jacor has grown from obscurity to the nation's second-largest radio operator with 1997 gross revenues of more than $600 million. ■ Jacor's explosive growth

has its roots in the Telecommunications Act of 1996. The act removed national limits on radio station ownership and, more important, increased the number of signals a company could own within a broadcast area. It paved the way for an unparalleled merger and acquisition frenzy that continues today.

"Jacor Communications was the first company to act after the Telecom act was signed—and the first deal included stations right here in San Diego," says Mike Glickenhaus, vice president and general manager of Jacor's FM stations in San Diego. "We announced the purchase of Noble Broadcast Group while the ink was still drying on the Telecom act. The Noble transaction increased our presence in San Diego to a total of three signals and gave us the base to begin building one of the nation's first regional clusters."

Today, Jacor's high-profile presence in the San Diego market is a blueprint for radio consolidation success. Growing from a single station in October 1995 to eight stations and two exclusive sales agency agreements at the end of 1997, Jacor San Diego is one of the most promising broadcast areas of Jacor's impressive portfolio of markets.

"San Diego provides all the right ingredients for postderegulation success in the radio industry," says Glickenhaus. "The active lifestyles in this Sun Belt market and strong economic growth are the perfect footers for clustering. Advertisers can reach our listeners—their customers—in their cars or outdoors, where San Diegans spend

so much time. We offer our advertisers specific, demographically targeted audiences. More than 1.5 million people listen to our stations every week, over half the city's population. That's powerful reach for our local and national advertisers."

Jacor's San Diego stations include KIOZ-FM (Rock 105), KGB-FM 101.5, KKLQ-FM (Q106), KHTS-FM (Channel 933), KJQY-FM 102.9, KOGO-AM News Radio 600, KSDO-AM 1130, and KPOP-AM 1360, plus an exclusive agreement to provide programming and sell advertising for Mexican licenses XTRA-FM (91X) and XTRA-AM Sports 690. Airwatch America, based in San Diego, is also under the Jacor umbrella, providing traffic, news, and sports reporting services to radio and television stations along the West Coast.

At year-end 1997, Jacor Communications, Inc. was the nation's second-largest radio company— measured by total stations—and was fourth ranked by revenues,

with 189 radio stations across 18 states in 41 broadcast areas. Jacor has also invested in high-quality, hard-to-duplicate programming, with rights to *The Rush Limbaugh Show*, *The Dr. Laura Schlessinger Show*, and *Medical Minutes with Dr. Dean Edell*, the first-, second-, and third-rated national radio talk shows in the country. In addition, Jacor owns Premiere Radio Networks in Los Angeles, the country's third-largest syndicator of radio programming, comedy clips, and jingles.

I N April 1996, Chicago-based Tribune Broadcasting Company, one of the largest broadcasting companies in America, purchased a local television station (KTTY) in San Diego. Known today as "San Diego's WB," KSWB 5/69 was relaunched with great anticipation in September 1996. The new station debuted with new call letters, a new cable position (channel 5), a new transmitter and antenna, improved technical facilities, and, best of all, new

programming. The impact of Tribune's transformation of KSWB has been widely felt and seen throughout the community ever since.

"In many ways, the birth of KSWB was similar to starting a television station from scratch," according to Lisé Markham, vice president and general manager of KSWB 5/69. "Everything from our programming to our staff . . . even our name was brand new. Our goal was to create a new local station that serves the many interests of San Diegans, from children

to adults. It was quite a challenge, but given the tremendous response from our viewers and advertisers, our first year proved to be very rewarding."

A Family-Friendly, Fun Alternative

From the very beginning, KSWB 5/69 has focused on programming that suits the entire family, but with special emphasis on entertaining children and young adults. The result is KSWB's unique family-friendly philosophy, a balanced

blend of high-quality children's animation, family-friendly comedies, original WB Network shows, blockbuster Hollywood movies, and more.

The emphasis on children's programming sets KSWB 5/69 apart from other local stations. "We take our family-friendly philosophy very seriously," adds Sam Bickel, longtime San Diego resident and KSWB's program director. "We screen not only our programming, but our advertising as well. Not everything on the station is for children, but we want parents to know KSWB 5/69 is a safe and fun place for them and their kids to watch TV." Putting this philosophy into action, KSWB airs no excessively intense or inappropriate commercials prior to 8 p.m., airs Public Service Announcements urging parents to monitor their children's TV viewing, and has adopted stricter-than-normal TV rating standards.

The Proof Is in the Programs

Entertainment is KSWB's specialty. For kids, the fun begins weekdays on KSWB with great animation from Disney, Steven Spielberg, and Kids WB. It continues with hit comedies such as *Full House*, *Boy Meets World*, and box office superstar Will Smith in *The Fresh Prince of Bel-Air*. And even though KSWB is programmed with children in mind, adults, too, find many of these entertaining shows hard to resist.

At 8 p.m., KSWB 5/69 proudly presents the popular WB Television Network. Praised by critics for its family-friendly, original, and entertaining programming,

Joining the KSWB All-Star Cheer Squad is the station's lovable mascot, Michigan J. Frog, a familiar face in and around San Diego.

Enhanced technical facilities, such as this state-of-the-art, nonlinear editing room, have greatly improved the image quality KSWB delivers to its viewers.

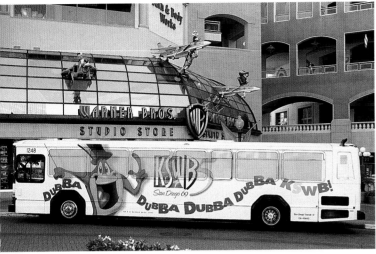

The WB is also recognized as America's fastest-growing new network. Monday night showcases The WB's signature family hit *7th Heaven*, while Wednesday and Sunday nights deliver plenty of laughs courtesy of the many WB comedies. In early 1998, The WB launched a new night of programming, Tuesday, led by one of TV's most exciting new shows *Buffy the Vampire Slayer*, followed by one of the most original breakout hits of the year, *Dawson's Creek*.

But KSWB 5/69 isn't relying solely on The WB for new and original programming. In October 1997, KSWB debuted X-Treme Saturdays, San Diego's first locally programmed complete night of adult action and adventure entertainment. Led by one of TV's most refreshing and thoughtful dramas, *The X-Files*, X-Treme Saturdays also features top-rated action series including *Xena: Warrior Princess* and *Hercules: The Legendary Journeys*.

Yet with all the success of the new KSWB 5/69, the station refuses to stand still. In 1998, KSWB will add two of TV's most popular comedies to its schedule: *The Nanny*, starring Fran Drescher, will be joined by one of the most successful and innovative TV comedies of the 1990s, *Friends*. Beyond new programming, KSWB will be moving into a brand-new, state-of-the-art broadcast facility as it prepares for future expansion, digital broadcasting, and more.

NATIONALLY RECOGNIZED, LOCALLY FOCUSED

Another aspect to Tribune Broadcasting's relaunch of KSWB 5/69 is the company's desire to prominently position the station as an active member of the local community. Perhaps the greatest of these local ambitions lies in the area of community fund-raising. Aided by the Robert R. McCormick Tribune Foundation, KSWB has founded the KSWB Cares for Kids Fund to raise moneys for select local charitable organizations that specifically serve to improve the mental, emotional, and physical well-being of underprivileged children.

"All of the new facilities, improved programming, and innovative marketing are designed to help the station do one thing: reach out to our customers here in San Diego," according to Will Givens, creative services director. "The KSWB Cares for Kids Fund is a proactive way in which we can help serve our customers. We are very excited about being able to give back to our communities in this new and important way."

The station promises to continue exciting community partnership events such as the popular KSWB Trick or Treat Street Halloween event for kids and families, as well as a more active KSWB Kids! club promoting a variety of activities and station programming developed exclusively for children.

KSWB 5/69 may also introduce a locally produced magazine show in 1998 that will cover a range of topics reflecting the diversity and interests of San Diego.

A BRIGHT FUTURE

Without a doubt, KSWB 5/69 has enjoyed a remarkable debut. Thanks to the favorable response from the community, KSWB has become San Diego's fastest-growing new television station. And the traits that helped to build the new station—original and entertaining programming, unique marketing, a responsible approach to children and family television viewing, and a desire to serve the community—will serve KSWB 5/69 well as it continues to build for an even brighter future.

CLOCKWISE FROM TOP LEFT: FROM CUSTOM TRANSIT BUSES, TO CHARITY FUND-RAISING EVENTS, KSWB 5/69 PROVIDES MORE THAN JUST GREAT TELEVISION TO THE LOCAL COMMUNITY.

MIXING THE BEST ENTERTAINMENT PROGRAMS ON TV WITH COLORFUL, INNOVATIVE, AND ORIGINAL MARKETING AND ADVERTISING HAS HELPED KSWB MAKE A STRONG DEBUT.

THANKS TO ITS STRONG APPEAL TO ACTIVE YOUNG FAMILIES, AS WELL AS KIDS AND TEENS, KSWB HAS QUICKLY BECOME SAN DIEGO'S FASTEST-GROWING NEW TELEVISION STATION.

PHOTOGRAPHERS

GRAHAM BLAIR, originally from the East Coast, moved to the San Diego area in 1958. Specializing in sports action photography, he also enjoys fashion, product, lifestyle, and portrait photography relating to sports. His photos have been published in numerous international surfing magazines and *Sports Illustrated*, and his clients include Billabong, Disney, Gordon & Smith Surfboards, and Anarchy Sunglasses. Blair's other interests include traveling to exotic locations, fly-fishing, off-road driving in the desert, gourmet cooking, and wine tasting.

JAMES BLANK began his career at age 15 by taking pictures of pro wrestling matches in Cedar Rapids, Iowa. After selling 40 pictures to wrestling magazines, he began a career in landscape photography. A resident of Chula Vista, Blank is employed by Scenics of America, and his clients include Kodak, Hallmark, World Book, *Reader's Digest*, and *Beautiful America*.

JOHN CLARK works at Aviation Photographics near Boston, and specializes in aviation and military photography. In December 1996, he photographed the last operational flight of the U.S. Navy's A-6E Intruder from the flight deck of the USS *Enterprise*. Clark's images were included in *Aviation Week*'s 1993 Photo Contest Issue. He also is interested in low-light photography and taking pictures of sunsets.

JIM CORWIN earned a bachelor's degree from the University of Washington and a degree in photography from Everett Community College. He spent 12 years working for photo labs in the Seattle area before opening his own business in 1990. A native of Portland, Oregon, Corwin specializes in travel, nature, people, and sports photography, and he has worked for such clients as The

Boeing Company, Safeway, U S West Communications, GTE, and Microsoft. His work has been published in *National Geographic Traveler*, *Audubon*, *Mother Earth News*, *Business Week*, and Towery Publishing's *Seattle: Pacific Gem*.

ROBERT FRIED has traveled on photography assignments to more than 50 countries. A graduate of the State University of New York with a degree in anthropology, he specializes in travel and editorial photography for advertising, corporate, and education markets. Fried's pictures have been published extensively in the travel/tourism industry, international magazines, guides/picture books, encyclopedias, and calendars, and his clients include American Express, *GEO* magazine, the *Los Angeles Times*, *National Geographic Traveler*, the *New York Times*, *Travel & Leisure*, UNICEF, and World Book. He currently lives north of San Francisco and enjoys growing tomatoes.

DAVID HARRISON is a lifelong San Diegan who specializes in studio product, architectural, and corporate photography. Since 1980, he has operated Harrison Photographic, where he works for clients in the biotechnology, building, and resort/hotel industries. Harrison has earned recognition within the local design and advertising community, and is a vital part of the music scene in San Diego and Los Angeles, playing harmonica in a blues band.

ML HART, who moved to San Diego in 1966, specializes in black-and-white documentary and entertainment photography, as well as portraiture. She has participated in numerous solo, juried group, and electronic exhibitions, and her special photography projects include Inside the Music, a photographic suite of portraits of jazz musicians and their instruments, and the Opera Project, a documentary

portrait of an entire season of the San Diego Opera.

SANDY HUFFAKER JR., originally from Raleigh, North Carolina, received a bachelor of fine arts in photography from Pratt Institute in Brooklyn. A resident of San Diego and a self-employed photographer, he has a particular interest in Latin cultures and specializes in documentary photography, photojournalism, and portraiture. His images have appeared in such publications as *San Diego Reader*, *USA Today*, and *Mother Jones* magazine.

KEN JACQUES, a professional photographer for 17 years, is a Seattle native who moved to San Diego in the late 1960s. The owner of Ken Jacques Photography, he specializes in performing arts, marine wildlife, and editorial images, as well as movie production stills. Among his most rewarding and challenging experiences is the time he spent photographing live whales. His clients include Saatchi & Saatchi, Rapp Collins Worldwide, the U.S. Navy, CBS and USA networks, Cox Communications, and the La Jolla Chamber Music Society. Jacques' images have appeared in *Time*, *National Geographic*, and *Sunset Magazine*.

ERIC LABASTIDA works out of his La Jolla-based studio, Labastida Photographics. He was awarded a one-week assignment from the Associated Press after attending the Eddie Adams Workshop.

JAMES LEMASS studied art in his native Ireland before moving to Cambridge, Massachusetts, in 1987. His areas of specialty include people and travel photography, and his work can be seen in publications by Aer Lingus, British Airways, and USAir, as well as the Nynex Yellow Pages. Lemass has also worked for the Massachusetts Office of Travel and Tourism, and his photographs have appeared in

several other Towery publications, including *New York: Metropolis of the American Dream*; *Treasures on Tampa Bay: Tampa, St. Petersburg, Clearwater*; *Washington: City on a Hill*; and *Orlando: The City Beautiful*.

TIM MANTOANI has lived in the San Diego area since 1991 and works out of his studio, Tim Mantoani Photography. Specializing in sports images and portraiture, he studied at the Brooks Institute of Photography. Mantoani's clients include No Fear, Reebok, Toyota, AT&T, MCI, and DirectTV.

BRAD MATTHEWS, a lifelong resident of San Diego, is a certified athletic trainer and a licensed physical therapy assistant who works for the Center for Sports Medicine and the California Ballet. Also a freelance photographer and videographer, he specializes in sports and dance photography, portraiture, and photojournalism. His work has been published in the California Ballet yearbook, the *San Diego Union Tribune*, and *San Diego Magazine*.

NICK NACCA, a native of San Francisco, moved to the San Diego area in 1967. A self-employed photographer and a mountain biking enthusiast, he specializes in advertising and digital imaging, and his clients include Airwalk and Huffy Bicycles. Nacca's images have been published in *Bike* magazine and *Troxel Sports & Fitness*.

ROBERT T. NOBLE, a tattoo artist for the past 20 years, served as the public information office photographer in Vietnam. In his spare time, he enjoys taking pictures of animals at the San Diego Zoo.

PHIL NORTON, a stock photo administrator and contract photojournalist for the *Gazette* daily newspaper, lives in Châteauguay,

Quebec, with his wife and their two children. Norton enjoys photographing rural and wilderness areas, and his images have appeared in *Time*, *Canadian Geographic*, *Adirondack Life*, and *Reader's Digest*, as well as with his own articles. He received National Magazine Awards in 1983 and 1985 for his pieces on the effects of acid rain on forests.

LOUISE PALAZOLA, a graduate of the University of Denver with a bachelor of fine arts in studio photography, specializes in black-and-white artistic works and environmental portraiture. Her work has been exhibited in galleries across the country, and her images were published in the book *Sister Stories*.

PHOTOPHILE, established in San Diego in 1967, has more than a million color images on file, culled from more than 85 contributing local and international photographers. Subjects range from images of Southern California to adventure sports, wildlife/underwater scenes, business, industry, people, science and research, health and medicine, and travel photography. Included on Photophile's client list are American Express, *Guest Informant*, Franklin Stoorza, and Princess Cruises.

PHILIPP SCHOLZ RITTER-MANN, an artist since 1977, began teaching photography at the Community College in Hannover, Germany, in 1979 before cofounding the Werkstatt fur Photographie and the Galerie Novum/Oktogon. With an interest in landscape and night photography, he has participated in more than 50 group shows and more than 25 solo exhibitions throughout North America and Europe. Rittermann's work is included in public, private, and corporate collections ranging from the Museum of Modern Art in New York to the Bibliothèque Nationale in Paris. He frequently leads lectures and workshops, and his photography is currently being shown in two traveling exhibitions and a solo exhibition at the McDonough Museum of Art in Youngstown, Ohio. Rittermann's work has been published nationally and internationally in books and magazines.

AL RODRIGUEZ, a lifelong San Diegan, teaches black-and-white photography and graphics at the San Diego School of Creative and Performing Arts. A member of the Photo Imaging Educators Association, his manipulated Polaroids have been published in *San Diego Magazine* and *San Diego Home/Garden*. A winner in 1964's National Newspaper Snapshot Awards, Rodriguez enjoys gardening, fishing, kayaking, camping, reading, playing classical guitar, and listening to music.

KIRK SCHLEA, a self-taught photographer, spent seven years traveling extensively throughout the world before returning to Southern California in 1980. He specializes in taking pictures of sports and people, and his interests include surfing, sailing, and fishing. Among his clients are Cadillac, Toshiba, Sears, Nike, Pepsi, and ESPN. Schlea has won awards for his work in *Sea* magazine and with First Interstate Bank, and his images have appeared in *Newsweek*, *Sports Illustrated*, and several international publications.

STEFAN SCHULHOF, a member of the Professional Photographers Association of British Columbia, Professional Photographers of Canada, and Canadian Association of Photographers & Illustrators in Communications, is an award-winning photographer whose work can be seen in *Visions in View* and the *Vancouver Sun*. His clients include BBDO Advertising, B.C. Telephone, Canadian Helicopters, Coldwell Banker, *Forbes* magazine, and Westin Hotels. Schulhof was born in Dublin, Ireland, and moved to Canada at the age of four.

BRETT SHOAF, a resident of San Diego since 1958, studied photography, telecommunications, and film production at City College and later at Grossmont College, where he earned an associate in arts degree. Shoaf is self-employed at Artistic Visuals, and his work includes stock, commercial, and instructional/tutorial photography, as well as ad design. His clients include Ivid Communications, Vortex Interactive, Shelter Island Inc., Bartell Hotels, and the San Diego Visitor Information Center. His stock photography has been published in the *San Diegan* and *San Diego Official Visitors Planning Guide*. With a special interest in nature photography, Shoaf has photographed the natural beauty of such places as Kauai, Switzerland, and Utah.

STEPHEN SIMPSON, a self-employed photographer and affiliate of stock photo agency FPG International, has lived in San Diego for 25 years. His areas of specialty include people/lifestyle, high-tech/biotech, corporate/international business, and travel photography, and his images have been published in *Time*, *Newsweek*, *People*, *Outside*, *Condé Nast Traveler*, *Wired*, and *San Diego Magazine*.

THOM VOLLENWEIDER has been the proprietor of Thom Vollenweider Photography since 1981. Specializing in editorial, commercial, and sports photography, he is the team photographer for the San Diego Chargers and publisher of the team's *Bolt Magazine*. Vollenweider's work has appeared in *Time* and *Newsweek*, as well as in several international magazines, and he was recognized by the San Diego Press Club for Best Sports Photography in 1995.

JOHN D. WHITFORD, originally from Dayton, Ohio, studied photography and art history in college. Now employed at Carlsbad Printing Services, Whitford intends to pursue a full-time career in photography. He enjoys taking both black-and-white and color images. Working extensively with the *Dayton Daily News*, the *Journal Herald*, and numerous other papers and periodicals, he specializes in pictorial and photojournalistic work. Whitford was the sole photographer for *The Lessons of Saint Francis*, a book featuring 20 black-and-white images taken at the Little Portion Hermitage in Eureka Springs, Arkansas.

MARSHALL WILLIAMS, a San Diego-based photographer, received a bachelor of arts from the Brooks Institute of Photography. Specializing in advertising and editorial photography, he regularly contributes to *San Diego Magazine* and *San Diego Home Garden & Lifestyles*. Fascinated by run-down movie theaters and motels, as well as dilapidated areas of town, Williams also enjoys photographing people, fashion, and food.

Other photographers and organizations that contributed to *San Diego: World-Class City* include Artistic Visuals, the California Ballet Company, Check Six Photo Archives, Christian Community Theater, Richard Cummins, Ron Garrison, Bob Glasheen, Olga Gunn, Howard Hall, Hillstrom Stock Photo, Roger Holden, Hotel del Coronado, Mark Keller, Matt Lindsay, Charlie Manz, San Diego Historical Society, San Diego Museum of Art, Scripps Institution of Oceanography, Rick Stangler, Joseph Woods, and Zoological Society of San Diego.

INDEX OF PROFILES

ERECTED IN 1910, THIS GREEK-inspired monument, designed by local architect Irving Gill, is the centerpiece of Horton Plaza Park (OPPOSITE). The world's first working electric fountain, it has been the source of much controversy over the years, as city leaders have debated whether to tear down the historic landmark.